# 50 STATES

# 50 WEEKS

# my American Adventure

## Amy Burritt

Foreword by Governor John Engler

Edited by Deborah Hawkins and Lynn Bowers

Ironwood Press
Traverse City, Michigan

PUBLISHED BY
IRONWOOD PRESS
P.O. BOX 4651
TRAVERSE CITY, MI
49685-4651

© 1998 by Amy Burritt

Governor's quotes are from interview tapes and may have been shortened or paraphrased for literary purposes.

LIBRARY OF CONGRESS CATALOGING-IN-PUBLICATION DATA

ISBN  0-9662840-0-3

Burritt, Amy Suzanne 1983 January 19-
My American Adventure/Amy Burritt

Non-Fiction 1. Travel-U.S.  2. Political-50 Governors
3. Government-Democratic process  4. Education

98-92529
CIP

PRINTED IN THE UNITED STATES OF AMERICA

Cover design/layout by Saxon Design, Traverse City, MI

Photographs copyright ©1998 by Kurt Burritt
Other photographs used by permission
Flag image © 1997 Photodisc, Inc.

10  9  8  7  6  5  4  3  2  1

# T H A N K S !

I WANT TO THANK MY LORD FOR ALL THAT HE'S DONE FOR ME. I WANT TO THANK HIM FOR HIS EVERLASTING LOVE AND FOR ALL THE AWESOME OPPORTUNITIES HE'S PROVIDED FOR ME.

Mom, co-writer, editor, you deserve a raise. Unfortunately I can't give you one yet. Thanks for having so much patience with me.

Mark and Shelly, thanks for your comments. I'll never forget, mist doesn't plink.

A special thanks to my own governor, John Engler. I appreciate your support.

A big 'thank you' to the Hilton Hotel chain for hosting us while we were in Hawaii.

*Angela and Erik Saxon. you guys are great. I love the cover. Please accept my profound thanks!*

Mom and Dad, thanks for being the crazy dreamers that you are and for living out those dreams.

Thanks to the campgrounds who hosted us along the way.

Dad, thanks for being there and for making me look at the 'big picture' of my life and this book.

Erika, I don't know how you got through that first draft. Thanks for your comments.

THANKS TO ALL THE GOVERNORS FOR MAKING MY DREAM A REALITY. AND FOR TEACHING ME PERSISTANCE.

Look Pastor John, you're in the book!

Melisa, you've been a great friend during this book writing process. Thanks a lot.

Lynn Bowers, thanks for devoting so much time to teaching me how to write. You're the best writer I know and maybe someday I'll be as good as you!

THANKS TO MY WHOLE FAMILY. YOU GUYS HAVE BEEN LIKE SANDPAPER ON MY 'ROUGH EDGES'. BY THE WAY, THAT'S GOOD!

Deb Hawkins, I don't mean to sound cliché, but you are so cool. Thanks a bunch.

Brittany, thanks for sticking with me through thick and thin (and orange and red if you know what I mean)!

Jon, what can I say? You're the best brother I've ever had. Thanks for showing me how to play Monopoly by myself, I shall never forget it (except how much money to deal)! Love ya buddy.

# contents

## tour three

## tour four

## tour five

# foreword

Charles Kuralt would have been proud of Amy Burritt.

The late newsman, known and beloved for his more than 25 years *On the Road* with CBS, lived a life of great adventure, traveling the back roads and small towns of America, and meeting many colorful and friendly folks along the way.

Like Kuralt, Amy and her family toured the country in a motorhome, discovering each day the fascinating diversity of the cities and states of America. From her travels, Amy learned what Kuralt knew: there is always another good story just around the next bend in the road.

In October 1995, Amy interviewed me in Lansing as part of her project, *America Through the Eyes of a Student*. She asked thoughtful questions and impressed me with her enthusiasm and persistence. I was happy to share with her why I feel Michigan is special. I could see why Amy was ultimately successful in her pursuit of all 50 states and their governors: she was having fun.

Amy has captured all of the fun and adventure of her family's extraordinary journey in this, her first book, *My American Adventure*. Her story is a compelling one and fulfills a dream that many people, young and old, have shared: to visit every one of the United States.

This book is more than just a good read. It is a testament to the power of education. By making learning fun, Amy's parents, Emily and Kurt Burritt, have opened the door to remarkable achievement by Amy and her brother Jonathan. Recognizing the importance of education and her own ability to read and write, Amy plans to contribute a portion of her book's proceeds to literacy organizations.

Kuralt would have been proud indeed.

—Governor John Engler

# my new home

"**J**on," I yelled, "It's here! It's here!" We both rushed out the door to see our new home cruising down the driveway. It was huge. It looked like a gigantic bus. It was cream with burgundy stripes, and the name on the side was *Bounder*. We waited by the driveway as it rolled to a stop.

"Can we get in? Can we get in?" Jon and I shouted in unison.

"Sure," Dad smiled as he opened the door. I stepped inside and looked around. It was a house on wheels. It had everything. A stove, refrigerator, two TV's, a VCR, and even a microwave. Above the steering wheel was a small television. "Dad," I asked, "is this your own little TV?"

"No, that's the back-up camera, so I can keep an eye on the car that we'll be towing behind us."

"Wow, they think of everything. Look at all the cupboards."

I walked down the hall and opened a door. It was the bathroom. At the back of the motorhome was a bedroom with a queen-size bed and more closets. Opening every door, I investigated each empty space. I knew this was Mom and Dad's room.

"But where will I sleep?" I asked Dad.

"Right here, Amy," he said, pointing to the table.

"On the table?"

"Yeah, look, it folds down into a bed." Dad moved the cushions and quickly changed the booth into a bed. "And Jon," he continued, "you'll sleep over there on the couch, and you'll both be able to use your sleeping bags."

"Awesome," I said, "now I won't have to make my bed every day."

I sat on the cushions and motioned for Max, our Springer Spaniel, to jump on my bed. "Max, you can sleep right here next to me."

Traveling in this motorhome was going to be a lot more fun than the Minnie Winnie we used to own. The Bounder was so much bigger. But then so was the trip.

I remember when I wasn't so excited about our trip, just a few months before, when Mom and Dad first made the announcement.

They'd called my younger brother Jon and me into the living room for a family meeting. That's when they told us what they were planning.

"You want to do what?" I shrieked. "You mean we're going to leave home? Just travel around the country for a whole year?"

"That's our plan," Dad smiled. "We want to take you to all fifty states."

"Why?" I asked, shocked that my parents seemed so nonchalant about such a crazy idea.

"Why what?" Dad's eyebrows raised.

I slumped back in my chair, a hundred thoughts running through my head. "Why do you want to do it?"

"For lots of reasons, Amy," Dad explained. "To begin with, your mother and I have always had a dream to travel and see our country. Plus, you and Jon are growing up so fast. Someday, in the not too distant future, you'll have lives of your own. I want to spend time with you guys now, so we can experience these things as a family."

"Are we gonna fly in a plane?" Jon asked. He was seven and loved airplanes. If flying was involved, Jon would go for the idea. I, on the other hand, wasn't convinced.

"Yes," Mom answered. "We'll fly to Alaska and Hawaii, and we'll travel in a motorhome to visit all the other states."

viii

"But what about my friends?" I asked. "And our store? Our house, what about our house?"

"Slow down, Amy," Mom laughed. "Those are all details we still have to work out, but we've decided to take the trip in tours so we can come home every ten weeks for a short break. You'll be able to see your friends then and share some of your adventures with them."

Ten weeks. Sounded like an eternity. I couldn't imagine a whole year.

"We also wondered what you thought about interviewing the governor of each state during the trip." Dad asked.

"Me?"

"Yes," Mom smiled.

"Why?"

"Because you'll be going to every state, and we think that by interviewing the governors and keeping a journal, you could share your experience with other kids," Mom explained.

"How would I do that?"

"Maybe you could publish a book about it."

"Me? Publish a book?" I was overwhelmed by all this news. "Can I think about it for a while?"

"Sure," Mom said.

I went for a long bike ride that afternoon. I was excited about the idea of trying to accomplish something as unusual as meeting every governor in the United States. It seemed like an unobtainable goal, but somehow that made it even more appealing. I wasn't sure where we would start, or how I could possibly accomplish something so big, but I did know if I wanted to do it, Mom and Dad would find a way to help me make it happen. And it would definitely be a new adventure.

As I explored our new motorhome, reality began to set in. We really were leaving. Maybe a year wouldn't be so bad. We would have all the conveniences of home, and there was plenty of room for Max.

I went to bed that night feeling confused. I was excited about the trip, but part of me didn't want to leave my friends. Maybe, if I had known then about all the new friends I would meet traveling over the next year, from prisoners and politicians to people like Captain Vectra and Dana with her dolphins, I wouldn't have felt so torn. That night, though, I could only picture my best friends, Melisa and Brittany, sleeping in the house across the road, and I didn't want to leave them. We did everything together.

I lay awake a long time that night, listening to the wind blow through the woods surrounding our house and thinking. Adventure was my middle name. I took every chance I could to explore new places. The woods to me were like the ocean was to Columbus. I spent every summer roaming those woods with Melisa and Brittany. We loved to stuff ourselves with wild blackberries and strawberries, build teepees, climb trees, share secrets and discover treasures, going home only after we were too tired and aching to go any farther. I tried to imagine the adventures I'd have on a trip across America. What would they be like without Mel and Britt?

I started thinking about the junkyard. The three of us had discovered it during one of our hikes through the woods. It was hidden down in a small valley, just beyond a ridge of pine trees near our houses. Since then, it had become one of our favorite places to go. We liked to think of it as our secret place, where we could go and no one could find us.

There was one object at the junkyard that sent chills down our spines. Near the bottom of the hill, there was a big wooden box that looked like a coffin. The box was latched shut, and the hinges on the top were rusted and falling apart. Our curiosity about what was inside the box had begun to get the best of us. Our imaginations would run wild with the idea that there might be a dead body inside. One time, we found a glass eyeball and set of false teeth nearby. Maybe they belonged to whoever was in the box. We were always trying to convince each other to open it.

One day, after not finding any new treasures, boredom drove us to the one last thing we had yet to uncover. We looked at the mysterious box. With no words spoken, we looked at each other in silent agreement. This would be the day. Shaking, we all walked down to the box, put our hands on the lid and counted.

"One ..." I slid my fingers under the edge, ready to pull it open.

"Two ..." I glanced up at Brittany. Her eyes scanned the box.

"Thr-"

"Let's wait," I interrupted suddenly. "We can look in there anytime."

I shivered in bed, remembering how scared we were about the box that day. "Anytime" seemed to be slipping away. I wondered if the girls would go to the junkyard while I was on my trip and open the box without me.

I walked over to my bedroom window and looked at Melisa and Brittany's house across the road. The moon cast a faint light on their porch. I put my hand against the glass, *would they miss me?*

A week later, Mom, Dad, Jon and I walked into the lobby of Traverse City's Park Place Hotel. "Do I have to talk to her?" I asked. We were meeting with our first dignitary, Michigan State Representative Michelle McManus.

"You might as well get used to it now, Amy. This is just the beginning," Dad said.

"Thank you for taking the time to meet with us," Mom said, shaking hands with Michelle. She was thin with dark curly hair and glasses.

"You're welcome. I'm happy to help," she answered. We told her about our plan to travel to all fifty states.

"Wow, you must be excited about this, Amy. What a project."

"Yes, I am."

"I think it's a great idea, but I'm not sure what kind of response you'll get from the governors' offices."

"Can you tell us where to begin?" Mom asked her.

"Well, I would suggest you start by writing letters to each of the governors. In fact, I'd be happy to write a letter of endorsement for you."

Her endorsement letter arrived in the mail a few days later, along with other letters from our State Senator George McManus, Lt. Governor Connie Binsfield, and Governor John Engler of Michigan. We included all of the letters in the request packets we sent to the governors.

We all worked hard making the project come together. After the request packets were addressed, we took them to the post office on May 19. I'll never forget that date. The postage came to over fifty dollars. I was so glad to be done with the packets. After they were mailed, we waited for the governors to respond.

Exactly one week later, Mom received a phone call. "Hello?" Mom's eyes widened and she signaled us to be quiet. We froze. I could hear my heart beating. "Yes it is ...." she said in her business tone of voice. All of a sudden, a big smile came across her face. "That's

*Assembling request packets.*

wonderful ...she'll be excited to hear that ...sure, that'll work out fine... Okay, thank you ...Good-bye."

"Who was it?" I asked.

"Oh, nobody special. Just the governor's office in Kentucky," she paused, then smiled, "and the governor said he would meet with you!"

We all screamed. You'd have thought we just won the lottery. But, no, it was better than that. My first meeting with a governor was scheduled. I couldn't believe it, a governor actually wanted to meet with me. I took a deep breath. It hit me then. We were committed to doing this trip, and I would have to be prepared for my meetings.

Over the next few weeks, the calls continued to come in. Before we knew it, thirty governors had agreed to meet with me. I was feeling nervous. I'd never done any public speaking before, let alone interviewing, but Mom and Dad assured me I'd be prepared.

I practiced my public speaking every night. For the fifth night in a row, I stood in front of my parents and read aloud from a book on the history of the state of New York. Why they chose that book, I don't know. It was hopelessly boring.

"Stand up straight," Dad said.

"Speak clearly and don't rock on your shoes," Mom added. "Amy, how many times do I have to tell you," she sighed, "don't chew your nails." I couldn't help it. It was one of my bad habits.

I felt like Melisa and Brittany were tired of hearing about the trip. They didn't want me to go, and every time we talked about it, they were reminded I'd be leaving soon. I didn't blame them. It had to be hard for them, too.

Four weeks before we were scheduled to leave, Mom and Dad called me into the living room.

"What's this all about?" I asked.

"Max," Dad said.

"Oh, I've already figured that out. He's going to sleep on my bed." I smiled.

"Well, Amy," Mom began, "we've realized we can't take Max with us."

"What? Why not? He won't be any trouble."

"Amy, it's not that he'll be any trouble," Dad explained. "He just needs a lot of room to run. Keeping him cooped up in the motorhome wouldn't be fair to him."

Max belonged to Dad, but he was special to me, too. I spent a lot of time with him when he was a puppy, teaching him tricks and playing ball with him. Max always followed me through the woods on my adventures. He loved to chase birds. Even when they were flying way up in the sky, Max thought he just might be able to catch one. (He could be pretty dumb sometimes.) I didn't think Max cared about what was "fair," he just wanted to be with us.

Dad told me that a family interested in giving Max a new home was on their way over to meet him. I was hoping the family wouldn't like Max and that we would have to take him with us, but that wasn't the case. They fell in love with him right away. He seemed to like them, too, although Max liked everyone. I was sick to my stomach.

I pulled Mom aside. "What if they're mean to him and don't treat him nice?" I asked, my voice quivering.

"Amy," Mom said softly, "they seem like nice people, plus they live on a farm, which would give him a lot of room to run." Somehow that didn't make me feel any better. I began to wonder if the trip would be worth all the sacrifices I was making.

When the time came for them to take Max, I cried. I tried to convince Mom and Dad we could manage with him on the trip, but they'd already made up their minds. I showed Max's new family all the tricks we taught him. With teary eyes, I gave him the commands, and he obeyed without hesitation.

"Sit Max," I said. He sat down. "Shake. Good boy. Lay down, roll over." Melisa, Brittany, Jon and I posed with Max for one last picture. We all put our arms around him and said good-bye. I gave him one final command. "Go for a ride, Max; get in the car." Once again, he obeyed.

*Melisa, Brittany, Jon, and me with Max.*

Even Mom and Dad were choked up as Max rode off with his new family. Everyone was silent, and my throat hurt from swallowing back my tears. I felt like part of me was gone forever. Our other dog, a Bichon Frise named Shasta, wasn't sure what to think. She wasn't even a year old, and Max had been like a big brother to her. I picked her up and held her tight. At least she was small enough that we could take her with us, I thought. I lay in bed that night wondering how Max was adjusting to his new home. My poor orphan dog. I hope they love him as much as I do, I thought, as I cried myself to sleep.

Time seemed to fly by. Before I knew it, Dad found renters for our house, so I had to pack up the stuff in my room. It was hard to decide what to take with me and what to pack away for a whole year. I pulled out a small wooden box from underneath my bed. Grandpa made it for my eleventh birthday. I'd memorized every line in the grain of the oak wood. Inside were my favorite treasures. I carefully wrapped the small glass bottles and broken pieces of porcelain in newspaper and set them back into the box. I poured the buttons and rusty metal pieces around the inside edge and shut the lid. I looked around my room as if I was saying good-bye to an old friend. It was strange to think about someone else living in my room, especially when I found out it would be a boy.

With just two weeks left before we departed, we moved into the motorhome. One morning, Dad had to take it to the RV dealer to get an awning attached. When he started backing the motorhome out from the campsite, he forgot to put down the TV antenna. It hit a big branch and broke off completely. It tumbled over the windshield and landed on the ground in front of the motorhome.

"Doggonit!" Dad said. "We haven't even left town yet and I have to repair something." I couldn't believe he forgot to crank it down. That was a one hundred dollar mistake, but I had a feeling he wouldn't do *that* again.

In the days just before we left, some of the local media, the *Traverse City Record-Eagle* and a few local television and radio stations, wanted to talk to us about our trip. Tom BeVier, from *The Detroit News*, interviewed us in our motorhome.

"How are you able to get out of school for a whole year?" he asked.

"Well, I'm homeschooled, so this is just part of my education," I told him. I also showed him the sweatshirts we'd made with our logo on the front, which read, *America Through the Eyes of a Student.* That was the name of our trip.

"I wish you luck, young lady," Tom said, shaking my hand.

WTCM, a country radio station, had asked us to do a live interview. We walked into the studio. The deejay was wearing headphones, and he was surrounded by a panel of buttons and flashing lights.

"Hello," he said, in a voice I recognized. It was Jack O'Malley, the host of the morning show.

*Jack O'Malley, WTCM*

"Hi, I'm Amy," I said.

"So, I hear you're going on a trip around the country. That sounds pretty exciting."

"Yeah, I can't wait to go."

Jack invited us to sit down in front of a big microphone. "I'm going to ask you some questions about your trip, so just talk into that microphone," he told me.

"What will be your job on the trip, Amy?"

"I'm going to interview the governors and write a book."

"Now, why do you want to do that?"

"Because, how many kids have gone to all fifty states, with a goal to meet all fifty governors and wrote a book about it," I answered. "I think kids like to read stories about other kids, at least I do."

The time went by quickly as Jack took turns asking each of us questions. "Emily," Jack said, looking at Mom, "would you be willing to call us with a live update from the road, say, once a month?"

"Sure, I'd be happy to," Mom agreed.

"And, Amy, maybe you could talk to us occasionally, too!" Jack smiled. *Me*? I thought. *I'll leave that up to Mom.*

A few days later, Aunt Sue threw a going away party for us at the beach. Friends and family came to say good-bye. My cousin Audrey gave me a silver pendant with a lizard on it for a going away gift. She knew I liked lizards.

"You know what, Audrey?" I said. "I'm going to take this lizard to every state with me and it will be a special souvenir." I thought it would be neat to have something special that traveled with me to all fifty states.

"Cool," Audrey said, with a smile on her face. I put the pendant around my neck and wore it for the rest of the day.

After all the anticipation, I was excited about our trip. I was ready for my new adventure to begin, but it was hard to say good-bye to everyone.

"Amy, do you really have to go?" Melisa asked.

"I wish I could say no, Mel," I said, trying to find a way to tell her and Brittany how much I was going to miss them, even if I was really happy about taking the trip. I never found the right words.

# hitting the road...

The following Saturday, Dad drove the motorhome to Grandma and Grandpa Peckham's house, where we would spend our last night. Early the next morning as I listened to Grandpa pray for a safe journey, my eyes filled with tears. My hands were sweaty and my stomach knotted. There was no doubt I'd need strength to make it through the entire year.

"Amen," Grandpa said, as we all squeezed hands. Grandma and Grandpa went down the line giving each of us a hug.

"We're going to miss you," Grandma said, choking back her tears.

"You, too, Grandma." I watched them waving good-bye from the edge of the road until they were out of sight.

It was July 30. Dad began singing *On The Road Again*. It's such an obnoxious song. Unfortunately, I'd hear it many more times over the next twelve months.

I walked back to the bedroom and flopped on the bed. I felt the pendant on my necklace fall across my neck. I ran my fingers over the silver and followed the design of the lizard. Dad had sold his business, we'd given away our dog and rented our house. My whole life was messed up. I tried to hold back the tears, but I couldn't. I was leaving behind so much of what was important to me, my room, my dog, my woods, and, most of all, my friends.

We drove for hours. I felt a little better by the time we stopped along the Ohio Turnpike to cook dinner at a truck stop. There were lots of motorhomes pulling off the highway and staying the night. While Mom cooked dinner, Jon and I played around the trees at the edge of the woods. We spotted a small toad and began chasing it.

Mom called us in. While I was eating, I looked down and noticed my lizard pendant was missing. I began frantically searching the floor and then the cushions. I couldn't find the pendant anywhere. I ran out the door.

"Amy," Jon called, "I'll help you find it." We searched the area where we'd been playing but couldn't find it anywhere. I was so mad at myself for losing it. Discouraged, I went inside, pulled out my sleeping bag and set up my bed. I lay there thinking about what I would say to Audrey. Maybe I would find the lizard the next day.

Early the following morning, I put my bed table up and went outside to look once more. I still couldn't find it. *How am I going to tell Audrey I lost her present on the very first day of the trip?* I was really mad at myself.

After everything was secured in the motorhome, Dad started to drive away. That's when we heard it. Crunch. We all looked at each other with wide eyes.

"Doggonit!" Dad said, pounding the steering wheel. He slammed the RV into park and stormed out the door. We looked at Dad through the windshield as he bent down to pick up his fractured antenna off the ground. I wanted to laugh, but then I saw Dad's face and I knew better. I managed a look of sympathy, but all I could think was, *I'm glad it wasn't my responsibility to lower the antenna.*

Dad and I both learned a valuable lesson our first day on the road. I learned to keep my special treasures inside the motorhome, and Dad put a post-it note on the dash, "Hey, stupid, is the antenna down?"

# tour one

new york

vermont

maine

new hampshire

massachusetts

rhode island

connecticut

new jersey

pennsylvania

ohio

michigan

# 1

# a bite of the big apple

**W**elcome to New York. We all cheered when we saw the green welcome sign. Dad stopped at the edge of the road to get a picture of Jon and me in front of it.

"Here we are, our very first state," Dad said, as he stretched and looked around the landscape. This was officially the beginning of our fifty state tour.

Our first stop was Niagara Falls. From everything I'd heard about them, I was expecting something really cool, but as I peered over the metal railing surrounding the falls, I was disappointed. Maybe they would have looked more impressive if I'd seen them from the bottom, during one of the boat tours that take you underneath the falls.

We walked back to the motorhome. I hopped in, grabbed a pop out of the fridge, and sat down at the table to drink it as Dad started to drive away. It was neat to be able to travel down the highway and sip a pop or eat snacks anytime. The big windshield allowed us to have a good view. It sure beat riding in the car and getting motion-sickness.

We stopped at a campground on Lake Erie to spend the night. Dad took our bikes off the rack so we could explore the area. It was pretty as the sun went down, its rays reflecting off the lake, first yellow, then orange. The horizon slowly darkened, and the colors eventually faded into the night. It was a picture-perfect ending to our first day in New York.

The next day we traveled through western New York. I was surprised to see rolling hills, trees, lakes, and vineyards. It didn't look much different than northern Michigan. I guess whenever I thought about New York, I'd only imagined New York City. I realized the state is more than just the Big Apple.

Dad was still adjusting to all the new sounds of the motorhome. Whenever the pots and pans rattled, he'd send me on a search to stop the annoying sound. Inserting rubber mats between the pots and pans quickly became part of our routine before hitting the road, along with securing the refrigerator, making sure nothing was sitting on the counters, and locking the motorhome door so it didn't fly open on the highway. Oh yeah, and lowering the antenna.

We were slowly making our way to New York City. We drove all day, until it was time to find a campground. That was Mom's job, to look through the campground guidebook, find one that was easy to get to and not too expensive. She found one that sounded really nice, so Dad turned off the highway. The paved road eventually changed into a dirt road that wound through woods and places that were barely wide enough for our motorhome. We drove for miles following the small wooden signs directing the way to the campground. Dad was beginning to worry we'd driven too far off the highway.

"Honey, where are you taking us?"

"I'm just following the directions in the book." Mom was funny. In order to read a map, she had to turn it in the direction we were traveling, which is probably why Dad was getting worried. He was almost ready to turn around when we finally found the campground.

It didn't look at all like the beautiful description in the guidebook. What I saw was more like a scene out of a horror movie. On a hill was an old hotel with lots of windows and broken shutters. The red paint was cracked, worn by the wind and rain. It looked deserted, haunted, and it gave me the creeps. As darkness set in, a light rain began to fall, making a plinking sound on the roof as we sat looking at the place.

Up another steep hill, a bunch of old camping trailers were lined up in rows. They looked like they'd found their final resting place. Mounds of clutter lying around the trailers made it look more like permanent housing than a campground. I had a weird feeling about this place. I didn't want to stay, but it was late and Dad was getting a headache. We didn't have any other choice.

The campground office was in a rundown trailer. Mom and I went in to pay for a campsite. Turning a wobbly knob, we opened the creaky metal door. The awful smell of cigarette smoke and musty carpet choked me. Behind a dark wooden desk stood a lady with pink curlers in her hair and deep wrinkles in her face. She was wearing one of those dresses that some grandmas like to wear, with big gaudy flowers and no sleeves. In the background, I could hear the murmur of a television. I glanced around the room. Piles of papers and dusty books cluttered the office. A sticky flytrap with ancient prisoners embedded in glue hung in one corner. I wondered how many years it had been there. Sunbleached blue curtains hung over the windows, making the room dark and dreary. Mom asked hesitantly about a campsite for the night and paid the twenty dollars. Anxious to get back outside for some fresh air, I stepped in front of Mom to get out first.

We drove the motorhome up to the top of the hill. I noticed a bunch of kids watching us. Their eyes widened as the RV came closer. Most of the kids were running around barefoot, wearing grimy tank tops and shorts. They didn't seem to care that it was raining. Dad pulled our shiny new bus into a site, turned off the engine, and went to lie down. The kids began surrounding the motorhome. They stood there silently, shifting their stares from the front of the motorhome to the back, as if it were a UFO that had just landed in their backyard.

Mom suggested Jon and I go play with them, but we were too chicken to go out the door. A freckle-faced boy in a faded blue t-shirt was inspecting us very carefully. He looked like he was about my age. I watched him as he slowly walked around the motorhome, his eyes scanning it from top to bottom. His straight brown hair was uncombed, and tattered jeans worn through the knees revealed a dirty gash. He stopped near the back of the motorhome. Slipping his hands into his pockets, he seemed to take a particular interest in my bike on the rack. I wondered what he was thinking. Maybe he didn't have a bike of his own. Maybe he wanted mine.

After a restless night, I woke up early, anxious to check the bike rack. I was happy to see that everything was there. We left as soon as the breakfast dishes were done and everything was secured, but the sight of that lonely looking boy in the faded blue t-shirt stuck with me.

Since May, when we had mailed the packets to all the governors, Mom's job had been to call their offices and arrange my interview meetings. She'd already been able to set up many appointments before we left Michigan, but here we were in New York, and she still hadn't been able to schedule a meeting with Governor George Pataki in Albany.

It takes a lot to upset Mom, but on her way back from the pay phone, where she'd made her tenth call to Governor Pataki's office, her face was a bit red. She looked as if she was ready to explode. Instead, she walked up to the side of the motorhome, looked me in the eye, and said calmly, "I think we'll let this one go for now."

"What happened?" I asked.

"We'll try again later." Boy, I knew she was mad when she evaded my questions, but I really wanted know to what Governor Pataki's office had said.

"What happened?" I asked again.

"Governor Pataki's scheduler just hung up on me."

"Oh, great," I said, waving my arms in frustration. "We're not getting off to a very good start!"

I took that first rejection very personally. It hurt my feelings to think the governor didn't want to meet with me. Suddenly, interviewing all fifty governors of the United States seemed to be an impossible dream. I worried if things didn't go better with the other governors, I was never going to reach my goal. Later in the trip, I would learn to roll with the punches better, knowing it was often the governor's staff making decisions, not actually the governor.

*August 4...Been through lots of New York. Finger Lakes, Ithaca, Plattekill. Visited Roosevelt's childhood home and Vanderbilt mansion. The Vanderbilts were a very wealthy family who made their fortune in the railroads. They have mansions all over the place. Tomorrow, the Big A.*

New York City. It's big. It smells. It's home to the Statue of Liberty, or so I thought. We met up with Gordon, an old friend of Mom and Dad's, who lives in the city. His blonde hair was a bold contrast to the rigid features of his face. His sharp jaw line and high cheekbones gave way to deep blue eyes that sparkled as he spoke.

"C'mon guys! We've got places to go and people to see!" Gordon said.

The first thing we did was eat a great breakfast at one of his favorite places. I learned one thing right away: New Yorkers love their food. New York City has every kind of restaurant you can imagine, from Chinese to Greek to Italian. You can eat in a small outdoor cafe or an elegant dining hall. There are so many choices. It's fantastic!

We moved fast through New York City. Gordon wanted to show us as much as he could in one day. After breakfast, we headed down the street to our first stop, the Museum of Natural History. I liked hearing all the sounds of the city: horns honking, the beeping sound of trucks backing up, people calling out for taxis, and street vendors selling their goods. There was a constant hum of activity. Gordon walked briskly. I was glad I wore my tennis shoes. We practically ran through the museum, snapping pictures as quickly as we could.

Forty-five minutes later we were walking through Central Park, the greenest spot you'll find in New York City. A man in old ragged clothes, looking as though he hadn't bathed in weeks, was digging through a trash can. I stopped to watch, curious about what he was trying to find. He just kept pulling out pop bottles.

"Mom, what's that guy doing?" I asked.

Mom looked at me sadly. "Amy, in New York a pop bottle is worth a nickel." I shuddered, and a sick feeling rushed through me. He must be collecting them to buy food, I thought.

"C'mon Amy, let's go," Mom said, pulling my sleeve. As we hurried along, Jon complained he couldn't walk anymore, so Gordon picked him up and carried Jon on his shoulders. Knowing he couldn't carry Jon all day, Gordon decided to get his car. He left us at the Metropolitan Museum of Art to wait for him. We had only forty-five minutes to tour the entire place before Gordon returned, so we only saw some of what was there. I wanted to stay longer to look at the armor display, but Gordon said, "We don't have enough time, if you want to see the rest of the city. Besides, it'll give you a reason to come back."

We spent the rest of the day cruising around the city in Gordon's green jeep, with the top off. Gordon turned on the radio, and we were driving through downtown Manhattan with the wind blowing through our hair just like in the movies. I felt as though I was on top of the world. Gordon was in the advertising business, but by the way he was swerving in and out of traffic like a maniac, Mom said he should have been a cab driver.

*Cruising through New York City in Gordon's jeep.*

We passed Trump Tower, Grand Central Station, and the marquee for the *Late Night Show* with David Letterman, displayed in big bold yellow letters. We saw the building where NBC airs the *Today Show*, and the spot where people line up every morning to try to get on TV. Next, we went to Wall Street to see the New York Stock Exchange. Wall Street is a narrow street with tall buildings along its curb. Gordon pointed out all the sites as we flew by. I noticed a sign that displayed a large number, somewhere in the trillions, and the last digit was spinning so fast I couldn't even read it.

"Gordon, what's that sign for?"

"It represents our national debt."

"You mean our country is that far in debt?" I asked in amazement.

"Yeah," Dad said, "and the worst thing about it is your generation has to pay for it."

"That's not fair!" I yelled over the noise of the traffic. "How do they expect us to pay for it?" I couldn't believe the government was spending money it didn't even have faster than I could count it.

In the distance I saw the one landmark I'd heard so much about, the Statue of Liberty. Gordon pulled over at the yacht harbor of the World Financial Center so we could get a good look. It was far away and seemed little compared to what I'd imagined. There was a misty rain falling, and fog was rolling into the harbor.

Finally, we took a break and had dinner at an outdoor cafe. I sank into a chair under a teal umbrella.

"When we're finished with dinner, I'll take you guys down to the Pier," Gordon said. He still had plenty of energy left to keep going. I think he was running on Energizer batteries. After dinner, I managed to find enough energy to walk along the Pier and look at all the shops. I leaned on the railing and gazed at the George Washington Bridge. I understood what "whirlwind tour" meant.

Although our day in the big city was coming to an end, Gordon wanted to send us off with one final, delicious memory. We stopped at another cafe for dessert. Mom and Dad reminisced about old times with Gordon while Jon and I scouted out the goodies. We decided on the super duper, triple-layer chocolate something-or-other-cake, made with several layers of different kinds of chocolate and topped with huge shavings of dark chocolate. It was the most awesome dessert I'd ever seen. Gordon was certainly a great tour guide, and his taste in restaurants was pretty good, too.

After an exhausting ten hours in New York City, I was glad to be in the car heading back to the motorhome. Staring out the window, I thought about the lights on Broadway and the fancy places like Trump Tower and Wall Street. I tried to remember the last number of the national debt, and I wished I would've saved some of the super duper, triple-layer chocolate something-or-other cake for the kid in the faded blue t-shirt back at the campground.

# 2

# texas falls

"**W**ow! Look at all the different flavors!" Jon exclaimed, running up to the brightly colored ice cream counter. "I want Chocolate Almond. No, I want Chunky Monkey. And ...and ...and can I have Mint Chocolate Chip, too?"

"You can have whatever kind you want," Dad laughed, as he rubbed Jon's bristly hair.

"How about Rainforest Crunch? Or Peanut Butter Cup?" I asked.

There must have been forty different flavors to choose from at Ben & Jerry's Ice Cream Factory in Stowe, Vermont, and, like Jon, I had a hard time deciding.

"Mom, can I have a double scoop? Please?" I batted my eyelashes, but it didn't seem to have the effect I was hoping it would.

"You better go with a single," she said, pointing to a small boy licking melted ice cream off his cone. "Look at the size of them."

"But, Mom, that's not very much."

"Alright," she gave in, "just this once!"

I pondered what flavors I should get as I walked around the outdoor area of the factory. It was set up like a fair. At one table, two little girls were making gigantic bubbles, at another someone was offering free face painting.

I returned to the counter where Dad was standing. "I've decided on Chocolate Chip Cookie Dough and a second scoop of Mint Chocolate Chip." It's my favorite.

"Coming right up!" Dad said in a deep radio voice. I leaned against the counter waiting for my ice cream.

"Oh, thanks!" I said, as the guy behind the counter handed me my double dip. I licked the top and let the cool minty ice cream slide down my throat. It felt good in contrast to the hot August weather.

We ate our cones while we waited in a line to take the factory tour. We were told that at the end there would be a quiz. Wait a minute, I thought, this sounds too much like school! I tried to pay attention anyway.

We watched a movie about the ice cream factory's early beginnings, and we walked through the factory. We saw how the ice cream is made. The quiz at the end of the tour consisted of one question: "What three ice cream flavors were named by people outside of the Ben & Jerry's factory?" I raised my hand. The guide picked the lady right in front of me, but she didn't have the right answer. Then he chose me.

"Chunky Monkey, Chubby Hubby, and Cherry Garcia," I answered.

"You're exactly right," said our guide, and he tossed me a frozen Peace Pop. I ate a few bites of it, but was too full to eat the rest. Jon was more than happy to take care of it for me. He's always so helpful.

At the end of the tour, we realized it was getting late. Dad was anxious to get to our next campground before dark.

"Guess what, guys?" Mom asked. "Our next campground is on a lake."

"That's just great," I moaned, as I lay on the couch in the motorhome, my stomach churning from too much ice cream.

I was feeling better by the time we pulled into Limehurst Lake Campground. Jon and I waited in the motorhome while Mom and Dad registered at the office. Out the front window I could see a beautiful lake with two diving boards.

"Yes!" Jon and I shouted, as we gave each other a high-five. Mom and Dad set up our campsite, and Jon and I ran for the lake. The diving boards were awesome. That was my idea of a great campground.

We'd received a letter before we left Michigan informing us that the governor of Vermont would be on vacation during our week in his state, but Mom still wanted to drive to Montpelier and meet with the governor's scheduler and tour the capitol building. Mom was hoping we could make an appointment for a later date. Dad had agreed it would be easy to return to Vermont later, since we were on the east coast and most of the states were small and close together.

Mom walked up to the secretary seated at the desk. "Hello," she said. "My name is Emily Burritt, and I'm here to make an appointment for my daughter, Amy, to see the governor."

"Well, his schedule is pretty full today," said the secretary.

"You mean he is here?" Mom questioned. "That's funny, the letter we received from your office said he was going to be on vacation this week, so we're here to see if we can reschedule the meeting for another time."

"Um, maybe I better let you speak with the scheduler." The secretary picked up the phone and made a call. "The scheduler will be with you in a moment," she told us as she put down the receiver. "You can have a seat." As we waited in the governor's reception room, I noticed several people looking at us through a small glass window in the door behind the secretary's desk.

"Mom, can I video tape those people looking at us?"

"No," she said, "I don't want to run our battery down."

Twenty minutes went by and several people were leaving the office. Finally, Mom walked over to the secretary.

"Is it going to be much longer?" she asked. The secretary called the scheduler again.

"I'm sorry, she went to lunch," the secretary told Mom.

"What do you mean she went to lunch?" Mom asked in disbelief. "We have been sitting here for twenty minutes waiting to see her, and she decided to take a lunch break?"

"I'm sorry, would you like to come back later?"

"No, just have her call me."

We gathered up our stuff and left the building. I felt really rotten. I couldn't understand why we were treated this way. Weren't they supposed to be serving the public? If this was how politics worked, I didn't like it.

"Don't take it personally, Amy. It's not worth getting upset about," Dad said.

Still I couldn't help feeling hurt. Why should a governor talk to me, anyway. I'm just a kid, I thought. The car ride back to the motorhome was quiet. It seemed to take forever. I was irritated and just wanted to take off my stupid dress.

After our family devotions the next morning, Jon and I dug into our school work. I was creating a timeline of American history on the computer. Mom was working with Jon. He was coloring pictures of historical figures like Paul Revere and George Washington and then pasting them on a timeline of his own.

*A typical school day.*

"Has anyone seen the scissors?" Dad asked. "They're supposed to be right here in the pencil box."

"They might be in the school bin," I said, pointing to the plastic container on the floor.

"You know, if everyone just put things back where they belong, it would make our lives a whole lot easier," he complained.

Dad is a neat freak. His motto is: "There's a place for everything, and everything should be in its place." Sometimes, it was hard to keep things organized in such a small space, especially when we were doing our school work, because our books were usually strewn everywhere.

"If you guys can get this place cleaned up and organized, maybe we'll go on an adventure," Dad said.

"No problem," Jon grinned, throwing his books back into the bin.

Jon and I had no idea where Mom and Dad were taking us, but we grabbed our backpacks and piled into the car. We followed the back roads through the towns of Roxbury, Warren, Grandville, and Hancock. We saw lots of dairy farms and old covered bridges. Everything was so green. The car whined to a stop at the side of the road.

"Where are we, Dad?" I asked. He pointed to a sign that read *Texas Falls*. "Why would Texas Falls be in Vermont?"

"Maybe it's the biggest waterfall in Vermont," Mom said, "and they decided to name it after Texas because everything is big in Texas."

12

The real reason didn't really matter, it was a great place to have some fun.

I looked at Jon and said, "Where there's water, there's got to be adventure!" I scrambled out of the car with Jon following close behind.

When I came to the edge of the bank, I could hear water rushing below. A slippery dirt path led down the steep hill, covered with knotty tree roots. I used them for steps, carefully edging myself down the bank.

I was doing okay until my shoe slipped on a mossy root, and I started sliding down the slope. I caught a glimpse of the path below as I slid faster and faster. I was headed right for the waterfalls. I tried to grab onto a root, but it slipped through my fingers. I reached out for another stick and missed again. Finally, I jerked to a halt when my hand caught the end of a long root. I stood up slowly, grabbed onto a low branch over my head, and took a minute to catch my breath.

*That was close, too close,* I said to myself. I looked up and saw Jon leaning over the bank.

"Are you okay, Amy?" he hollered.

"Yeah, I just slipped." I climbed carefully back to the top.

"Your arm is bleeding," Jon said, pulling me up the last few inches. I looked down at it.

"I know. So is my knee." I brushed the dirt off my shorts, determined not to let a few cuts keep me from exploring. "C'mon Jon, let's go climb those rocks on the other side." We ran across the bridge to the large rocks near the river. From there we could walk to the river's edge. The water was crystal clear.

"Jon, feel the water, it's really nice." Jon reached his hand down into the river.

"Brrr!" he shrieked. "It's freezing, Amy!"

I took off running and laughing. I love it when I get him like that.

*Texas Falls.*

# 3

# thunder hole

"Flatlanders, that's what we call the tourists," said the waitress in a faded pink uniform. She poured coffee into the two white mugs on the table. Her dark hair was pinned back, revealing tiny age lines in her face. The bell on the door rang out, announcing a customer's departure.

"See ya tomorrow," the waitress called out cheerfully. Nodding his head, the customer smiled back. Boothbay was a friendly town set in a small harbor along the Atlantic coast. I could smell bacon frying and fresh coffee brewing. It made me hungry.

"Could you tell us about some of the things to do in the area?" Mom asked.

"Where ya stayin?"

"Down at the Ponderosa Pine Campground."

I liked the campground. It had tall pine trees, a big game room, and a miniature golf course.

"Take the kids to the aquarium, they'll love it. It's a hands-on aquarium where they can pick up creatures and look at 'em up close." Jon and I looked at each other, our eyes lighting up.

"Yeah, let's go there," said Jon. We finished our breakfast and paid the bill.

"What do you call the tourists who visit Michigan?" she asked Dad, chomping on her gum with every word.

"Fudgies," he told her. She laughed as we walked out the door.

"This is my kind of schoolwork," Jon smiled as he picked up a star fish.

I picked up a giant clam and set it on my hand. I watched as it opened, I could see its muscle inside. Suddenly, it clamped shut. The clam did this over and over, and it made me jump every time.

I noticed something that looked like a pickle in another spot in the tank. I reached over and picked it up. It was squishy, and slumped over the sides of my hand. Chris, the guy working at the aquarium, was watching us.

*Holding a horseshoe crab.*

"That's a sea cucumber," he said. "Squeeze it."

"Squeeze it?" I echoed. "What happens if I do that?"

"You'll find out," Chris laughed.

I wasn't sure if I should squeeze it or not. I didn't really want its guts on my hand. I decided to give it a try. Pointing the sea cucumber at Jon, just in case something happened, I closed my eyes and squeezed. Jon screamed and I opened my eyes. His shirt was wet. He picked one up, and the next thing I knew, we were having a water fight with sea cucumbers.

We walked around the aquarium looking for more excitement. The building was made of cement, and the inside was painted blue like the ocean. It smelled fishy. In the middle of the room was a small indoor pool filled with creatures that looked like tiny sharks.

"Hey, Jon!" I yelled, my voice echoing off the cement walls. "Come here and look at this." The sign read: *Spiny Dogfish.*

"What are these, Chris?" I asked.

"Sharks. Go ahead and pet them," he smiled.

"No way, I'm not puttin' my hands in that tank."

"They won't bite you. They love attention," he assured me. I slowly put my hand in the water. I touched one as it swam by. It didn't seem to mind. It came back and rubbed against my arm like a puppy wanting attention. I told Mom and Dad I wanted one, but they only laughed. Parents are just too practical.

Our campground wasn't far from Boothbay Harbor, a small village with lots of shops selling expensive little trinkets. Mom and I were in a shopping mood, and the guys came along to make sure we didn't spend too much money. All of us walked through town, down to the marina where several boats were unloading the day's catch of clams. I didn't like the smell, a strong fishy odor. There were two seals playing in the harbor. The fishermen said the seals liked to hang around the boats when they're being cleaned, to eat the little pieces of fish that fall into the water.

That night, Mom decided it was finally time to have the lobster dinner she had dreamed about for so long. Ever since she was a kid, Mom wanted to come to Maine and eat lobster. We were told we could experience the local flavor if we went to the Fisherman's Co-op in Boothbay. When we arrived at the restaurant, Dad took one look and frowned.

"Let's wait," he said.

"Wait?" Mom exclaimed. "I've waited long enough." The restaurant, owned by the local fishermen, was rustic-looking with picnic tables lined up along the dock. "I think it's quaint."

Dad rolled his eyes and followed Mom down the stairs to the pier. We walked by some big kettles full of boiling water.

"What are those for?" I asked.

"That's how they cook the lobster," Mom said. "You pick out the one you want to eat and they throw it into the pot. Amy, go find a table while I order the lobster."

After quite a long wait, our number was called. Mom set the tray in front of me.

"What are those things?" I leaned back from the table.

"Those are oysters," Mom said.

"They look disgusting."

"C'mon," Dad said. "Remember we were going to be adventurous and try different foods on this trip."

I took one tiny bite just to say I'd tasted one. It was gross. I decided not to try the clams. The lobster was good, but it was the messiest food I've ever eaten. I cracked open the hard shell of the lobster with the plastic pliers to get the meat out. The juice ran down my arms. It took a lot of work just to get a little bit of meat. There must be easier ways to eat lobster, I thought. Mom was happy, though.

"I could eat lobster all the time," she smiled contentedly.

The rest of us decided one lobster dinner was enough.

The coastline in Maine is very different compared to the sandy shoreline back home. Maine's beach is lined with massive boulders, and the waves crash onto the shore like exploding bombs. We were hiking along jagged red rocks in a section of Acadia National Park, just north of Boothbay. I could feel the spray of the water hitting my face. It was refreshing after working up a sweat from the hike.

"Shh, listen," Dad whispered.

I stood still, wondering what I was supposed to hear. In the distance, people were screaming, then it stopped.

"What's going ..."

"Shh," Dad interrupted.

We listened. It happened again, the voices grew louder and I could hear an explosion and then more screams.

"Let's go see what it is," Dad said. The screams grew louder as we moved closer. We realized they were screams of excitement. Peering over the edge of the cliff, we saw a crowd of people standing below us.

"What's going on?" Mom shouted to a lady just below us.

"We're watching the water shoot up from that crack in the rocks. It's called Thunder Hole!" The lady pointed toward the rocks.

We stood there for a moment to see what she was talking about. The waves from the ocean began to swell and grow larger as they came rolling toward the shore. The closer the waves came, the louder the crowd would yell. Finally, the wave exploded into the crevice and gushed fifty to one hundred feet into the air, drenching the enthusiastic on-lookers below.

"That's awesome!" I yelled. "Mom, can Jon and I go down there?"

We'd heard people talking about a hurricane that was offshore creating colossal waves along the shoreline. The park rangers in Acadia National Park had roped off a section of walkway because of the danger. Another wave was rolling in, and people were rushing down to get closer. I couldn't stand just watching other people have so much fun without being part of it. I asked Mom again if she would go down.

"No, Amy, I don't want to get all wet. Besides," she said, pointing to the scab on my arm, "look what happened to you the last time you got near raging water."

"Oh, Mom, that's different."

Kaboom! The water crashed against the rock. It sounded like a bomb going off, and it made my heart race. Mom's adventurous side finally got the best of her, and she agreed to take us down.

"You stay right behind me, and hold on tight to the railing," she instructed.

We followed her to a spot just far enough to look down into the crevice. We

*Thunder Hole.*

stood there waiting for a wave to come in. I looked up at Dad perched on the rocks above. He had the video camera balancing on his knee, determined to get our adventure on tape. We waited. A few small waves came in, but nothing exciting. Then we saw a wave bigger than all the others. The crowd began to roar. By the look on Mom's face, I could tell she was having second thoughts. I held on tightly to the railing. The wave hit. It splashed against the rock with such force, I could feel the ground beneath me shaking. Suddenly, I felt a stinging sensation all over my body. The salty ocean water made all my mosquito bites sting, and I had plenty of them. We were all soaked.

"Oww," I complained, not enjoying the burning sensation.

"You asked for it," Mom laughed. "Now we get to ride all the way back to the motorhome in our soaking wet clothes."

It was worth it.

"Beep, beep, beep...," the alarm screamed in my ear. I squinted at the clock. It was 5:00 am.

It was the day of my very first interview, and I wanted to make sure I was ready on time. I climbed out of bed to get the first shower. That morning, my mind was filled with all kinds of questions about the interview. How long would it take? Would there be security guards all over? Would Governor Angus King be easy to talk to? My stomach began to knot up. I wasn't sure I could even eat the donut Dad gave me. I said a quick prayer and asked God to calm my nerves.

With four of us all trying to use our little bathroom at the same time, morning could be a little crazy. The motorhome was a mess. Mom had the ironing board set up on the table, and Jon was playing with his Legos on the couch. I pulled out the dress Mom and Dad had chosen for me the night before. Dresses just aren't me. Wearing them means I have to sit a certain way, walk a certain way, and wear stupid nylons. It was going to be hard enough just getting through the interview, but now I had to think about my slip showing or a run in my nylons. Being a girl is pretty complicated sometimes.

Finally, we were in the car driving down the road. "Oh, no, the sweatshirts!" I shouted from the back seat. Dad slammed on the brakes.

"What about the sweatshirts?" he asked, looking back at me with that annoyed expression he sometimes has when things aren't in order.

"We forgot them."

Dad spun the car around, all the time mumbling under his breath something about being unorganized. I wanted all the governors to sign the sweatshirts. They were going to be souvenirs for Jon and me. Going back to the motorhome put us twenty minutes behind schedule. This also really bugged Dad. He lives by another important motto: "If you're not five minutes early, you're ten minutes late." Whatever that means.

As we drove into Augusta, Maine's capital, I felt excited and nervous, happy and tense, all at the same time. I stepped out of the car and straightened out the wrinkles in my dress. There were butterflies, no, more like a flock of birds, in my stomach. I stretched and looked up at the towering capitol building in front of me. It was surrounded by a manicured lawn and hardwood trees. The outside was made of granite, and a green dome was perched on the top. We walked through the front doors. I could hear the echoes of children laughing. I thought they were probably on a field trip to the capitol.

Mom led the way to the governor's office. She checked in with the secretary. A moment later, a man from the governor's staff introduced himself and apologized for the governor, who was running behind.

"The Governor was scheduled to have lunch with a group of school kids, and it's going a little longer than we planned," he told us.

I didn't mind the wait. I figured it would give me more time to study my questions. In the background, I could hear the kids singing songs led by Governor King. It sounded like he was having fun. He must like kids. I peered around the corner to see the governor sitting among the students. He was wearing a blue dress shirt and a colorful tie. He smiled as he ate cake and ice cream with them. I started pacing the hall, thinking about my questions and trying to convince myself that I'd be fine. Knowing that Governor King actually wanted to meet with me boosted my confidence. Mom and I made one more trip to the bathroom so she could mess with my hair, even though I thought it looked fine. Finally, they called my name. The governor's aide led the way through the narrow hallway and into his office.

"Governor King, this is Amy Burritt."

"Hello, Amy, how are you?" he asked.

"I'm fine," I said, taking a deep breath. He shook my hand, then looked down at Jon.

"Who's this young man?"

Jon, who's pretty shy, managed to squeak out, "I'm Jon."

"Well, hello Jon, are you here to help your sister?" the governor asked.

"Yep."

"Well, Amy, I understand that you want to interview me. What is it you'd like to know?" I unfolded the sheet of paper with my questions on it, and I started at the beginning. I was shaking like the cowardly lion in the *Wizard of Oz*.

"We've been traveling around Maine, and from what we've seen so far, it's a beautiful state. We were ...I was ...I wanted to know, um

... what ...I mean ...why would someone want to come and live in your state?"

I was so flustered, I couldn't even talk. Governor King must have been relieved when I finally finished my question. I'm sure he knew I was nervous. He smiled.

"Oh, that's easy. Because it's beautiful, and we have very nice people." I told him I'd noticed how friendly everyone was to us.

"Why did you choose to be an independent governor?" I managed to ask, still very nervous.

"Because I thought that the parties were playing too many political games, and I wanted to come from the outside and say, 'Enough of this bickering, let's get on with it.'"

"Okay," I said. "What are your state's greatest needs, and how do you plan on taking care of them?"

"More jobs. And, you and I don't have time enough for me to explain how I'm going to take care of that, but one of the things we're doing is ..."

I drifted off in thought. If I ever became governor, I would have to take care of a lot of problems in the state, and I wouldn't be like the governors who didn't meet with me. I would let kids come and visit me anytime, like this governor. My train of thought was interrupted by silence. Oops, the governor was done with his answer, and I hadn't heard a word he said. Quickly, I asked my next question.

"One of my goals is to meet all of the governors. What is your greatest political goal?"

"To leave Maine better than it was when I came into office. More jobs, better schools, cleaner environment."

After several more questions, I finished my interview.

*Governor King, our first signature.*

"Well those are all the questions I have, Governor. But we have two sweatshirts that we'd like all the governors to sign, and we were wondering if you would sign them for us."

"Sure," Governor King said. "How many have you seen?"

"You're the first one," I smiled, feeling relief for the first time since the interview began.

We took a picture with the governor and thanked him for his time. Walking out of the capitol, Mom and Dad told me I'd done a great job.

"The funny thing is, I don't remember any of it," I said. "I was so nervous that my mind just went blank. I don't remember any of his answers to my questions."

"That's why we're video taping each interview, Amy," Mom said, "so you don't have to worry about trying to remember everything. You just need to concentrate on the governor's answers at the time, and, of course, on standing up straight." We laughed. My project was finally underway. One interview done, only 49 more to go.

# 4

# puppy love

Daniel Webster. Here was a guy who really did some interesting things during his lifetime. Webster was born on January 18, just one day before my birthday, but about 200 years earlier. He ran for president as a Whig candidate against Martin Van Buren in 1836, but lost. One of Webster's most important accomplishments was settling a dispute with Great Britain about the Maine/Canada border in 1842.

Webster's boyhood home was a little brown log cabin with small windows and simple furniture. A humble beginning for a man who accomplished so much. As I peered through the little glass window into the old living room, I wondered what Daniel Webster did for fun when he was my age. I didn't see any toys laying around, but I figured he must have liked to explore. How else would he have discovered the Old Man In The Mountain? The Old Man, as it's often referred to, is a naturally formed rock, sitting at the top of a mountain, and looks just like an old man's face.

One of the things I learned about Webster was when he was young, he was too shy to stand up in front of his class and give a report. Also, since he was such a scrawny kid, he was the only one in his family who didn't have to do the hard work necessary to survive in that era. It sounded like he probably got picked on a lot, too. I liked knowing he overcame all that to make a difference in the world.

We enjoyed the rest of the day, driving all over the back roads of New Hampshire. The mountains and hardwoods make it green, like Vermont, and the lakes and mountains are very scenic. New Hampshire sits along a small strip of the Atlantic Ocean. It has a lot to offer for a small state.

I took Shasta for her afternoon walk the next day through the Mile Away Campground. With all of the trees, it reminded me of the campgrounds in Michigan. Shasta spotted another dog and started going crazy, barking and pulling away. I had to yank her leash to make her behave. The man walking the other dog stopped to talk with me for a minute. His name was Henri, and his dog, Alex, was a beautiful Bichon Frise like Shasta, except much taller. The two dogs seemed to like each other, and they wanted to play.

When I got back to the motorhome, I asked if we could invite Henri and Alex over for dinner. Since Mom and Dad had already met Henri, they said that would be fine. Henri was an older man who lived alone in Rhode Island. He spent every summer at the campground and knew most of the regulars there. He was retired from the United States Air Force and very proud of it. Alex was his constant companion.

I created a formal invitation to Alex from Shasta on our computer, inviting the Bichon and his Human to dinner. Henri cracked up when I delivered it to him and said he'd be happy to come. Shasta and Alex spent most of the evening chasing each other up and down the hall in the motorhome. They had a great time playing together, and they entertained us all evening.

After Henri and Alex left, all we had to do was mention the name Alex and Shasta would bounce up onto the motorhome dashboard to look for her special friend.

The day of my meeting with New Hampshire Governor Stephen Merrill was approaching quickly. A few days before, we'd received a call from Governor Dean's office in Vermont. They decided to schedule a meeting with me after all, but the only time they could do it was on the same day I was scheduled to meet with Governor Merrill. I wasn't very happy about the conflict when Mom first told me.

"Two states in the same day?" I shrieked. "How are we possibly going to do that?"

Dad pulled out the map and started adding up the mileage between the

*Jon and me on a rock in the mountains.*

two capital cities. He was always calm in these situations. He was the one who reassured us everything would work out fine.

"We'll be cutting it close," he said. "If we don't waste any time, we should be able to make it."

Dad spent a lot of time studying the maps, planning the roads we would take to get where we needed to go. Usually, we'd take the scenic route, but not this time. We'd have to hurry to make it to Vermont to meet Governor Dean.

My first meeting was at eleven in the morning with Governor Merrill in Concord, the capital of New Hampshire. On the way there, Mom and Dad were figuring out how much time I'd have to talk with the governor.

"We'll have to leave the capitol no later than noon," Dad said, "or we'll miss the meeting with Governor Dean. Okay, let's move it." He parked the car at the capitol.

The secretary greeted us inside the governor's office. "It'll be a few moments before the Governor is ready, so you may have a seat."

We set up our camera equipment and waited for him to arrive. A few minutes later, he came out of his office to greet me.

"Hello, Amy, I'm Governor Merrill, how are you?"

"I'm fine, thanks. Congratulations, Governor, I heard your wife just had a baby. You must be really happy."

"I sure am," he said, smiling. He was excited. We shook hands, Dad took some pictures, and the governor signed my sweatshirts. He told me I could ask his press coordinator my questions.

"Thank you, Governor, for taking the time to meet with me, I really appreciate it."

"You're welcome, young lady," he said, as he handed me a small black notebook with the state seal on the cover and a pen that read *Stephen Merrill, Governor, New Hampshire*. "I think this will be helpful for taking notes during your interviews with the other governors."

"Thank you, this will be great." I never expected to receive gifts from a governor.

We then met with the governor's press coordinator, and his answers were very thorough. I noticed Dad was tapping his black dress shoes and checking his watch.

"It's almost twelve o'clock," Dad mouthed anxiously. "We have to get going."

Feeling rushed, we packed up our equipment and hurried to the car to begin the two-hour journey to Montpelier. My meeting was scheduled for two thirty, so we didn't have time to goof around. A quick stop at Taco Bell and a reminder from Mom, "Don't spill on your dress, Amy," and we were on our way.

I was excited that Governor Dean had called back and wanted to meet with me, especially after all we went through the first time we were in Vermont. All the way there I was rehearsing my questions, trying to memorize them. I really wanted to be prepared for the interview. This time, the scheduler was there to talk with us when we arrived.

"I'm sorry for the mix-up last time you were here," she said. "Things have been hectic around here because of the flooding in Vermont. Governor Dean even had to postpone his vacation. He will be with you in a few moments."

I picked up a magazine and leafed through it. Mom was setting up the video camera, and Dad was fidgeting with his own camera. Jon was stretched out on the couch, bored to death. Finally, Governor Dean walked in the room.

"Hi Amy, I'm Governor Dean." He shook hands with all of us. "I'm in the middle of an important meeting, but I have time for a quick picture."

I could see the frustration in Mom's face. She didn't say a word. I wondered why they would schedule my interview with the governor in the middle of an important meeting? Even Mom is more organized than that.

As he signed the sweatshirts, he asked, "Where are you headed next?"

"To Massachusetts," Mom said, trying not to reveal any anger.

"Oh, well, you'll have a harder time getting in to see Governor Weld than you did me," he stated in a very matter-of-fact manner. He said good-bye and disappeared as quickly as he'd arrived.

"We came all the way here for that?" Mom asked angrily.

"Honey," Dad said to her, "just let it go."

We packed up the equipment and stepped onto the elevator.

I had an uneasy feeling about the next governor. I didn't have a meeting scheduled with Governor Weld. If it was going to be harder to get in there than it was at Governor Dean's office, things weren't looking too promising. I had to remind myself that part of an adventure is the challenge.

# 5

# mayflower journey

Istretched sleepily. Barely awake, I stood in front of the cooler doors at the campground store. The sliding door squealed as I opened it to pull out a gallon of milk. The chill of the cool air blew over me, and I slid the milk carton off the shelf. My arm dropped abruptly. For some reason, the milk felt heavier than usual. We'd traveled from Concord, New Hampshire to Boston, Massachusetts, the previous day. It wasn't very far, but Dad took the scenic route again. We'd been doing so much lately, I was exhausted. We were settled in at the Boston Hub KOA. I could already hear loud noises coming from the game room where kids were allowed to play video games for free. I wondered how they could stand all that noise so early in the morning.

After breakfast, I continued my schoolwork. I was learning about the early beginnings of America, but it was our visit to Boston that brought things to life for me.

Our first stop in Boston was the capitol. We weren't able to arrange an interview with Governor Bill Weld, which didn't surprise us, but he did agree to sign the sweatshirts. I was beginning to feel discouraged about my plans for the trip, but my emotions would end up being minor when compared to how I would feel in Alaska. It also made me mad that Governor Dean had been right. I wondered why the governors in the east seemed so difficult. I had meetings scheduled with many governors in the south and the west, but these governors were very difficult to reach. Still, I decided a signature was better than nothing.

A security guard was sitting at a desk when we walked into the governor's reception room. He wore a uniform like a police officer, but I didn't think too much about it since I'd seen guards at the other capitols. We were walking by him to see the secretary, and all of a sudden he jumped up out of his seat and asked us what we were doing. A little startled by the guard, Mom explained.

"Do you have an appointment?" the guard asked sternly.

"Well, no," Mom said, "but the governor agreed to sign Amy's sweatshirts, so we're dropping them off." He looked through the bag before he allowed us to pass. *Boy, they don't trust anyone around here*, I thought. We left the shirts behind and headed out to explore the city.

Boston is an amazing city. There are so many buildings from different time periods. There's a three-mile historic path called the *Freedom Trail* that winds through the city past many interesting and historical places. This would be like an adventure through history. Beginning in downtown Boston, and ending at the edge of town at Bunker Hill, we followed the red line painted on the sidewalk that designates the *Freedom Trail*.

During our walk, I saw where the Boston Tea Party took place. On the night of December 16, 1773, a group of colonists snuck down to the Boston Harbor disguised as Indians and dumped 342 chests of tea into the harbor. They committed this act to show Britain how angry they were about the taxes on tea being raised without their approval. I saw Paul Revere's home and saw the tombstone under which he is buried. I walked aboard the *U.S.S. Constitution,* one of our country's first naval ships. It was launched at Boston in 1797 and carried forty-four guns.

We walked to Quincy Market. It reminded me of something called a Greek agora, which was one of the things we studied in school the year before. In ancient Greece, people would gather together in what would probably be called a farmer's market in modern times. Everyone brings stuff they've made to sell, like jewelry, food, or clothing. In Quincy Market, we also enjoyed watching street performers entertaining the crowd with juggling and music. There were all kinds of things going on. It was a fun place.

Mom and I were having a great time shopping, but Jon complained, "I can't walk any more or my legs will fall off." I wish I had a dollar for every time Jon said his legs were going to fall off during our entire trip. I would be a millionaire. Since he was tired, we waited for a bus back to the capitol so we could pick up the sweatshirts.

"Let me give you some advice," the secretary said to Mom, as she handed Mom the sweatshirt bag.

"Sure, what is it?"

"Don't give up so easily."

"Thank you," Mom said with a smile, "I won't next time."

That's all Mom needed to hear. She'd been very nice to all the governors' staff when they gave her the run around. She didn't want to force her way into their offices. This secretary made her realize, though, that it was probably the staff that was being difficult, not necessarily the governor, and that maybe she'd have to get a little tougher.

The next day, we visited *Plimoth Plantation,* a living historical site where people reenact the pilgrims' way of life. Plymouth was the first permanent European settlement in New England. The pilgrims sailed to America on the Mayflower and founded Plymouth in December of 1620.

*Plimoth Plantation*

Watching the pilgrim reenactment made some of the hardships that America's early settlers suffered seem more real to me. It was amazing to think they went through all that just to have the freedom to worship God in their own way, something I take for granted.

Driving back to the motorhome that night, I felt blessed to be with my own family and to be free to learn and grow in my own way. I

*Checking out the pilgrim's tools.*

was like a pilgrim, too, taking this journey across America. As I fell asleep that night, I tried to imagine what it would've been like to have been sleeping on the Mayflower, instead of in my comfortable motorhome. The next day, I wrote my thoughts down in my journal.

*October 14, 1620*

*Dear Journal,*

*We've been on the Mayflower for about a month now. Nearly everyone is seasick, even me. The ship moves along slowly. Below deck, where I have to spend most of my time because of the orders from Captain Jones, it is very dark and difficult to see. The Captain may allow us to walk the deck for a short time, but the danger is high. Just yesterday, John Howland was tossed into the ocean, but he was lucky enough to have been seen and rescued.*

*The smell from dirty clothes and pails of vomit burn the nostrils, so we open the hatches for a moment and even though the salty ocean water brings a chill to my spine, the fresh air revives us for a time. Fresh water is scarce and we are not allowed to wash.*

*For the morning rations I was given a hard biscuit, some cheese and salted beef. Once in a while, we get a warm meal and it brings back good memories of the home I left behind.*

*Sometimes when the sea rages against our ship, the caulking breaks loose and the crew comes running with rags to plug the leaks.*

*Many people who wanted to go to the New World could not fit on the ship, so many of us had to leave close friends behind. Now I am making new friends with the other children on board.*

*Mr. Fuller's servant, William Butten, died a few days ago. I'm guessing it was from scurvy but I can't be sure. I wonder what they did with his body?*

*I am anxious to see what the New World will be like, but I also feel afraid. We had to hire a soldier by the name of Miles Standish to come along and help us fight the Indians. We are risking our lives for the freedom to pray and worship God where and when we desire. King James I doesn't permit freedom of religion, he believes everyone should belong to the official state church, the Church of England. That is why we are on this journey to a new land, a land where we can build our own church and worship God without persecution. We have sacrificed so much. Dear God, help us to reach our new land.*

# 6

# junkyard blues

"Hello," the voice on the line said. It was Brittany.

"Hi Britt," I said eagerly.

"Amy?" she questioned.

"Yeah, it's me."

"Where are you?"

"I'm in Rhode Island."

"Melisa," she yelled out. "It's Amy, pick up the phone."

"So, what are you doing?" she asked.

"Oh, lots of stuff. I'm having a great time."

"Hi Amy," Melisa cut in.

"Hi, Mel. How are you?"

"Okay, I guess."

"What have you guys been up to?" I asked.

"I'm taking an art class and learning how to paint with watercolors," Melisa said.

"That's neat."

"Guess what?" Brittany jumped in.

"Ummm, you're taking piano lessons," I said, knowing she was already.

"No," she blurted out. "I mean, yes, I am, but that's not what I meant."

"You cut your hair?" I guessed again. Brittany was always asking me to guess something, so I usually chose an obvious answer. It always drove her crazy.

"No, I joined a basketball team," she said.

"Oh, you're lucky. I want to do that, too," I said, wishing in a way that I could be part of her team.

"Have you guys been to the junkyard?" I asked.

"No. We've been too busy," Mel said.

If I were home we would've gone lots of times, I thought. I remembered one time, when we were searching for things to take back to our tree fort, we found the glass eyeball. We didn't know if it was a real one or not. I put it up to my eye and squeezed my eyelids together to hold it in place. "You look like a mad scientist," Brittany laughed. Melisa tapped me on the shoulder and I turned around to see what she wanted.

"Ahh!!" I yelled, as she thrust a set of false teeth into my face. She and Brittany rolled back on the grass laughing. I grabbed the teeth and said, "I think the gums look a little pale." I picked up a bottle of hot pink nail polish lying in the junkyard, and painted the gums of the dentures. My paint job didn't make them look much better, but we sure had fun that day.

I hung up the phone feeling lonelier than before I'd called. I walked back to the motorhome. Mom asked how it went, but I didn't feel like talking.

"It was okay," I said.

"How are the girls doing, Amy?"

"They're fine," I mumbled.

"What's wrong?"

"Oh, nothing. I just miss them."


It was Labor Day. The only holiday kids don't really like, because it signals their return to school. I'd been in school and studying hard for over a month now, so the holiday didn't bother me. One of the things I liked about homeschooling during the trip was that I did my book work for a few hours in the morning. When I was done with that, we would go out for some sightseeing and hands-on learning in the afternoon, my favorite part of school.

On this Labor Day, though, it was hard to concentrate on my book work with all the commotion from campers staying at the Whispering Pines Campground for a final summer getaway. I sat and watched a family getting ready to leave and packing up their pop-up camper. Dad calls these kind of campers "popovers" because of what can happen when they're in a windstorm. I'm glad we didn't have to travel in one, because we would've spent forever setting up and taking down.

Another family, on the other side of us, was yelling at each other. *Sounds like they're having a lot of fun,* I thought. Their TV blared from the picnic table, where dishes and cardboard boxes heaped with food were piled high. I tried not to stare, but it was too much fun watching. People-watching is one of my favorite pastimes. Parked next to us was a couple in an older motorhome. We named them Wild Wayne and his sidekick Susie. Wild Wayne liked talking to Dad, and he loved telling cowboy stories about the old west. He looked like an old cowboy with his worn jeans, dusty boots, and a wide leather belt with a silver and gold buckle. His wife wore nice, new jeans and her long brown wavy hair was pulled back in a clip. They seemed like really nice people.

After I finished writing a paper on the presidents, we cleaned the motorhome, at Dad's request. When we finished, we went to the beach. Rhode Island is called the Ocean State because much of the state is surrounded by ocean. Swimming in the ocean is entirely different than swimming in Lake Michigan, a freshwater lake. I was playing in the sand when a huge wave came up from behind and knocked me down. The undertow was so strong that it dragged me down the sandy shore and into the water. I didn't get pulled under, but I did get a bad scratch on my leg and it hurt. The power of the ocean is unbelievable.

*A Kodak moment!*

The next morning, Shasta's wet tongue licking my eyelid woke me. It was five-thirty a.m. Mom shook me. "Amy, it's time to get up."

"Mom," I said in a sleepy voice, "Shasta needs a bath."

"There's not much I can do about that right now, Amy. Remember, you have a governor's meeting today."

Before we piled into the car, I checked off our exclusive *Governor's Day Checklist*. We learned, after our first mishap with Maine's Governor King, that a checklist was a good idea, so we wouldn't forget anything. Dad went down the list and called off the items.

"Sweatshirts?" If they were in the car, I would say "Check."

"Video camera?"

"Check."

"Battery?"

"Check."

"Camera?"

"Check."

"Film?"

"Check."

"Tripod?"

"Check."

*Rhode Island's Capitol.*

"Gum?" When Dad got to the gum, I flipped the cupboard door open, grabbed three packs of Big Red and slammed it shut.

"Check," I said and was out the door and into the car.

The front doors of Rhode Island's capitol in Providence were large and heavy. We stepped inside and stopped to admire the elegant building. It seemed as though everything was made from marble: the floors, the walls, even the stairs. The huge staircases were lit with soft-glowing lights that made the lobby feel warm and comfortable. I think, considering Rhode Island is such a small state, it should receive an award for having one of the most beautiful capitol buildings. The governor's reception room was like a palace, decorated with royal reds and golds. The ceiling was high and the wood trim around it had a beautiful design covered with gold leaf. A life-size painting of George Washington loomed over the fireplace. Jon and I sat in the oversized chairs covered with red velvet. I felt small.

"Amy," the secretary announced, "I'd like you to meet Governor Lincoln Almond." He walked over to shake my hand. He was very tall. With my head tilted back, my eyes focused on his white hair.

"Hello, Amy, nice to meet you," he said in a deep voice. His large hand swallowed mine as he shook it firmly.

"Thank you for giving me an interview," I said quietly. He invited me to sit down. I waited for Mom to set up the microphone for Governor Almond before I began my questions.

"What is the main industry in Rhode Island?"

"The main industry in Rhode Island is the health care industry. But, we also have significant interest in jewelry. We're the jewelry capital of the United States, and we're a strong manufacturing state."

"What is the most fascinating attraction in your state?"

"We have a lot of things: a beautiful bay, beautiful beaches, and we have Block Island and Newport."

"What are your greatest personal and political goals?"

"My goal is to do the best possible job that I can for the citizens of the state of Rhode Island." During the year, I would discover that pleasing their citizens was usually a big priority with governors.

"We have two sweatshirts that we're going to have all of the governors sign, and I would love it if you would sign them for us," I explained.

"Amy, how did you feel about that interview?" Dad asked, while we were driving back to the campground.

"It was great. Governor Almond was so easy to talk to, and I felt like he really cared about the people of Rhode Island."

"I was thinking the same thing," Mom said.

Back at the campground, two young boys were waiting for Jon at our picnic table.

"I'm going to get my tennis shoes on," Jon told them, "then I can play."

"You have sneakers?" one of the boys asked.

"Yeah," Jon said, "don't you?"

"Nope," the boy answered, "we don't have any money." Jonathan looked at me. He didn't know what to say to the boy.

"Where do you live?" I asked him.

"We live here," he said.

"In Rhode Island?"

"In the campground. We don't have a house."

"Oh." I felt bad for the kid, the only shoes he had were the vinyl sandals he was wearing.

That night, Jon and I talked with Mom and Dad about the boys. "Can I give some of my clothes to that boy?" Jon asked.

"Sure," Mom said. "You go through your drawer and take out anything you would like to give him, and I'll see that he gets it."

The next morning, Mom took the bag down to the camp office. She asked the lady there to give them to the boys. Mom learned that the father lost his job and then they lost their home. I was glad we could do something to help their situation. This wasn't the first time I'd heard about kids living in a campground. I remembered those kids in the campground back in New York. Seeing somebody like that little boy, who'd be happy with just a pair of sneakers, made me realize how blessed I was.

# 7

# security check

"You'll be speaking to about 200 kids," my great uncle said, as we walked down the school hallway. "I've been telling my classes that you're coming, and they're looking forward to meeting you."

"Really?" I asked, my voice echoing through the halls. I started to feel butterflies fluttering inside me at the thought of such a big group. Students were getting out of their classes, and I noticed they were looking at me. Some girls came up to me and asked, "Are you Amy Burritt?"

Surprised they knew my name, I managed a weak, "Yes."

"I can't wait until you speak." "How many states have you been to?" "Which one did you like the best?" "Have you met our Governor?" "How do you like homeschooling?" It was noisy in the hall, and I was bombarded with questions. Some I answered, some I couldn't quite hear, but it helped calm my nerves to know the kids were excited to hear about my trip.

I was at the William J. Johnston School in Colchester, where my Dad's Uncle Richard was a teacher. He's about 6'5" and towers above everyone at the school. He also has an accent, although he argued with me on that point. He said we were the ones who talked funny. Uncle Richard had asked me to give a presentation to his classes about my adventure.

Our display for the presentation showed some of the things we'd collected so far: granite from Vermont, broken bones, a piece of a lobster cage, state pins, and flags. I also showed slides of the things we'd seen and done. I spoke, Dad operated the slide projector, Mom ran the video camera, and Jon watched over the display table. Near the end of the program, I gave everyone time to ask questions. The kids had so many things to ask that we ran out of time before I could answer all of them. Even though I had fun, I was relieved when the presentation was over. It took more energy to do that than interviewing the governors.

I had my interview with Governor John Rowland at Connecticut's capitol in Hartford. After an hour drive there from the Odetah Campground, Dad took the exit for the capitol. He drove the car around the building, looking for a parking spot and ended up back on the freeway.

"Kurt, where are you going?" Mom asked.

"I don't know, I was just trying to find a parking spot," he said, frustrated.

"Dad, we don't have time to goof around this morning," I told him. "I have an interview in just a few minutes." Mom and Jon laughed at my humor, but Dad didn't think my remark was funny.

"The roads in the East are confusing, you guys. Give me a break."

He took another exit, turned around, and headed back to the capitol. This time we found a parking spot. The capitol was huge. It looked like a gothic castle. Inside was a statue of Nathan Hale. He was the guy who said, "I only regret that I have but one life to lose for my country." Out of all the capitols I'd seen so far, this was my favorite.

We checked in at the governor's reception area and sat down to wait.

It was only eight-thirty in the morning, so it was quiet. While we were waiting, Governor Rowland walked past us to his office. He was smiling and joking with the secretaries and security men. He looked like he was in his thirties, clean shaven and cheerful. I had a feeling it was going to be a fun interview.

The secretary announced the governor was ready to see me. As I walked through the large cherry wood doors, I saw him walking toward us with his hand outstretched and a huge smile on his face. He greeted me with a handshake and then leaned down to shake Jon's hand. Pointing to me he asked Jon, "Is this your wife?" Jon laughed and shook his head. The governor teased him, saying he had a daughter about his age and wondered if Jon would like to meet her. Jon shook his head again. He's pretty shy, especially when it comes to girls. We chatted about our trip and some of the places we'd been. Then the governor and I sat down to begin the interview.

I started to ask my first question, but Governor Rowland jumped up out of his chair and said, "Wait a minute, I want to show you and your brother some stuff." We followed him around the room as he showed us pictures of his kids and his wife. He pointed to a picture of himself on a roller coaster.

*Jon and me with Governor Rowland.*

"I don't even like roller coasters," he said. "There was a theme park that was closed for remodeling, and I made a promise to the people that I would be the first one to ride the roller coaster when it reopened." The picture showed his security guys with their hands in the air and a few other people screaming. The only person who didn't look like he was having any fun was Governor Rowland. He was crouched down in the seat looking petrified. "They printed this picture on the front page of the newspaper," he said. "That didn't make me look too good."

We were just about to sit down again when he asked me, "Should I wear my suit jacket?"

"It doesn't matter," I laughed. I liked how the meeting was going.

"Would you like some coffee or tea, or maybe a Coke?" the governor asked. I smiled. "No, thank you."

"Good, 'cause we don't have any, anyway," he joked. "I don't know what to do here," he confided. "I'm a little nervous."

He made me feel comfortable, I wasn't nervous at all. I was thinking to myself how nice it would be if all of the governors were as easy to talk with as Governor Rowland.

During the interview, the governor noticed I was using a note pad from New Hampshire.

"Where'd you get that notebook?" he questioned.

"Uh, Governor Merrill gave it to me," I smiled.

"What else did they give you up there?" Governor Rowland inquired. I held up a pen with Governor Merrill's name on it.

"Anything else?" he asked, as though he was a cop searching for weapons.

"No, that's all," I assured him.

"That's all they gave you? They're cheapskates up there. You aren't allowed to use those things in my office," he said with a smile. He turned to a staff member and said, "Get a Connecticut book, no, get two Connecticut books and some flags and pens and pins. Whatever we have." Then he turned toward me. "We'll fix you up good!"

Like many of the governors, Rowland spends a great deal of time traveling throughout his state, promoting jobs and economic opportunities.

"What's the most fascinating attraction in your state?" I asked him.

"Besides me?" he joked. "No, I'm kidding. Probably Mystic Seaport, although our capitol is really beautiful."

Governor Rowland was so funny, and he made me feel important. I think that's what I liked most.

42

After the interview, we took a tour of the capitol. Lafayette's Bed was preserved there, and our guide told us the story behind it. Lafayette was a soldier in the Revolutionary War. His full name was Marquis Marie Joseph Paul Yves Roch Gilbert du Motier de Lafayette. His friends called him Gilbert. Gilbert's bed was a canvas cot, and canvas stretches so much that it would sag and be uncomfortable. He would call over a couple of guys and have them tighten the canvas on his bed by pulling the strings on the sides of the cot and tying them. That's where the saying "sleep tight" originated.

Governor Rowland invited us to tour his mansion that afternoon. The mansion was on the other side of town, and on the way there, we got lost and ended up in downtown Hartford. It was a very poor part of town, and I started to get worried when we began seeing houses boarded up and bars on the windows.

"This doesn't look good, Dad," I said. On the news the night before, I had seen a story about all the crime in Hartford. "I don't like it here at all."

"That's good," Dad began.

"What do mean that's good?" I interrupted.

"Maybe someday you'll do something to change it."

We made it to the governor's mansion just in time for our appointment. As we followed the tour guide, I noticed there was a security man following us.

"Hi, how are you doing?" Dad asked him.

"Good," the man answered. "How's the trip going?" Mom and Dad looked at him.

"How did you know about our trip?" Mom asked.

He told them he knew everything about us. He has to do security checks on everyone who visits the governor or his house. This security guard must have done his homework. He even knew my Uncle Mike is on a Bomb Squad. It was really strange. I was amazed to think they knew so much about us, but we knew nothing about them.

*September 15...I saw Yale University and Mystic Seaport this week. It's a tourist attraction where they reenact historical things such as boat building. I was asked to play the piano in a restaurant while the regular pianist took a dinner break. It was fun.*

# 8

# mr. swan and the great seal

Atlantic City, where all your dreams come true. Not. Many people come to Atlantic City to gamble, with big dreams of making a fortune. The majority of them go home with less money than they had when they came. We arrived in Atlantic City around noon and we walked along the wooden pier known as the Boardwalk for over two hours. We picked up shells and threw clams back into the ocean. We were surrounded by casinos, but there wasn't much happening. Probably because it was the middle of the day and things don't start hopping there until night. I think gambling is a complete waste of money. Working hard is a much smarter way to make money rather than leaving it up to chance.

Since there wasn't much for us to do in Atlantic City, except gamble, we got back in the car and drove south to Cape May. I liked this town. It sits right on the ocean. People can rent bikes to ride along the sidewalks, which wind all over town. I think it would be a fun place to stay for awhile.

New Jersey is basically flat, but it has a lot of Atlantic shoreline like Rhode Island. It also had the only female governor in the United States when we visited, and I couldn't wait to meet her, Governor Christine Whitman.

The capitol building in Trenton was being renovated when we arrived, so it was quite messy outside. When we found the governor's office, Mom asked to speak with the scheduler. A staff member asked us to have a seat while they looked for her. As I sat in the small office, I noticed a nice-looking woman standing in the doorway. She was medium height, blonde hair, thin and pretty. The blue skirt and jacket she was wearing looked sharp. She must be the governor, I thought.

Surrounded by staff and security, she started walking my way. I scrambled to get the sweatshirts out of the bag, but Dad said to wait. He figured it was lunchtime, and if she was going out, that meant she'd probably have to come back in. So we waited. And waited. And waited.

Finally, after what seemed like hours, we heard a group of people walking down the hall. The governor was coming back from lunch. I had the sweatshirts out and ready. She was walking past us and suddenly stopped and walked right over to me.

"Hello," Governor Whitman said. "How are you?" She reached out her hand to shake mine.

I was so surprised, I didn't know what to say. Mom saw that I was speechless, so she jumped in to help.

"Hello, Governor, I'm Emily Burritt from Traverse City, Michigan, and we're on a year-long tour of America to visit all fifty states. This is our eighth state. My daughter, Amy, has a goal to interview all 50 governors, and we wondered if you would be willing to sign these sweatshirts?"

"Of course. I'm sorry I couldn't meet with you. Please leave me your questions and I'll return them to you," she said, as she signed the shirts. "I'm just on my way to a press conference, would you like to join me?"

"Sure, I'd like that," I said, able to speak once again.

We followed her into a room full of reporters. I watched as she answered questions. It was cool to think she was the only woman governor in office, and I was watching her in action.

When the press conference was over, we went down the hall to the Secretary of State's office. Because the governor wasn't available for an interview, Mom had arranged for me to interview Lonna Hooks, New Jersey's Secretary of State. We agreed it would give me the opportunity to learn about some of the other jobs in government. I even prepared a new list of questions.

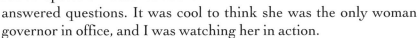

*Interviewing Lonna Hooks, New Jersey's Secretary of State.*

"What are your duties as the Secretary of State?" I asked, from across the large wooden table. She spoke calmly as she answered my question.

"Well, as Secretary of State, I have a lot of responsibilities. I am the keeper of the Great Seal of the state of New Jersey," she began. "I keep track of all the businesses in the state and also the state elections. I also run the Division of Archives. We have an original signed copy of the Bill of Rights, which many people from around the country and the world like to borrow, and I keep track of that. I am also in charge of improving our roads. We have a lot of traffic coming through our state, so we have to keep our roads in good shape. New Jersey's Constitution is different from other states. We don't have a Lieutenant Governor, so I take on those responsibilities, along with my other jobs."

I liked talking with Lonna, and I appreciated the fact that she took my project seriously.

I woke up early the next morning, pulled out my journal, and tried to catch up on the day before. After my interview with Lonna Hooks, there was a lot to write about, and I'd already learned if I didn't write each day, I'd forget details and funny stories. I turned the coffee pot on and looked at the clock. It was only 5:00 a.m. Mom and Dad wouldn't be up for two or three hours. I looked out the window and watched the leaves swirling around the ground. I must be the only one awake in the whole campground. We were at the Tip Tam Campground. The camping season was almost over since everyone was back in school. We practically had the whole place to ourselves. Journaling was the hardest job I had on the trip. Writing down everything that happened and my thoughts and feelings about them took a lot of time and energy, so moments like these were good for catching up.

After Jon and I finished our schoolwork for the day, all four of us climbed into the car for a drive to the western side of New Jersey.

A sign marked the spot where General George Washington crossed the Delaware River. It read *Washington's Crossing*, so it wasn't too hard to figure out what it meant. Before we crossed the river, we stopped at the Visitors Center. Ivy was growing all over the sides of the building. It reminded me of the book, *The Secret Garden*.

We went inside and watched a movie showing a reenactment of the Revolutionary War. After the movie, we toured the historical museum. A big collection of artifacts from the war were on display. There were guns and bullets that were actually used in the Revolutionary War, medical kits, gun powder pouches, and a handwritten note from General George Washington. Those were the treasures I liked the best.

As I gazed at the different artifacts, I wondered if any of them had been discovered by kids horsing around the way Melisa, Brittany and I did in the woods behind my house in Michigan.

Mr. Swan owned most of the stuff in the museum, and he proudly showed us around. When we came to a glass case, he said, "I have something very special in here for you to see that very few people have ever touched." He reached into his pocket and pulled out a key and proceeded to unlock the case. With great care he handed a metal object to Mom. "Do you know what that is?" he asked.

"No, I don't think so," Mom said.

"Look closely at it. What do you see?"

"Uh, an eagle and ..."

"That's right," he said. "It's the Great Seal."

Mom looked at him with a puzzled expression on her face. Then Mr. Swan turned to me and asked, "Do you know what the Great Seal is, young lady?" His dark eyes seemed to look right through me, and the only answer I could think of was the great seal I saw at Sea World. I shook my head.

"Well, I'll tell you what it is," he said slowly. I didn't have any doubt he would, either. He'd told us about everything else in the museum. "The Great Seal is what they used to put the stamp on the dollar bill, and there are only a few of these around. Do you have a dollar bill?" he asked, turning to look at Dad. Dad reached into his wallet and handed Mr. Swan a dollar. "See, here on the back is the stamp of the Great Seal."

He was right, it was the same stamp. He looked at Mom and said, "Why don't you take a picture of the little girl and boy holding the Great Seal?"

*What?* I thought. *I'm not a little girl, I'm almost thirteen.*

At the end of our week in New Jersey, our answers from Governor Whitman arrived in the mail. Aunt Sue gathered our mail in Traverse City and mailed it once a week to the campground where we were staying. The governor's letter read:

Dear Amy:

I am glad we had a chance to meet, even if it was only briefly. I will try to give you concise answers to all the questions you asked.

... New Jersey is known for its high technology and for being the home of some of the largest pharmacy and biotechnology companies. We also have some of the world's premier boat-building facilities in New Jersey ...

The most fascinating attraction in our state is its diversity. From the highest point of Sussex County to the lighthouse in Cape May, New Jersey offers endless fascination.

The best known historical site is Washington Crossing, scene of the famous battle that represented Washington's first significant victory over the Hessian troops ....

I hope this information is helpful to you. All the best.

Yours sincerely,

Christine Todd Whitman

*September 20...As we've been traveling I've noticed that it's hard to find a decent radio station; I don't have all the ones I'm used to from home. I didn't know that the Statue of Liberty was actually in New Jersey. Went to the campus of Princeton. Told Dad I wanted to go to college there. He said, "Start saving your money." Bought a sweatshirt instead.*

# 9

# one soldier's struggle

I felt like I was traveling through time as we drove through Lancaster County, Pennsylvania, where a small community of Amish live. Because of their religious beliefs, the Amish people live very differently than most of us. They believe in being independent from the world, living in this world, but not of it.

We were exploring the back roads on our way to Pennsylvania's capital, Harrisburg. We drove past plain Amish farms. The Amish don't use electricity in their homes or barns, though some use generators, and the houses are very simple. The paint on the walls of their homes is glossy blue, green or brown. They do this because glossy is easier to wipe clean than flat paint and because those are nature's colors. Green for grass, blue for the sky, and brown for the soil.

It must have been wash day when we drove by, because lines of black and white clothes were strung from houses to barns. Instead of cars, we saw horse-drawn buggies. At one point, we saw two young children walking beside the road dressed in traditional Amish clothing. Dad slowed our car down. The little boy wore black pants, black shoes, and a white shirt. He also wore a black hat with a flat top and wide brim. The little girl had on a long dark dress with a white apron over it, and on her head was a white cap with the

strings dangling on her shoulders. She was barefoot, and in her hand she carried a small basket. As much as we wanted to take a picture, we didn't, because we knew it was best to respect their beliefs. The Amish don't want their pictures to be taken, because they believe it would be disobeying the commandment of the Bible, "You must not make for yourselves a graven image."

Arriving in Harrisburg, I felt confident about meeting Governor Tom Ridge. We were realistic enough at that point to know he probably didn't know anything about my project, but his staff had told us there would be no problem scheduling an interview with him. When we arrived at the governor's office, however, they had a different story.

We waited in the large reception room for about ten minutes before a woman came out to talk with us. "I'm sorry," she said. As soon as I heard those words, I knew what it meant. "Governor Ridge just doesn't have time for an interview."

"Then why were we told all this time that it wouldn't be a problem to schedule an interview?" Mom asked.

"Well, I don't know who was telling you that, but they were wrong."

*Oops! Where's the governor?*

"Why don't I give you his name, and we can call him out here and ask him personally," Mom stated in a matter-of-fact manner. It was obvious the woman didn't want to discuss it any further, and I could tell she was getting a little frustrated with Mom's persistence.

"That won't be necessary, because the Governor still doesn't have time in his schedule." I decided maybe I should say something to help Mom.

"Do you think the Governor would be willing to at least sign my sweatshirts?" I asked, flashing my best smile.

"Yes, I think he would do that for you." When she brought the sweatshirts back, I looked at his signature. The front of the sweatshirts were filling up. I was only missing one signature, but I still wished I had more opportunities to actually meet the governors and talk with them.

We finished studying the Revolutionary War a few mornings later, and Mom read the story, *The Winter At Valley Forge*. This was an account of how General George Washington and his army tried to survive a long winter with very little food and supplies during the Revolutionary War. The men remained committed to George Washington and the cause of freedom, despite the fact they didn't have the right tools to fight a battle or even shoes for their feet. Things were so bad, the men were forced to live off tasteless "fire cakes" (primitive biscuits made from coarse flour and water) and drink melted snow water. Many of them suffered from smallpox and "camp fever," otherwise known as typhus. The saddest part about the whole story was that just a few miles away, thousands of barrels of flour sat, spoiling, on the banks of the Susquehanna River, and huge supplies of beef and pork meant for the army were rotting in New Jersey. Unfortunately, there was no way to transport the supplies to the hungry troops due to great amounts of snow piling up, cutting off the roads to Valley Forge.

We walked through the tiny cabins at Valley Forge, where men had eaten and slept on dirt floors. There weren't even windows in the small cabins. It was amazing to see it all and then realize that, against all odds, this poorly suited, all-volunteer army conquered the British during the worst winter our nation had ever seen.

As I walked around the grounds, along the paths once walked by those brave soldiers, I tried to imagine what it must have been like for them. To be away from their families, living in such disgusting conditions. What kept them going?

Not long after the Revolutionary War ended, this new nation adopted the U.S. Constitution. It was a set of rules that were created by delegates from each state to form a stronger government. The colonial leaders (the guys with the funny wigs) were afraid that they didn't make a set of rules for every state to follow, the whole Union would fall apart. Their other worry was giving government too much power, which would take away the rights of the people. So all the guys in the wigs agreed that a balance of power between three branches of government would be really important.

The Constitution gives the government the power to raise taxes, regulate trade, and build an army. To be sure these things were done rightly, the early leaders put together two groups. One is called the Senate, made up of two people from every state who are called Senators. The other is the House of Representatives, and the number of Representatives is determined by how many people live in each state. The Senate and the House of Representatives, also called Congress, make up the Legislative branch of government.

The second branch is called the Executive branch. It has a President and Vice President. The President is in charge of executing all the rules. He is also in charge of the army, and he picks the judges for the third branch, called the Judicial branch.

It's simple, I thought. They're like clubs. If I wanted to form a club with a bunch of my friends, we would definitely need to create some rules.

The people who created the Constitution knew it wasn't perfect, and in time realized they had to make some changes. They got together and came up with ten changes to the Constitution they called the Bill of Rights. These ten rules keep Congress from passing any laws that hurt a person's rights and guarantees many of the freedoms we enjoy, such as freedom of speech.

For one assignment, Mom had Jonathan make a tree out of construction paper with three big branches to help him remember. He labeled them the Executive, Judicial, and Legislative.

Pennsylvania sure has a lot of history, I thought, as we pulled out of the Spring Gulch Campground. We were back in the car headed to Gettysburg, where many Civil War battles were fought. The Civil War was the war that split our country in half from 1861 to 1865. The country was divided on states' rights, slavery, and other issues. The northern states, or the Union, wanted to abolish slavery, while the southern states, called the Confederacy, depended on slavery for their cotton farming, the key to their strong economy.

I walked along the rows of cannons where thousands of young men lost their lives and I wondered how it felt to be faced with something as terrifying as war. Later, I wrote about it in my journal.

*The deafening sound of the blasting cannons pierces through my soul. Suddenly, a bullet penetrates the soldier next to me, and I watch as he stumbles to the ground. I am afraid for my life. Another bullet whizzes past my ear. I fire a shot. At who or what, I don't know, but fear pulls the trigger. The open field around me is littered with dead and wounded soldiers. I have to keep a sharp eye, for the smoke from the guns is blinding. I am one of the infantry men in the United States Civil War, fighting in this battle of Gettysburg. This war between the North and the South has been raging for some time now. I may give my life in battle, but so have many of my friends.*

# 10

# something
# is different

I remember Ohio as a long turnpike leading me home. During our trip, we would travel through Ohio several times and experience interesting adventures, but on this first visit, I just wanted to go home.

We'd been gone for almost ten weeks, and I was so homesick. I was actually relieved when Governor Voinovich's office said no to my request for an interview. I believed we'd find a way to catch up with him later.

We stopped at a gas station to fill up the motorhome, and Mom called home to tell her sister Sue when to expect us. As we traveled down the highway, I thought about all the fun things I'd done and seen on this first tour. Visiting the spider web farm in Vermont, going down into a rock quarry, swimming, hiking in the mountains, and getting the eight governors' signatures on my sweatshirt.

I sat on the couch looking out the side window of the motorhome. Northern Ohio is flat with miles and miles of farmland. I saw a billboard advertising Sea World. It reminded me of the time I went there with Melisa, Brittany, and another friend, Kahla, last summer. We had a blast. There was so much to tell Melisa and Brittany about this trip. I couldn't wait to share my adventures with them.

We were back on the turnpike with the campground where I lost my lizard pendant at the beginning of the trip.

"Dad, can we stop and look for my lizard pendant?"

"We can't, Amy," Dad said. "We're on the turnpike, it's on the other side and we can't cross over."

"But, we're right here, Dad," I pleaded.

"Amy, someone probably already found it, anyway."

I leaned back in my seat, folded my arms and stared out the window. The hum of the tires made me sleepy. Before long, everything went black.

It was late when we pulled into Traverse City, so Dad made me wait until the next day to call the girls. The next morning we made plans to get together for an overnighter.

Mom drove down the gravel road past our house to Melisa and Brittany's. Even though we weren't living there, it felt good to see my house and woods again. Everything looked just like it had when we left. Dad would be happy to know the renters were taking care of his manicured lawn. For a moment, I thought I saw Max on the front porch.

I stood at Melisa and Brittany's door anticipating our great reunion. Brittany answered the door. "Hi!" I said excitedly.

"Oh, hi, Amy," Brittany said, with little feeling.

I looked up the stairs. There sat Melisa, chin in hand. "Hi, Melisa!" I was still enthusiastic.

"Hi."

I waited for her to run down the stairs to greet me. Instead, we all just looked at each other and said nothing. *What happened?* I thought. *This isn't the response I expected.* Finally, Brittany broke the silence. "Long time, no see," she said.

"Yeah, no kidding. It's been ten weeks," Melisa added.

"Where do you want these?" I held out my pillow and sleeping bag.

"Bring them in my room," Melisa said. I followed Brittany up the stairs.

"What's new?" I asked, as I sat down on Melisa's bed.

"I moved up a level in my gymnastics," Brittany said.

"I'm going to a youth group now," Melisa interrupted. "I'm making lots of new friends."

"Cool, sounds like fun." I was trying to sound happy, but suddenly it was hard. I felt left out. They were going on with their lives without me. It didn't even feel like they'd missed me. I wanted to tell them about what I'd been doing, but it didn't seem important and they didn't seem to want to know.

Melisa put in a CD and hit the play button. "This is the latest Newsboys release," she explained.

Feeling confused, I folded my arms and looked around Melisa's room, searching for something to talk about. "Uh, so what do you guys want to do?"

"Hey, let's go to the junkyard," Brittany grinned.

"But what about my CD?" Melisa asked.

"We can listen to that later, let's go to the junkyard before it gets dark," I suggested. I was eager to do something we'd always enjoyed together.

Melisa gave in. "Okay, let's go." We all jumped up and bounded down the stairs.

That night, as we lay on the floor in our sleeping bags, I tried to figure out why things between us felt so different. Even at our special place, the junkyard, our conversations didn't feel natural. It was like we were all holding back something. Maybe they were afraid to get too close to me, knowing I was leaving again. Part of me wanted to stay and forget about the trip, but a bigger part wanted to leave right away and get on with my adventure. Maybe it's just too hard to share someone else's dream. I guess you have to find your own.

# 11

# my governor

There's no place like home. I love Traverse City. After traveling to so many strange new places, it felt good to be back in familiar territory. Driving downtown the next morning, I smiled as I caught my first glimpse of beautiful, blue Grand Traverse Bay at the edge of town. I soaked up the sight of the storefronts of my favorite shops and restaurants and smiled when I saw Burritt's Market, our family's store. Even the green and white street signs made me feel better.

On our return home, we had parked the motorhome at our friends' beach in Suttons Bay, just north of Traverse City. We stayed there for about 10 days until we left again for Indiana. There were so many things we had to accomplish during our short time home. We had several media interviews scheduled, a presentation at one of the elementary schools, doctor and dentist appointments to attend, visits with family, unpacking and repacking for cooler weather, and our trip downstate to interview my own governor, John Engler.

As busy as we were, though, there wasn't a day that went by when I didn't think about Melisa and Brittany. Our reunion hadn't been what I thought it would be. I really don't know what I expected; I just wanted things to be the way they were before I left. But they weren't. Over the next year, the word friendship would come to mean many things to me, but during my first trip home, I still thought time and distance couldn't have any effect on real friends.

A few days later, we drove to Lansing for my interview with Governor Engler and stayed in a hotel near the capitol. Early the next morning, we walked into his office. All of the cameras and media people gathered around the table made me nervous. This was the first time I had interviewed a governor under such scrutiny. A crew from CNN was there, as well as the Traverse City television crew from TV 9 &10, and a reporter from the Associated Press. As I gazed around the governor's office, I caught glimpses of his personal life. I knew he and his wife, Michelle, were parents of triplets. On one shelf sat three little pairs of ski boots, on another bookcase a teddy bear. A basket full of toys sat on the floor, for the triplets, I guessed, when they came to see their dad.

Jon had the sweatshirts spread out neatly on the dark wooden table. His job during the interview was to make sure the sweatshirts got signed. I wasn't the only one who was nervous. He sat next to me with his legs swinging wildly under the table. I glared at him. He stopped fidgeting and sat still, but glared back at me. The new shoes Mom bought me were pinching my feet. I coughed. I smiled at a reporter, then looked down at my watch. I still had a few minutes to wait. These moments were the hardest, when I had time to stop and think about what I was doing. A twelve-year-old interviewing the governor, was I crazy? I wanted to make this a good interview, because I realized it would be all over the country in newspapers and on TV the next day. I swallowed hard and sat up straighter.

I heard voices in the hall and the shuffling of shoes. The doors opened and in walked Governor Engler. Suddenly, the camera crews hustled over to their cameras, and I stood up to meet my governor.

"Hi, Governor Engler. I'm Amy Burritt."

"Hello Amy. It's nice to meet you," he smiled. He shook hands with me, Jon, and then Mom and Dad. He motioned for me to sit back down. The bright lights from the cameras blinded me for a moment. They didn't seem to bother Governor Engler, he just squinted slightly. He was very professional, more serious than Governor King or Governor Rowland had been. I looked around at the room full of reporters. Was he thinking the same thing I was? Wanting to do a good job representing Michigan?

"Thank you for giving me the opportunity to interview you."

"You're welcome," he said smiling. I felt my body relax a little and I smiled back. He took an immediate interest in my questions. Soon, we were both focused on the interview, forgetting about the media, except for the occasional camera flash.

"What are your duties as governor?"

"I'm the Chief Executive of the state. My most significant duty is to set the tone and direction of government policy."

"What is Michigan's greatest attraction?" I asked.

"The Great Lakes," he said. He folded his hands on the table and leaned closer. "They're the signature of Michigan. From space, astronauts can always see Michigan ... nothing defines us like the Great Lakes."

I thought for a second about what my state looked like from outer space. Everyone pictures a big mitten, but when he said that, I realized Michigan really was one of the few states you could see from such a distance. I knew it was a special place.

"What is Michigan's most interesting historical site?" I asked, glancing up at the big television microphone with a fuzzy gray cover, hovering just inches above my head.

"Greenfield Village has more of what built America," he said, "but Mackinac Island is also interesting."

"What are Michigan's greatest needs and how do you plan on taking care of them?"

*My interview with Governor Engler.*

"To improve the education system and fix the problems with welfare, but our greatest challenge as a nation is the strength of the American family and there's only so much government can do ..."

"What are your personal and political goals?"

"To do the best I can for the people of Michigan ... "

Before I knew it, the interview was over. I had one last request. "Governor Engler, could you help me with the governors of Ohio and New York? I'm having trouble getting them to agree to meet with me."

"Sure, I can drop them a note; that would be the easiest thing," Governor Engler smiled. This would be the second time he had written a letter of support, and I felt as though he really believed my project was important.

The governor set two white boxes on the table. "These are for you, Amy," he said. One was a Michigan paperweight, and the other was an official governor's pen. He then signed a copy of his book, *The Journey of John Engler.* Inside he wrote, "To Amy, with hopes that your journey ends as well, John Engler." I looked forward to enjoying his journey, too.

*most supportive Governor John Engler award*

"Thank you so much," I said, shaking his hand. I watched as he signed the sweatshirts. By being so professional and thoughtful about answering my questions, he'd made me feel important. I now had a better understanding about why he was such a popular governor.

The media surrounded me, and, for a second, the interview tables were turned. They asked me how I thought the governor had done.

"He's great," I told them, and after a few more questions, we were on our way out the door. I took a deep breath. Mom and Dad put their arms around me.

"We're so proud of you Amy," Mom said.

"Amy, you did an excellent job," Dad said, as he squeezed me tight. That made me feel really good. Sometimes, I don't remember much about the interviews. But I did know one thing: I really liked my governor.

"Mom," I asked, as we walked back to our hotel, "can I take these shoes off now?"

"Sure."

We packed our things and headed home.

The next morning, the car phone rang and Dad answered. "You won't believe who that was," he said, hanging up the receiver. "CNN News. They covered the interview with Governor Engler, but now they want to come to our motorhome to interview us."

"Oh no," Jon moaned, "Not another interview." We all laughed. He always said that.

It was exciting to realize the story about our trip was going to be on national news, but ironic that even though we had already traveled almost 10,000 miles, they were going to interview us at home. It was as if we never really went anywhere.

The following week the CNN camera crew arrived. Three people climbed out of a big, gray van, dragging tons of equipment with them.

"Amy, hi, I'm Joan MacFarlane," the reporter said, as she shook my hand. She was tall, had sandy blonde hair, and wore a brown suit. "What a great experience you've had so far. Why don't you have a seat over there by the water? And your little brother, too. What's his name?"

"That's Jon."

"Okay, Jon, you sit here, next to your sister. Now just relax, I'm going to ask you a few questions about your trip. Amy, I'll start with you. Do you like traveling?"

"Yes," I said. "It's a lot of fun exploring new places."

Joan glanced down at her note pad for a moment, then looked back at me. "I understand you're studying history on this trip. Why do you think it's important to learn about history?"

"I think it's important to know what happened back then, so we can be prepared for what might happen in the future, because history repeats itself," I said. What I didn't say, maybe because I was so nervous, was that I used to think history was really boring. It was always the same kind of stuff over and over again. A war here, a takeover there. Then I learned to look at history as a way to learn from our mistakes. That's when history became interesting.

She went on to ask Jon, Mom, and Dad some questions, and after two hours of video taping in the motorhome and at the picnic table, it was over.

The next day I gave a presentation at the Glenn Loomis Elementary School. While we were waiting in the school library, the CNN report aired for the first time. It was weird, but fun, watching myself on television. The segment about our trip only lasted two minutes, but Mom and Dad said that was long for a broadcast news story. Still, I was surprised because we'd spent such a long time talking with the reporter. I realized then how much time and work it took to review all the tapes and edit the parts together to tell our story. It must take someone like Steven Spielberg years just to make one movie.

When I finished my presentation to the kids, many of them raised their hands, eager to ask questions.

"Did you get to go to Disney World?" one girl asked.

"Not yet," I smiled.

"Have you been to the Everglades?" a boy asked.

*Glenn Loomis classes.*

"No, I haven't been to Florida at all yet."

"Do you ever miss your friends?" asked another girl.

"Yes," I paused. My throat tightened. "That's the hardest part, leaving my friends."

# tour two

indiana

kentucky

west virginia

maryland & washington, d.c.

delaware

virginia

north carolina

south carolina

georgia

# 12

# dream list

"Now, that would be a nice way for us to travel," Mom joked, as she pointed to a shiny black limousine. We were sitting outside a coffee shop in downtown Indianapolis, enjoying frozen mocha drinks and waiting for Governor Evan Bayh to sign the sweatshirts.

"Is it on your dream list?" Dad asked.

"No, I'm just kidding," Mom said.

The "dream list" was Dad's idea. One day, during our first tour, Dad gave each of us a note pad and pen with some categories to use as a guide. He told us to list the places in the world we wanted to go, people we'd like to meet, things we wanted to have, and what kind of person we wanted to be. He said not to be concerned about how much it would cost, just write down any dreams we had. It was fun thinking about the things I wanted to do in my life, and it didn't take me long to fill up an entire page. When I read aloud the list of things I wanted to buy, Dad joked, "You'd better include a rich husband on that list, Amy."

I add new dreams to my list all the time. I have everything from getting a new pair of roller blades and hang gliding over the Grand Canyon, to climbing to the top of a mountain and flying a helicopter. As for what kind of person I want to be, it took me a while to come up with something. After seeing that boy in the blue t-shirt back in New York, though, I realized I wanted to be the kind of person who could help make a difference in people's lives. I wrote down *generous* and *helpful* on my dream list. I also dream about meeting Jonathan Taylor Thomas, Jane Seymor, Robin Williams, and, of course, the President.

The best part about my list is when I mark off a dream I've achieved. I put a check next to it and dated it. During the trip I marked off a lot of dreams. The dream list is a great way to keep track of everything I accomplish and to focus on things I still want to do. Nothing is too strange to put on the list, and just because I write it down, doesn't mean I have to do it. My dreams give me a path to follow and great things to anticipate.

"I've added some things to my list," I said, joining in the conversation.

"What are they, Amy?" Mom asked.

"I want to swim with dolphins, go parasailing, stand on top of the Statue of Liberty, and explore Australia."

"Those are great dreams, Amy," Mom said. "I've added going to Europe to my dream list."

As hard as it was to leave my friends and family after our week in Traverse City, it felt good to be back on the road. I was beginning to like the routine of our traveling lifestyle, and I was ready to continue my adventure. We'd all agreed the first tour was too exhausting. This time, we decided to travel at a slower pace and not squeeze in as much activity as we had during the first tour.

The first city we visited was Indiana's capital, Indianapolis. It's the home of the Indianapolis 500 Motor Speedway, where the Indy races are held every spring.

After picking up our sweatshirts from the governor's office, we went to the Children's Museum. Governor Evan Bayh said this is the largest museum of its kind in the world. Jon and I had fun trying out all the unique hands-on activities. Jon loved the airplane cockpit. He sat inside maneuvering all the gadgets, dreaming he was the pilot. Flying airplanes is big on Jon's dream list. I liked the planetarium. It reminded me of all the glow-in-the-dark star stickers I had on the ceiling in my bedroom back in Michigan. I wondered if they were still there.

Traveling south on Highway 65, we passed Franklin, Columbus, Scottsburg, and then Sellersburg. Slowly, the landscape began to change from flat and open to hilly and wooded. We were coming into one of Dad's favorite states, Kentucky.

After we left Indiana, Governor Bayh mailed his answers to my questions. In response to my question about the state's most interesting historical sight, the governor wrote, "Since Indiana was one of the first states beyond the 13 original colonies and was originally the gateway to the west for all Americans, there are many historic sites in Indiana." He mentioned several of them, but one that caught my attention was Conner Prairie. Governor Bayh described it as "an 18th-century village that allows modern visitors to experience colonial life in modern-day Indiana."

One of my questions was about the governor's personal goals. He was the father of twin baby boys, so I wasn't surprised by his response. "I believe my greatest personal goal is to be the best father and husband that I can possibly be, to provide for and support my family to the absolute best of my ability, and to be a positive role model for my sons. There is no job in the world that is more important."

*October 19...Pendleton, spent the night at a fishing lake. Didn't catch a thing. Finally found a packet of Big League Chewing Gum in the camp store, been looking since we left home.*

# 13

# a purpose greater than myself

I checked something off my dream list today: visit Mammoth Caves in Kentucky. It's the longest string of caves in the world. The walls in the caves rise 120 feet in some places. The largest of its chambers covers over an acre. I brought my survival backpack with me for the cave tour. My pack was filled with snacks, a flashlight, ten dollars, and my brand new, black Tomahawk pocket knife. I had bought the knife at a shop just down the road from the Jellystone Park Resort in Cave City where we were staying. The knife cost six dollars. I also bought a four dollar leather case. It was expensive, but considering I was embarking on an hour-long journey into the unknown, I thought it was worth the money. I was about to become a spelunker. That's what you call someone who explores caves.

Our guide carried a bright lantern and explained all the rules before we walked down the steep path to the cave entrance. I could feel the temperature change as we descended into the cave. The air was hot and humid outside, but the lower we went, the cooler the air felt. It took a minute for my eyes to adjust to the darkness.

"Dad, what are those things hanging from the ceiling?" I asked.

"Those are called stalactites. There are stalactites and stalagmites. You can remember the difference between the two, because stalagmites grow up from the ground and hope that they *mite* make it to the ceiling someday. The stalactites grow down from the ceiling, so they have to hang on *tite*."

The tour guide held the lantern in front of him as he explained the different parts of the cave. His khaki-colored uniform made him look like a boy scout. I didn't like following a tour guide. I wanted to explore the caves myself and have a real adventure. He told us about an Indian woman who'd been found in the cavern, wrapped in cloth with a special preservative. She'd been in the cavern for a long time, and her body was well preserved, so they sent her to a museum to be put on display. Maybe she didn't have a tour guide.

In the middle of the tour, when it was the darkest, the guide asked us all to be silent. Then he turned off the light. It was blacker than black and so quiet. I couldn't see anything at all. It was an eerie feeling. I felt all alone, except for Mom who was gripping my arm, probably making sure I wouldn't try to scare her. I was relieved when the guide turned on the light. I think everyone took a deep breath, I know Mom did. As we walked out of the cave, I had to squint until my eyes adjusted to the bright sunlight.

That night, Jon and I sat around the campfire carving wood. I was trying out my new knife. Jon made a corn cob pipe. I carved a pencil from a twig, hollowed it out and added a piece of lead from Dad's mechanical pencil. It worked pretty well.

"Time for bed, guys," Mom said. "We have an early day tomorrow."

"Oh, Mom, do we have to?" I pleaded. I loved sitting around the fire late at night.

"Amy." That's all Dad had to say. I carefully closed my knife and put it in my pocket.

"Good night," I said. I gave Mom and Dad the usual bedtime hug and kiss.

The next morning, I woke up to a terrible sound. I lifted my head off the pillow. It was Dad singing again.

"Ohhhh, Dad, please stop," I moaned.

"Time to get up," he sang in a deep operatic voice. I buried my head under my pillow, hoping the noise would go away.

"I'll stop if you get up," he continued to sing.

"Okay, okay, I'm up." Dad could really be annoying sometimes, but he had made his point.

A light rain was falling as we drove the scenic Blue Grass Parkway to Frankfort, Kentucky's capital. Governor Brereton Jones had been the first governor to answer my request for an interview, so I didn't feel quite as nervous about meeting him as I did the East Coast governors. I sensed he was sincerely interested in my project, but I still had some butterflies.

"It will all be fine," I told myself, "you've done this before, you can handle it."

I was still working on building up my confidence when we walked through the doors of Kentucky's capitol.

I wondered if I'd ever get over the nervousness completely. Usually, as long as Jon didn't do something to distract me, I felt more at ease after the first or second question. Mom told me that when she had sung in front of audiences, she was nervous until after the first few songs. Mom traveled all over Michigan, Indiana, and Ohio when she was a teenager, singing at youth rallies and coffeehouses. If Mom had been able to overcome her shaky nerves, I knew I could too.

The floors and the walls of the state capitol were made of marble. It's interesting that many of the capitols around the country use marble, probably because it lasts so long. In the governor's reception room, we were welcomed by the secretary.

"Hello, you must be the Burritts," the secretary smiled. "We're so glad you're here. The governor has been looking forward to this meeting. He'll be ready in just a few minutes. You're really going to like Governor Jones; he's very friendly."

"Thank you, I'm looking forward to meeting him, too," I told her. We sat down on the sofa. As we waited, a man in tattered clothes and a long gray beard walked into the office.

"Can I help you, sir?" the secretary asked.

"I wanna speak to the govenah," he said slowly with a southern drawl. I smiled. If only it was that easy. The secretary took the man's phone number and said the governor would call him.

I straightened Jon's tie and grabbed another mint from the bag. There's nothing worse than talking to a governor when you have bad breath. Just as I put the mint in my mouth, the secretary opened the door.

"He's ready for you, Amy." I chewed as fast as I could to get the mint down before I had to say hello.

"Welcome to Kentucky," Governor Jones said, greeting me at the door. He was friendly, just as the secretary had said. I guess this is what people mean by southern hospitality, making people feel welcome. Governor Jones invited me to sit next to him at his desk. We talked about my trip before I started the interview. I liked him from the start. He seemed genuinely interested in me, and I loved listening to his accent.

"So, Amy, what would you like to know about Kentucky?"

"Governor, can you tell me, why would someone want to come and live in your state?"

"Because it's the greatest state in America," he said proudly. I laughed and thought to myself how many governors might answer that question the same way, each loyal to their state. As the interview continued, it felt almost as if we were sitting in rocking chairs on an old southern front porch just shootin' the breeze. By the way he took

time answering my questions, I sensed that Governor Jones would be at ease talking with just about anyone.

"What are your goals?" I asked, nearing the end of my questions.

"Not long ago I was in a helicopter crash that I should have died in, but didn't. It changed my outlook on life. I learned that in everything we do, we have to have a purpose greater than ourselves. Instead of worrying about what people are saying about you, take what you know you should do, and do it," he said. I thought about that statement during the rest of the interview.

"What's your favorite part about being governor?" I asked.

"I would have to say the program I started called *Open Door After Four*. One day a month, starting at four o'clock in the afternoon, we open the door to anybody who wants to come in and talk with the governor," he explained. "It's a first-come, first-serve basis. So, if a person has a problem that they don't know how to deal with, they can come in, and I will sit down with them personally, listen to their problems and try to help them solve it. I go home at night and feel like I really have helped somebody. That's become the best day of the month for me."

"Wow, that's really neat," I said. I now understood why the man in the reception room was so bold about asking to see the governor. "That's all the questions I have, Governor, thank you for your time."

"Amy, it's been a pleasure," he said, shaking my hand. "I think what you're doing is great. Keep up the good work. So, where are you headed next?"

"West Virginia," I told him.

"Well, say hello to Governor Caperton for me. He's a good friend of mine."

"I will."

In the car, Mom and Dad talked about the statement Governor Jones made regarding a purpose in life. "You know, Amy, Governor Jones is right. No matter what you do, you need to have a purpose greater than yourself."

The next morning, Mom shook me from my sleep. "Amy," she whispered, "get up." I glanced at the clock on the microwave. It was 7:30.

"I'm too tired, Mom." After getting up at five-thirty yesterday morning, I just wanted to sleep in.

"Amy, we could sneak off to breakfast."

That got my attention. I love it when Mom and I sneak off to-gether. I dressed quietly so I wouldn't wake Jon, but I'd forgotten Mom had scheduled a radio interview for me. Before we could leave for breakfast, I had to call radio station WIOG, in southern Michi-gan, and do a live interview with Mike and Karen, the hosts of the morning show. We went to the pay phones in our sweatshirts, coats, and gloves. It was only thirty degrees outside, so I kept it short and to the point. I was amazed at how easy it was becoming for me to do interviews, like it was no big deal. I jumped back into the warm car.

Mom drove to a country restaurant down the road. She told me about how Grandpa used to wake her early in the morning and take her to breakfast, too.

"It was one of the neatest things my dad used to do," she said, "and I love the fact he still takes me to breakfast."

It's great how Mom spends this time with me. We talked about when she was a little girl, the "when I was your age" stories parents like to tell. It was fun, too, because I've discovered that in many ways Mom was like I am now. She liked to explore and climb trees and ride dirt bikes with her younger brother, Jim. Grandpa even built a dune buggy out of an old car. Mom was allowed to drive it all over their property. What a blast that would be. I can't wait until I can drive. That's on my dream list, too.

*October 27…We visited the Governor's horse farm, the Corvette museum in Bowling Green, and I won second prize for my Halloween costume in a contest at the campground. I was Miss Camper U.S.A.*

# 14

# dog smuggling

**"D**ad, will you pull off the highway so I can climb those rocks?" I asked, pointing to the mountain of rock along the roadside.

"No," Dad said. "I want to get to Wilderness Water Park and Campground before dark." I liked the name of our

*Seneca Rock*

campground. It sounded like a fun place to stay. We turned off the main highway and took a winding road through the woods, down into a valley where it was located. There must have been a lot of rain, because the valley was full of mud. Dad said it was called a bog.

We were disappointed to discover the campground was being remodeled, so the water slide was closed and the game room was under construction. The only thing we could do was go hiking in the mountains, but the rain had started again. The pitter patter on the roof made me want to snuggle up on the couch with a good book. I never lacked good books to read. We had over 30 Landmark books when we left on our trip. They're a family favorite, and we're always searching through used bookstores to find more. Some of them are very hard to find, but one of Mom's dreams is to collect all of them. The Landmark books are a series of about 185 books written by different authors about people and events in history. We read them as part of our history class. I was ready to start a new book, and since we had been studying the Civil War, I chose a book I found at the book store called *Behind Rebel Lines*. It was a story based on the true account of a young girl who, dressed as a man, enlisted in the army and became a spy. I love those kinds of stories.

Jon was playing another game of Monopoly with himself. He likes playing all the various roles, especially the banker. None of us were very surprised when Jon exclaimed, "Mom, I won the game!" I can't imagine him losing.

It rained most of the week, so I was looking forward to getting out of the motorhome for my meeting with Governor Gaston Caperton. At the capitol, we were directed to a conference room and a woman there invited us to take a seat. The room was full of people. After waiting for a few minutes, we heard someone say, "Ladies and gentlemen, please welcome the Honorable Governor Caperton." The governor walked into the room and stood behind a podium. He was tall and thin, with slightly graying hair. He welcomed everyone to the awards ceremony and began handing out awards and grants to people in the room.

"Mom," I whispered, "why are we here for this?"

"I don't know, Amy, they just told us to be here."

"I hope I don't have to go up front."

"Don't worry, even if you do, you'll be fine," Mom assured me.

All I could think about was how much I didn't want to do the interview in front of all these people.

"We have a special guest with us today from Traverse City, Michigan. Amy Burritt, would you come forward, please."

Mom stuck her elbow in my side. "Go on," she whispered. I walked to the front of the room, my knees shaking and my palms sweating. I hope he doesn't shake my hand, I thought, or he'll discover how nervous I am.

"Now, Amy is a creative and smart young woman," the governor began, "who's taking a very interesting approach to education. She is taking a trip to all fifty states, and her goal is to write a book based on her learning experiences. I'm a little nervous, because she is going to be interviewing me after this presentation."

Everyone laughed, and I was relieved to know we'd have a private interview. He handed me a plaque that read, "Certificate of Friendship" and labeled me an "Honorary Mountaineer." A photographer took pictures. Smiling, I went back to my seat and listened to the rest of the ceremony.

Later, inside his office he offered me a Coke and sat down in the chair next to me. I liked his office. It was smaller than the others. It was cozy; I felt like we were sitting in someone's living room.

"Governor Caperton," I asked, "why would someone want to come and live in West Virginia?"

"West Virginia is a state of the future. With its remarkable natural beauty and central location, it offers a good quality of life. With skiing and whitewater rafting, there is so much to do. And our capitol building is probably the most fascinating attraction in West Virginia."

When the interview was over, Governor Caperton handed me two gifts. I thanked him and said, "Oh, and Governor Jones said to say hello to you." I was glad I remembered the message.

"Governor Jones is a great friend," he began. "You know, we are godparents to one of each other's children."

"That's pretty neat," I said.

In the car, I opened the small white boxes and discovered a shiny brass paperweight in one and a letter opener with the words *West Virginia* on it in the other. I liked getting things from the governors.

"I think that was a good interview," I said. "Don't you, Mom?"

"Yes, you did great."

We drove two hours back to the motorhome in Clarksburg, we changed into our exploring clothes, and I packed up our dog Shasta for a ride in the car. Shasta loves going for rides. As soon as I ask her if she wants to go for a ride, she gets excited and starts jumping on us before she runs to the door to wait. Dad suggested we pack an overnight bag just in case we decided to stay in a hotel.

We traveled the back roads with no particular destination in mind. We spent the whole afternoon traveling the scenic route along Highway 219, all the way to southern West Virginia. We came to a place called Pipestem Lodge and Campground, and we drove into the parking lot. The Lodge overlooked the New River Gorge. It looked old and mysterious, surrounded by a thick band of clouds.

"Dad," I said, "can we stay the night here?"

"Yeah," Jon echoed, "this place looks cool." Dad looked at Mom, and without saying a word, they were talking to each other. It's funny how parents do that.

"Okay," Dad said. "Let's go check it out." Jon and I were excited. It wasn't very often that we stayed somewhere other than our motorhome.

At the front desk, Mom asked how much a room cost for the night. "What about having pets in our room?"

"We don't allow pets," said the lady at the desk.

"But we keep her in a kennel."

The lady looked at Mom, and with a grin on her face, she whispered, "Well, just don't let me see it." We realized this was her way of saying it was okay.

"Great," Mom said. On the way back to the parking lot, we discussed how we were going to get Shasta inside without being noticed. We unloaded the car and left Shasta behind while we carried the luggage up to our room.

Along the way, we searched for a place to sneak her inside. We found a quiet entrance at the back of the lodge that didn't look like it was used much.

"That's where we'll bring her in," Dad said.

After we took our things to the room, Mom sent Dad and me down through the "secret" passages of the hotel to get Pookie (that's my nickname for her). Dad and I were trying to pretend Shasta was a little baby, so we wrapped her in a blanket. We must have looked really strange. In the parking lot, we had to walk past some people while we tried to keep Shasta in the blanket, without bursting out laughing. To avoid as many people as possible, we walked into the basement through the "quiet" entrance. Bad choice. A conference was just ending, and a group of businessmen were walking our way. Dad was trying to keep

Shasta's black nose hidden under the blanket, and, at the same time, keep her tail from sticking out the other end. We could barely contain our laughter as the situation intensified. Just as we were passing the last person, I noticed Dad had Shasta's dog leash dangling from his back pocket. I wondered how many people had noticed it. We heard one of the men say, "Oh, somebody has a tired baby all wrapped up." Dad, whispered under his breath, "A little baby covered with hair!" That's when we both totally lost it. There was absolutely no way we could contain our laughter. Just as the guy approached, Shasta popped her little black nose up out of the blanket. I think he was going to say something about our "baby," but decided against it.

We finally made it to the safety of our room. Mom was busy unpacking. Without looking up, she said, "Shasta could use a walk. Why don't you take her back outside, Amy."

After a great dinner in the lodge restaurant, we walked to the lobby to browse through the gift shop. It was quiet. There were only two other couples hanging around. Dad was talking with them and telling them a little bit about our trip.

"Oh, my gosh!" one of the ladies gasped. "I saw your picture in our newspaper in North Carolina last week. You were interviewing the governor of Michigan."

"Really?" I asked, surprised that I was featured in their newspaper.

"Maybe we should get an autograph," the other lady smiled.

It was unbelievable. I had no idea how far-reaching my project was. I was in the middle of nowhere, and a stranger recognized me. It was a weird feeling.

*November 2... Drove all day in the car sightseeing. Saw Seneca Rock, a huge rock formation in West Virginia. I just wanted to climb it, but we didn't have time for that stop. Had a good dinner at Oliverio's.*

# 15

# dinner at
# the mansion

"I'd like to meet and interview the President," I told our congressman, Bart Stupak, who'd invited us to visit his office while we were in Washington, D.C.

"Well, I'll see what I can do for you Amy," the congressman told me, "although this is a campaign year and that will make it very difficult."

I knew arranging a meeting with the President was nearly impossible, but I wasn't going to let that stop me from trying. The worst thing that could happen was that the President would say no. I could live with that. I might not have believed that philosophy a few months before, but on this trip I was learning that not trying was the worst thing I could do.

Allison, Mr. Stupak's secretary, offered to give us a personal tour of the Capitol. We followed her through the maze of underground tunnels leading to the building. It was a long walk. Security was tight, and the guards wouldn't let us just walk into the House of Representatives or the Senate. Even with a special pass, they still made us leave all our bags outside and wouldn't allow us to bring in our cameras.

We were glad to be able to observe a session of the House and the Senate. After my studies about the Constitution, it was exciting to see firsthand how the government works. I sat in the balcony above the Senate floor listening to one Senator debate a bill. I looked around. It reminded me of a schoolroom, with each Senator sitting at his or her own desk. The Senate chamber was comfortable, full of dark rich wood and carpeting. The Senators took turns going up to the front of the room to give their opinion of the bill being discussed. I noticed some teenagers, dressed in blue oxford shirts and dark pants, coming in and out of the room.

"Mom, who are those kids? What are they doing?" I asked.

"They're called pages," she whispered. "They work for the Senators, delivering documents and sending messages back and forth."

"That would be fun," I said.

Watching the Representatives and Senators debating issues on the floor helped me understand more about how a bill becomes a law. I figured it's like being part of a club. You elect Representatives, Senators, and a President to represent the club and your ideas. If somebody decides the club should add a new law or change an existing law, they write up a document called a Bill. First, the Bill goes to the group, or House of Representatives, where it is debated. Then, the Representatives vote on it. If the majority, or most of the Representatives, vote yes, the Bill goes to the Senators who debate it and vote on it, too. If the majority, or most of the Senators, also vote yes, then the Bill goes to the President. He can either sign the Bill into law or veto it, which means he votes no, and the Bill dies. Sometimes, a Bill is rewritten and resubmitted. Then the process has to start all over again.

After our tour of the Senate, Allison guided us back to her office. I could hear the echoes of people scurrying through the marble-lined corridors. Everyone seemed to be in a hurry to get somewhere. As we turned a corner, I could see a mob of people standing around someone. I recognized the man. It was Bob Dole.

"Mom, Dad, look—it's Bob Dole!" I exclaimed. I saw other familiar faces, but I couldn't remember their names. I was so excited to be there, on Capitol Hill, standing in the midst of people I had only seen on TV.

When we returned to the motorhome that night, I turned on the television to watch the news. I wanted to see if I recognized anyone I'd seen during the day, but Mom wouldn't let me stay up long enough to watch. We had to wake up very early the next morning. We had a big day planned, from a White House tour to my interview with the governor of Maryland.

During the two-hour drive to Annapolis for my meeting with Governor Parris Glendening, Mom and Dad prepped me. They were helping me think of some lead-ins for my questions. It had been a long day already, and I was tired. We woke up at five-thirty for our White House tour, only to be disappointed. We'd been hung up in traffic in downtown D.C., just five miles away from the White House, and we completely missed the tour. It seemed like we'd spent the whole day in the car. I had trouble concentrating, but I knew my interview skills improved every time my parents worked with me.

"Instead of just asking a straight question like, 'What are your personal goals?'" Dad suggested, "tell them one of your personal goals and then ask them about their goals." Dad pretended he was the governor, and I asked him my questions.

"When I grow up, I think I want to be a veterinarian," I said. "What did you want to be when you were my age?"

Dad answered in a deep voice, "Well, when I was your age I wanted to be a fireman."

"Dad," I said, "be real." He just laughed.

We were an hour early for my meeting, so we walked through downtown Annapolis. Maryland's capital was the cutest town I saw on the whole trip. The brick streets, lined with neat little shops, led us down to the shore of the Chesapeake Bay. The harbor was dotted with boats, reminding me of my hometown. It was very clean. I liked the capitol, too. It was plain, small, and the oldest state house still in use. It was built in 1772.

Waiting in the Governor's reception room, Jon began to act goofy. He does that when he gets tired or bored, and I think he was a little of both. He started making funny faces at me and coming over to give me hugs. Mom and Dad noticed a camera up in the corner and pointed it out to Jon. At first, he didn't believe it was on, but Dad told him it was a security camera, and that the people in the office had been watching him. Jon's face turned instantly red.

The governor's secretary came out to tell us he was ready. We gathered up our equipment and followed her into the office. As we were walking past the other secretaries, we noticed they were all smiling at Jon. We saw the screen for the security camera. One of the ladies said, "Those were some pretty funny faces you made out there." He was so embarrassed, I think he could have crawled under a desk and died right there. They really had been watching us on the camera. I tried to remember if I'd done anything stupid.

The governor's big office with its tall ceilings made me feel small, but the walls were a soft cream color which gave the room a warm feeling.

"Welcome, Amy," the governor said, as he reached out to shake my hand. Governor Glendening was tall, with gray hair and glasses.

"Thank you, Governor." I introduced him to my family. Just as other governors had, he took a liking to Jon.

"Why don't you come on over and sit down here, and you can ask me your questions." I told Jon to sit down next to me. "You know, Amy, I think your project is so fascinating. How about if I take two weeks off to travel with you?"

"Sure, we'd love to have you come!"

Governor Glendening used to be a teacher, and he said when he's finished being the Governor of Maryland, he would like to return to teaching. What would it be like, I wondered, to go back to a regular job after being the governor of a state?

"What is the most fascinating attraction in your state?" I asked him.

"The Chesapeake Bay is very unique. It's the largest bay in the country."

"When I grow up, I think I may want to be a veterinarian. When you were my age, what did you want to be?"

coolest invitation
Governor
Parris
Glendening
award

"As a young boy, I probably wanted to be a fireman and all that sort of stuff, and that's kind of traditional." I looked over at Dad in disbelief.

He continued on with his answer, "But, then when I was in college, I started teaching and I really liked it. I grew up in a very poor family and, as a result of that, I didn't think of long-term, college-based careers."

He showed us around his office and pointed out some pictures of his family. Then the secretary motioned to him that it was time to go. "Well, I have another group of people waiting for me, but I would like to ask you something, Amy. You probably won't have the chance to do this with another governor. How would you and your family like to join me this evening for a dinner reception celebrating my first year as governor?"

I wasn't sure I had heard him right, so I looked at Mom and Dad to see their reaction. They were smiling and nodding their heads.

"That would be great," I said, trying to keep calm. I was so surprised by the invitation, and I knew Governor Glendening was right, I probably wouldn't get another offer like that.

He told his secretary to escort us over to the mansion and make sure we didn't have any problems getting in. As we followed the governor's secretary out of the office, Mom began to worry we weren't dressed well enough for an evening reception. Mom and I were both wearing blazers and dress pants, Jon and Dad were in casual suits with ties. The secretary assured us we looked fine.

The mansion was located across the street. After receiving clearance from security personnel at the gate, we were allowed inside. We stepped in the front door and stood there for a moment. The house was beautiful. A huge crystal chandelier lit up the entire foyer, where a crowd of people were hanging out.

"Everybody's all dressed up," Mom said. "I feel so funny."

"You look fine, honey," Dad assured her.

We walked through the mansion, admiring all the artwork hanging on the walls and the expensive knick-knacks on display. I felt awkward. It was strange to be at a party with people I didn't know. Jon and I were the only kids in the whole place, so they were probably wondering what we were doing there. The governor rescued us from the strangers' stares and walked us through the crowd to introduce us to his wife and son. They were very nice and made us feel welcome. Governor Glendening sent us to the food table to get something to eat and told us to have a good time. The table was lined with silver trays and so much food that I didn't know where to begin. I picked up a set of silverware wrapped in a decorative napkin and a china plate and filled it with roast beef and other finger foods. I stood over the baby grand piano eating and saw my reflection in its high-gloss shine. I was trying to be careful, I didn't want to embarrass myself by spilling on my clothes. Jon was sitting on the floor eating over the coffee table. I bet all the people staring at him were wondering if he'd spill all over the carpet. I was glad Mom had spent so much time teaching us proper etiquette over the years. I think I would have felt more out of place if I hadn't known how to handle the situation. Still, trying to cut roast beef without a knife was a challenge. The food was so good, I wanted to go back for more, but I knew it wasn't the proper thing to do.

It was getting late, and Dad said it was time to go. We said good-bye to the governor, but he stopped us. "Wait, before you leave I want to show you something. Not many people get to see this part of the mansion, but I thought you might enjoy a tour." I was amazed that the governor would take time away from his friends to show us around. The private quarters were set up like a house within a house. We followed Governor Glendening into his private dining room. He carried his dinner plate in one hand and described the pictures and knick-knacks with a wave of the other. In the living room, he told us, "This is where my son and I watch football games on Sunday afternoons." It was a comfortable room with a big sofa and plump chairs. What a neat place to live, I thought.

I hoped the governor knew how much it meant to me that we were asked to attend such a special occasion. We all thanked him and waved good-bye at the door. The street lamps lit up the sidewalk along the street. The day had been one of the longest I'd experienced on the trip, but as exhausted as I was, I felt great about my evening with Maryland's gracious governor.

I was happy to have a break the next day. We were camping at Snug Harbor KOA. It was a fun place to stay, with a playground and a river running beside it. Jon and I spent the day catching frogs in the river and making a movie with the video camera. It was a mystery. I think someday I might want to be a movie producer. I'll add that to my dream list.

Sitting around the campfire that night, we watched a family next to us. It was a large family with five kids. They were trying to cook dinner over their fire, but their father was having trouble keeping the fire going. Every time he laid the kabobs on the grill, the fire would start to smolder. They were trying everything they could to cook their food, but nothing seemed to work. We felt sorry for them as we sat around our crackling fire. Finally, Mom said to Dad, "Honey, go ask them if they want to use our fire."

Dad walked over to their site. "I see you're having some trouble with your fire."

"Yeah," the father said, exasperated. "I just can't get it going very well."

"It might just be your fire pit," Dad said. "Would you like to cook your dinner over our fire?" The kids all looked at their father with eager faces, waiting for his answer.

"Well," the man laughed, "this isn't our dinner, it's our lunch, and we've been trying to cook it for a few hours. We would sure appreciate using your fire." The kids smiled and began moving their chairs over to our campsite. Their father carried over the tray of kabobs and set them on our fire ring. Immediately, they began sizzling.

"Oh, that sounds so good," said one of the girls.

"Thank you," the man said as he reached out his hand to Dad. "By the way, my name is Dick."

"Nice to meet you. I'm Kurt, this is my wife, Emily, and my children, Amy and Jon."

Dick introduced his family. "This is my wife, Marie, my son Dan, and our daughters Sarah, Rachel, Ruth, and Lydia."

We could see that they were really hungry, so Dad offered the potatoes we had wrapped in tinfoil and cooked in our fire pit. They didn't want to take them, but Dad insisted.

We sat around the fire for much of the evening, becoming acquainted and telling them about our trip. It was fun having people over and making new friends. Sarah, who was about my age, wanted to see our motorhome, so I gave her a tour.

"We stayed in one of the KOA cabins last night," she told me, "but I wish we could camp in something like this."

"Well, we're not really camping in it, we're living in it."

"I'd like to do that, too."

The rest of the family all piled in the motorhome, and Mom made hot chocolate for everyone. They were such a nice family. I wasn't surprised to learn they were Christians. It was getting late and the kids had to be at school the next day, so we all said a prayer and hugged each other good-bye. It was strange, we spent so little time together, but by the time they left we felt like they were old friends. Being around Sarah made me realize how much I missed Melisa and Brittany.

# 16

# lost pocket knife

"How long has Jon been your brother?" Delaware's Governor Tom Carper asked. I stood there for a few seconds, wondering if I'd heard him right. Then I smiled.

"Seven years," I answered.

"Okay, just checking," laughed the governor.

We talked before I began the interview about his kids, my trip, and his favorite baseball team, the Detroit Tigers.

"Why would someone want to come and live in Delaware?" I asked.

"People like Delaware because it's small and personal."

That's true, I thought. It's kind of like a small town. "We came into Delaware on Sunday, but we haven't done much yet, because it's been raining. We're staying in Townsend," I explained, practicing my new interview lead-in tactics. "I hear there may be some flooding in that area, but right now, what would you say are your state's greatest needs?"

"We need water," the governor replied. We all laughed at the irony. Boy, did I feel dumb. I was thinking they might need help with a flooding problem, but what Delaware really needed was water! He explained they didn't

*Governor Carper signs my sweatshirts.*

have much rain through the summer.

When I finished my questions, Governor Carper suggested we might enjoy touring Dover and visiting the old capitol. We decided if the governor thought it was worthwhile, we would head over there.

What interested me the most about the historic building was an old tablet used by the court scribe, probably in the 1800s. Using a quill pen, the scribe would neatly record everything that was said during the proceedings, similar to a court reporter's job today. The writing was so perfect. I wondered how someone could write so beautifully. I thought the quill pen might be the reason, so I decided to see what it was like to write with one.

When we returned to the motorhome, I pulled out a gull feather I'd found on the beach and cut the end to a point. Next, I took an ink pen apart and dumped the ink into a paper cup. I dipped the pen into the ink and tried to write a sentence. The paper I used was more like a piece of cloth, and it soaked up the ink. I couldn't read the words. I tried smoother paper and the pen worked, but it was a pain. I had to dip the pen every two or three letters. No matter what I did, it was hard to write neatly. I decided to stick with my Papermate.

*Trying my hand at court scribe.*

"**I** can't believe we're halfway through the second tour already," I told Mom, as we packed the motorhome for our drive to Virginia. I was getting used to our daily routines. Each of us had special jobs to help make things run smoothly. Dad made sure of that. He likes organization.

At lunch time, Dad pulled the motorhome off the highway. As soon as he turned off the engine, Jon and I were out the door in search of adventure along the Atlantic shoreline. I had my trusty survival kit, the same one I took to tour Mammoth Cave. I kept my backpack ready, filled with food, string, wire, and my pocket knife.

The Delaware beach was an explorer's dream. It was covered with huge boulders, creating lots of nooks and crannies where trea-sures could hide. At first, we only found a rusted fish hook, some bottle caps, and a tangled fish line. I reached into my backpack for my pocket knife, so I could cut the fish line, but the knife wasn't there. I snapped the fishing line with my hand, wondering if my knife slipped to the bottom of the back-pack. I checked again, but it wasn't there. It must be in the motorhome, I thought. Con-tinuing our search for more treasures among the rocks, I soon forgot about my pocket knife. Jon and I discovered some small buoys, bobbers, and our most exciting trea-  sures of all, two horseshoe crab shells. One was cracked and broken, but the other was in perfect condition. We hauled them carefully back to the motorhome and packed them securely in our bin, alongside the other treasures we'd gathered during our trip.

While Jon put the bin away underneath the motorhome, I went inside to look for my knife. I looked everywhere: in the cupboards, under every seat, and between all the cushions. I checked the pencil box, the battery box, the toy box, and even Mom's makeup box. I couldn't find it anywhere. I tried to remember if I'd left the knife anywhere during the previous weeks, but I couldn't think where.

# 17

# time to leave

"I just wanted to cross the bridge. I didn't want to buy it!" Dad joked with the lady in the toll booth as he handed her the money. We were about to cross an awesome bridge that connects Maryland with Virginia called the Chesapeake Bay Bridge. It's a toll bridge, and since we had a motorhome and a car, the toll came to almost thirty dollars just to cross it.

We were halfway over when Dad hollered back to the bedroom, "Hey guys, come and look at this!" We ran to the front window to see what he was talking about. Up ahead, the bridge turned into a tunnel and we drove under the water.

"Maybe that's why it costs so much to cross the bridge," I said.

"Yeah," Jon piped up, "and they probably make you pay at the other end before they let you out!"

I was looking forward to our next campground, the Colonial Campground in Williamsburg, Virginia. We would spend Thanksgiving there. It was a great campground with a pool, recreation room, basketball court, and bike trails. While we were setting up at our site, I noticed other campers pulling in with kids. Great! I thought, maybe I would meet someone my age.

The second day, I did. His name was Matt. His family came to the Colonial Campground every year for Thanksgiving. He hung around our camper all the time, wanting to do things with me like ride bikes or play on the computer. I liked hanging out with Matt, he was really fun, but he didn't know when to leave. One night, it was close to eleven o'clock, and he was still in our motorhome.

"You better go back to your camper now," Dad said, "your parents might be getting worried about you."

"Nah, that's okay, I'm out this late all the time."

"Well, Amy and Jon need to get ready for bed, so you'd better go now."

"Can I play the computer while they're getting ready?" Matt persisted.

"Matt," I interrupted, "you should go home now, but maybe I can play tomorrow."

"Okay," he sighed, "see ya later."

" 'Bye Matt."

That was not fun. We practically had to kick Matt out the door. If it'd been his choice, I think he'd have stayed and played the computer all night. Of course, that wouldn't have gone over well with Dad.

"Okay, Amy, my little boy magnet, I think it's time to pack up and leave," Dad joked. "The boys are starting to hang around our motorhome."

I wonder if Dad will ever let me get married. Every time a boy starts hanging around the motorhome, Dad decides it's time to move. And whenever I tell him I met a boy, he asks, "Did you tell him your Dad's a butcher?" He hopes it will scare them away. Poor Matt.

Over the next few days, I continued searching for my knife, hoping desperately it was somewhere inside the motorhome. I was mad at myself for losing it. Dad said I should keep looking, because I just hadn't looked everywhere. I'd already turned the place upside down.

The campground hosts a Thanksgiving Dinner every year, and we were invited to join them. It was our first Thanksgiving away from our family. Dinner in the recreation hall was different than what we were used to doing, and eating with 150 strangers felt funny. Matt sat next to me, though.

Early the next morning, there was a knock at our door. "Can you play?" Matt asked.

"No, I have to go to the capitol today, but maybe when I get back."

Governor George Allen's staff had told us to visit Richmond and they'd try to work out a meeting. I'd heard that line before, so I was skeptical. Still, I wasn't going to give up trying even though my expectations about governor meetings had become more realistic. After we arrived, I wasn't surprised when the governor's assistant told us Governor Allen didn't have time for a meeting.

"Could I just get a picture with him?" I asked her.

Just then a woman walked into the office, and the secretary introduced us to her.

"Kay, I'd like you to meet the Burritts. They're from Michigan, and they're traveling to all fifty states. Amy is trying to interview all the governors," she explained. "Amy, this is Kay Coles James, she works for Governor Allen."

"Yes, I saw your story on CNN," she said enthusiastically. "I think what you're doing is great." After seeing Kay's excitement, the secretary left the room and came back a few minutes later.

"Amy," the secretary said, "I just made arrangements for you to meet the governor outside the building, but we'll have to hurry so we don't miss him."

We said good-bye to Kay James and rushed through corridors and passages, and out the door just in time to meet Governor Allen before his next meeting. I stood on the steps of the capitol feeling like a reporter who had just chased someone down for a big story.

He welcomed the opportunity to answer some of my questions, but when I asked him, "What is the most fascinating attraction in Virginia?" he turned the question back to me.

*quick quip*
*Governor George Allen award*

"What do you think it is?" Governor Allen asked.

Since I hadn't seen much of the state before the interview, I didn't have a clue as to what Virginia attractions I liked.

"There are so many that I can't pick just one," I said, thinking that would be a safe answer.

"You're a true politician," Governor Allen laughed. I guess hanging out with governors was beginning to rub off on me.

The next day, we visited Jamestown, the first permanent English settlement in North America. Due to a federal government shutdown at the time, we could only see a portion of it. Mystery seems to surround this famous historic site, as well as the story of Pocahontas.

The story is that a group of colonists left England in 1606 and landed on the shores of North America five months later. They named it Jamestown after King James I. Unfortunately, they landed in a swamp and it was too late in the year to plant crops. Within a few months, half of them died, either from malaria, starvation or at the hands of the local Indians.

The Indian princess, Pocahontas, was kidnapped by the colonists during one of their raids. While she was held prisoner, a man named John Rolfe fell in love with the princess and married her, bringing a temporary peace between the colonists and the Indians. John Rolfe planted a new tobacco crop by crossing two different seeds and created a mild tobacco leaf that became very popular. This helped the nearly extinct and desolate colony survive. John Rolfe later sailed with Pocahontas to London where she was cherished by royalty who renamed her Lady Rebecca.

*November 22...Saw* Toy Story *movie. Went to Fort Monroe, Williamsburg, Fredericksburg and George Washington's birthplace.*

# 18

# when life hands you lemonade
## (clean up the mess)

Our trip to North Carolina didn't get off to a very good start. After I waved good-bye to Matt, we pulled out of the campground. It was hard enough feeling separated from my best friends back in Michigan, so saying good-bye forever to a new friend made me sad. I stared out the window, feeling lonely as I watched other motorhomes pass us on the highway. I thought all those people were probably going south to Florida, but I figured they would only go away for a few weeks, not an entire year. Sometimes traveling isn't all it's cracked up to be.

Dad pulled off the highway to get some gas. As he made the sharp turn into a gas station, we heard a loud crash. I looked back. The refrigerator door was wide open, swinging back and forth. Food was flying everywhere, and stuff was sliding out onto the kitchen floor.

"Oh no! Amy, quick, grab a towel!" Mom shouted, as we simultaneously sprang out of our seats.

We had just done our grocery shopping for the week, so the fridge was loaded. It just kept spilling out container after container, until Dad brought the motorhome to a complete stop. I looked down at the disgusting pile of broken eggs, yogurt, and leftover pasta laying on the floor in front of me. Our plastic beverage container was gushing pink lemonade all over the kitchen, and punctured pop cans rolled everywhere, spraying a sticky mess. This wasn't the first time the refrigerator door had swung open, but we'd never had such a horrible mess to clean. On top of it all, a bottle of garlic lay broken on the floor. The smell was nasty.

"What a mess," I said.

"I can see we need to add another item to our checklist," Dad noted, as he stepped out the door to pump gas.

Nearly twenty minutes and several kitchen towels later, we'd cleaned up the mess. Dad paid for the gas, and we relaxed back onto our seats. Pulling away from the gas station, the pungent smell of garlic lingered in the air.

"Honey," Mom's voice wavered, "there's a lady running after us waving her arms and screaming." Dad pulled over to the side of the road and stepped outside to see what the lady wanted. She was out of breath from chasing us.

"Sir, something went wrong with my credit card machine," she panted, "and your payment didn't register. I need you to come back and run your card through again."

"Sure, no problem," Dad shrugged, almost resigned to the idea that things just weren't going to run smoothly.

"Oh, I'm so glad I caught you or else that ninety dollars would have come out of my paycheck," the woman said. At least our inconvenience helped someone. That was nice to know.

**W**e arrived in Raleigh, North Carolina, a day early. We went to the capitol to confirm an appointment Mom had arranged on the telephone. The secretary told us we didn't have an appointment, because we never called her back to confirm it. Mom was frustrated since she'd never been told to call back. She would have done that if they'd asked.

We happened to have the sweatshirts with us, so Mom tried to convince the secretary to have the governor sign them for me. If he would just do that then we would be on our way, insisted Mom. Reluctantly, the secretary took the sweatshirts and asked us to stop by the next day to pick them up. I was disappointed I wasn't going to be able to meet Governor James Hunt. If something didn't change, he would be the sixth governor I missed.

We walked around the small capitol and took pictures. A few minutes later, the secretary tracked us down and said the governor would like to meet with me. Mom and I looked at each other and smiled. We knew what had happened. We figured the secretary probably looked at the sixteen signatures on the sweatshirts and decided she'd better give her governor the opportunity to meet me. I was really glad we had the sweatshirts, because they'd become much more than a souvenir. I think that's called leverage.

While we waited to see Governor Hunt, the secretary brought us a bunch of North Carolina pins and flags. Although my meeting with Governor Hunt was brief, I enjoyed it. He was friendly and joked with us. I left my questions with him, and he said he would send his answers to me. These were a few of his answers:

Dear Amy,

...I enjoyed meeting you and your family recently. Your ambitious project is certainly an inspiration to students throughout America, and I am glad I have the opportunity to contribute to your endeavor.

*1. What do you enjoy most about being governor?*

It is difficult to choose one aspect of being governor I would call my "favorite." However...I treasure the chance to interact with such a diverse group of citizens throughout the state, and to have the opportunity to hear their concerns and suggestions.

*2. What draws people to come and visit or want to live in North Carolina?*

...abundant natural resources such as pleasant climate and geographic features ranging from the coastal regions to the mountains. In addition, our state has friendly people, a thriving economy and a high quality of education.

*3. What did you want to be when you were a kid?*

I have always wanted to serve the public. During my childhood, my parents instilled in me a strong sense of community responsibility. I learned that the best use of one's talents is to better the lives of others. This philosophy motivated me to enter public life.

I liked Governor Hunt's answers, especially the part about using our talents to better the lives of others. I hope I can use whatever I learned on this trip to make a difference in another kid's life. I don't really know how I will, I just know I want to be able to make a difference.

*November 30...Dad wanted to travel to Asheville, and Mom wanted to see the lighthouse at Cape Hatteras, but we didn't have enough time. They're in opposite directions. Mom and Dad said we'd have to come back again. When? I wondered. Were they planning on more traveling after this trip was over?*

# 19

# toasted
# tomahawk

I could see Governor David Beasley standing inside the doorway of the governor's mansion. We'd been invited to a Christmas Open House to meet the governor. He was a young guy with curly brown hair and an outgoing personality. He was shaking hands, talking and laughing with people as they came through the receiving line at the front entrance. As I watched him, I thought the governor seemed like the kind of guy who would be fun to hang out with.

The mansion was decorated for the holidays. A big courtyard with a water fountain sat in front of the house. Large trees with Spanish moss surrounded the yard, and two carriages sat at the front of the house, decorated with those big red flowers you see everywhere at Christmas time. It was really beautiful.

Suddenly, it was my turn to "be received."

"Hello, how are you?" he asked, as he shook my hand.

"I'm great, Governor Beasley. My name is Amy Burritt, and I'm

from Michigan. I'm doing a special project this year," I said, continuing to explain about my trip. "I tried to get an interview with you, but you didn't have time, so I wonder if you would sign my sweatshirts?"

"Amy, that sounds like a great project," he said with enthusiasm, "and I'm sorry my schedule didn't allow time for the interview. Can I answer your questions and mail them to you?"

"Sure," I said, "we'll leave a copy of them with your scheduler." Working out details with schedulers was becoming second nature to me.

Governor Beasley signed the sweatshirts in the reception line, and I thanked him. We had been holding up the line, and people were becoming restless, so we moved on. I wished more and more that I could have interviewed Governor Beasley. He was very friendly, and I know it would have been a fun meeting.

I received Governor Beasley's answers to my questions in the mail a few weeks later.

What draws people to come and visit or live in South Carolina?

"... low taxes, jobs, southern hospitality."

What do you feel your state's greatest needs are?

"... jobs—working with economic development, and strengthening the family unit."

When you were a kid, what did you want to be when you grew up?

"Governor."

And as for his greatest political goal?

"To possibly run for a higher office."

The next day, it was chilly outside, about 45 degrees. The cool weather put Dad in the mood for a pot roast dinner. He turned on the oven to preheat it while he prepared the food. A few minutes later, we noticed a strange odor. Dad opened the oven door and looked inside. Nothing seemed to be out of the ordinary, but as the oven got warmer, the smell grew stronger. We opened the windows to air out the motorhome from the terrible odor, and Dad investigated further. He opened the oven door, again, and with two hot pads, pulled out the oven rack.

"Well, well, well," Dad exclaimed. "What do we have here?"

We all walked over to see what he was talking about. "I don't believe it! How did it get in the oven?" I asked in amazement.

There, between the grates on the oven rack, was my toasted Tomahawk knife, leather case and all. I was so excited to have my knife back, but confused. How in the world did it get in the oven? I guess Dad was right, I hadn't looked everywhere. I never thought to look in the oven, but then again, who would?

# 20

# christmas catastrophe

The Christmas season took on a different feeling while we lived in the motorhome. Mom insisted on hanging up Christmas lights, pointing out, "Just because we're not in our house, doesn't mean we can't decorate for Christmas." She even wanted to buy a tree, but Dad told her she would have to enjoy the one in the campground.

"Merry Christmas, guys!" Dad announced one night. He stood with a big red package in his arms.

"It's only December second," I said, pointing to the calendar. "It's almost a whole month until Christmas."

"I know," Dad said, "but after you open it, you'll understand why we're giving it to you now. Sit on the couch. I'm going to put it on your laps so you can open it together. Close your eyes."

That was torture for us, but the suspense made it more exciting. When we thought we had most of the paper off, we opened our eyes.

"Cool!" Jon shouted. "What is it?"

"It's a metal detector, Jon. You use it to find treasures buried beneath the ground," I told him. Jon was so excited he could hardly sit still.

"We wanted to give it to you here so you could take it to the beach," Mom explained. We were staying at the Rivers End Campground on Tybee Island, not far from Savannah, Georgia.

"It looks confusing, how do you use it?" Jon asked. We read the instructions and learned the basics of running it. Then we went outside for the trial run. The campground was pretty full, so we had to find a place where we wouldn't bother anyone.

"It's supposed to beep when it finds something," Dad said after a few minutes. "I guess we just have to keep going."

Suddenly, it beeped

"Dad, stop!" Jon squealed. "There's something there." Jon dug until he pulled our first treasure out of the ground, a rusty tent stake.

"This could be handy," I said. "Can that detector find money?" I asked Dad.

"Well, let's see." He threw a dime on the ground and ran the detector over the area where it had landed. Sure enough, it beeped. Jon and I jumped for joy.

"We're going to be rich!" Jon shouted.

We were five hours from Atlanta, Georgia's capital city, and the drive there was long and boring in the car. I was relieved when Dad finally parked. I jumped out and stretched my legs. We had Shasta with us, because she couldn't stay in the motorhome for the eleven hours we would be gone. Mom wanted to bring Shasta into the capitol for our meeting with Governor Zell Miller. She was worried someone might take "Pookie." Since Dad had veto power, though, we ended up putting Shasta in her pink kennel in the back of the car. That's one thing we hadn't done yet. We hadn't taken Shasta into a capitol. I guess we could've wrapped her in a blanket again and smuggled her in, but I think the security guys would have been on to us.

*Mom and Dad.*

The capitol was decorated for Christmas with big red bows lining the gray marble stairs. The most beautiful and unusual Christmas tree I'd ever seen stood in the center of the reception room. The tree was covered with fishing lures, deer antlers, bird feathers, and other kinds of hunting stuff. At the very top of the tree, a bunch of cattails were perched straight up and spread out like a fan. I had the distinct impression Governor Miller liked fishing and hunting.

We were escorted into the governor's office where he stood in his blue suit and cowboy boots. His hair was pure white.

"Hi, what's your name?" he asked, reaching his hand out to me.

"Amy Burritt," I said confidently.

"Well, I'm glad to know you. Where do you want to do this interview, Amy?"

"Over here is fine," I said, pointing to a leather couch.

"What have you got in that briefcase?" he asked Jon.

"Sweatshirts," Jon said quietly.

"Oh," Governor Miller smiled.

"So, what are you going to do with all this information you're collecting?"

"I'm planning on putting it into a book for students," I explained. "I understand you've written a few books. What are those about?"

"One was about my growing up in the Appalachian mountains and the culture, one is about great Georgians, and the other is about all the musical artists who have come from Georgia."

"I hear you also wrote a couple of country songs?"

"Not very well," he laughed.

"What's your favorite part of being governor?" I asked, as our conversation naturally progressed into the interview.

"Getting good tickets to the Atlanta Braves baseball games," he chuckled. "But seriously, I think being able to improve the education in my state, I think that gives me the greatest satisfaction."

"So, you're into baseball?"

"I'm a lot into baseball," he said firmly. The governor told me that he'd been a baseball coach at one time and had met Hank Aaron and Mickey Mantle.

"Why did you want to be governor?"

"I got into politics because I wanted to change the educational system in Georgia, and we have been pretty successful in doing some things. We have a scholarship program where if you graduate from high school with a B average, you get free tuition into college."

"Wow," I said.

I noticed his desk was covered with papers. I've heard that a messy desk is a sign of a hard worker. I wonder if that statement could apply to my bedroom.

"What is the most interesting historical site in Georgia?"

"Probably Stone Mountain or the Okefenokee Swamp."

"What about your state's greatest needs?"

"Education," he stated without hesitation. "Most of the states in the south have not put education as a high priority for a long time ... if we're going to continue to compete globally, we will have to have the educated workers."

"What did you want to be when you were my age?"

"A baseball player."

"Did you do anything to pursue that dream?"

"Yes, and I soon found out that I wasn't good enough. So, I became a teacher."

"Governor Miller, thank you for taking the time to meet with me, I appreciate it."

"You're welcome, young lady."

Over the next few days, the weather turned colder than we expected, but Jon and I continued searching for treasures with our metal detector. We found some nails, pop bottle caps, and some change on the beach. Not quite enough to consider ourselves rich.

One evening, during dinner, Dad surprised us with the news that we'd be spending the next two weeks at Disney World in Florida. Jon and I had so much fun when we went there, but the time passed quickly. Before I knew it, we were packing up for our second trip back to Michigan. Dad didn't want to drive the motorhome in the snow, so he moved it to a storage area until we returned.

Our little car was so loaded down, we looked like the Beverly Hillbillies. Three days cramped in the car with all our junk, Christmas gifts, the dog, and my brother was going to be a long trip, but I was happy to be going home for Christmas.

The farther north we drove, the colder it got. We came to Findlay, Ohio, where we encountered a huge snowstorm. It seemed to come out of nowhere. Suddenly, we were driving in fourteen inches of snow and slush. Creeping along at 20 miles per hour, Dad couldn't see very well. He was getting tense. He told us to be quiet. He was looking for an exit ramp that wasn't blocked with cars, because vehicles were strewn all over the freeway and down in the ditches. The freeway had suddenly shrunk to one lane. We were low on gas and I was hungry. Dinner time had passed, but we hadn't been able to get off the road to find a restaurant. We passed a semi-truck jackknifed in the road, his trailer hanging in the ditch. It was an unbelievable mess.

Dad finally spotted an open ramp and stepped on the gas pedal to pick up speed. He didn't want to get stuck like the others. We made it to the stop sign. We just had to find a hotel. Dad turned toward the first one he saw. We all went in to see if they had a room available. A group of people stood in the lobby, watching reports of the blizzard on a big screen television.

"I've got two rooms left," the clerk said.

"We'll take one," Mom said, relieved we didn't have to continue traveling. While she filled out the registration card, another couple came through the door.

"Got any rooms?" the man asked, with hope in his voice.

"One left," the clerk said.

"Great, they're closing down the roads, so we were forced to get off and find a hotel."

"Is there a restaurant nearby?" Mom inquired.

"They're all closing down due to the storm."

"How about pizza delivery?"

"Nope, they're also closing up for the night, but," the clerk hesitated, "let me just check one place. You might be able to get one last delivery on his way home." She picked up the phone and dialed. We all looked at each other with hungry eyes. "Okay, they'll take one last order, what do you want?" Dad looked around the lobby at the other guests.

"We'll take five, that should be enough for everyone," Dad said. "Just order a variety."

We unloaded the car, fed Shasta and put her to bed. By the time we returned to the lobby, the pizza was just being delivered. Dad gave the driver a hefty tip and thanked him for driving in the blizzard. Dad set the pizzas out and invited the other guests to eat. It was kind of fun being stranded with a bunch of strangers. Normally, when we stay at a hotel people don't talk to each other, but this situation was different. Everyone had something to say.

The next morning, the blizzard had passed and the roads were clear. I was anxious to get home and see everyone, especially Melisa and Brittany.

I only had time to spend an afternoon with them, but I was sure it would be enough time to get caught up with each other's lives.

Mom drove me over to their house. I think she missed our house and was anxious to get another look at it. When Mom picked me up, I sat silently in the car.

"What is it, Amy?" she asked.

"I don't know," I hesitated, pulling the strings on my coat. "The girls are different." I stared out the window, not sure of my feelings and not sure I wanted to share them with Mom.

"What do you mean?" she pried. In a way, I wanted to tell Mom every detail and have her explain it all to me, but I couldn't.

"I mean, things aren't the way they used to be. Melisa and Brittany are different."

"In what way?" she insisted.

"Like the way they talk and their attitudes. I just don't understand it."

"Amy, things are going to be different because all of you are growing up."

"No, Mom," I said, fighting back the tears. "You don't understand. I feel like I don't know them anymore, and I don't like it." I began crying. I felt like I'd just lost something special. Mom grabbed a tissue out of her pocket and handed it to me.

"If I hadn't left, things would still be the same," I said. "If we'd never left, I'd still have my friends."

"Amy, you can't blame yourself because things are changing. And, I bet it's just as hard for them as it is for you."

I didn't say another word all the way back to Aunt Sue's house. Mom sang along with the Christmas songs on the radio, but I just wanted to curl up in a corner somewhere and cry. I wanted my friends back.

Christmas Eve came quickly. We went to Grandma and Grandpa Peckham's house. I tried not to think about the girls too much. I wanted to enjoy Christmas with my family, because I wouldn't see them again for five months.

We all crowded into the small living room. Aunt Sue and Uncle Darryl were there with their children, Laura, Austin and Kelsey, and Uncle Jim and Aunt Sally had their five kids, James, Nicholas, David, Andy and Katie. Gifts were piled high under the tree, and we were anxious to open them.

"Wait," Grandma said, trying to get our attention. Grandma was tall and thin with short brown hair and glasses. She was always happy. With ten anxious grandkids in the room, she had to speak up. "What do we do first?" she asked at the top of her voice.

Andy, my little cousin, raised his hand. "Okay, Andy, what is it we have to do before we open our gifts?"

"Sing happy birfday to Jesus," he smiled. Andy was only three, but he already knew the routine. We sang our song, then Grandpa gave Andy's older brother, James, the honor of handing out the gifts.

"Pass out those gifts next to the tree first," Grandpa said, pointing.

"Okay, Grandpa," James said. The gifts were from Grandma and Grandpa. Grandpa was good with his hands, and every Christmas he made something special for each grandchild. I wondered what it would be this year. I quickly tore off the wrapping paper. It was a beautiful wooden box with handles on each side and a gold latch.

Grandpa made one for each of us. It was just what I needed, a special place to store my treasures.

The next day we spent Christmas at the farm with Dad's family. It was cold out, but Grandpa Gene had a fire blazing in the wood stove. I was sitting in the living room, glad that I'd worn socks instead of nylons, because the hardwood floors were cold.

Across from me sat Uncle Mike, a detective with the state police. He was talking to Uncle Ken, my dad's twin brother, who was sitting next to him on the worn, green couch. As usual, the topic was football. I think sports is all they ever talk about. Next to them sat my two oldest cousins, Annie and Jim. They were both about sixteen. Annie was Uncle Mike's daughter. She was tall with long silky black hair. Jim was Uncle Clif's oldest boy. He had short wavy black hair and a stocky build. I really like Jim. He is always willing to help out in any situation, and even though he is four years older than me, he never makes me feel like I'm too young to talk with.

At the other end of the living room, my Uncle Clif was lying on Grandma's nice red sofa watching TV. Aunt Becky and Aunt Teri were in the kitchen helping Grandma Kay cook our Christmas dinner. The smell of turkey filled the house. I hoped we were having cranberry sauce.

The fluorescent light above me was humming. This was the only light in the room, except for the small lamp on Grandpa's cluttered desk and the glow from the television.

"Donnggg...donnggg...," the big grandfather clock in the corner rang out the six o'clock hour.

I heard stomping upstairs where the rest of my cousins were playing, so I decided to go see what they were doing.

"Hey guys, what's going on?"

"Watch," my younger cousin Jake said. He stomped over to the black grate in the floor and pretended to fall through it. I remembered Dad once said that the grate was there to let heat upstairs, where he used to sleep as a young boy. We call it our spy grate, because we can look downstairs and watch everyone. Sometimes, we even hear them talking about us.

"No. You've got it all wrong," Jake's older brother Joel said. "You have to take off the top part of the grate, so your foot can go partway through it. Then it looks more real." Joel took the top grate out of the floor and covered up the hole with a pink rug.

"Amy," Mom called from downstairs, "could you come walk Shasta, please?"

"Why do I have to walk Shasta? Why can't Jon do it?" I complained.

"Because I asked you to do it," Mom answered. I reluctantly left my cousins to their mischief and took Shasta outside.

When I came back in, my fingers were numb. I unhooked Shasta's leash and walked over to the wood stove to warm my hands next to Aunt Julie and Uncle Adam. They were tired after their long drive from Tennessee. Mom and Dad were telling them about the snowstorm we'd been caught in. They'd just missed it.

I sat down in the vacant oak chair next to the desk. My stomach was growling, and I hoped we'd eat soon. I noticed a tray of cookies on top of the piano. One of those would hold me over, I thought. I jumped up and headed for the tray. Just as I picked up a Christmas cookie, I heard a loud crash behind me. I spun around to see what it was. Tiny pieces of shattered glass were flying everywhere. Uncle Ken and Uncle Mike jumped back from the edge of the couch. Grandpa Gene had been almost asleep in the old blue chair next to the wood stove, but now he was standing on his feet. Grandma, Aunt Becky, and Aunt Teri came running from the kitchen to see what caused the noise.

Everyone froze. There on the floor lay the mangled and broken eight-foot fluorescent light. Somehow, it had fallen down on the oak chair where I'd been sitting just seconds before, and then onto the wood floor. Slowly, everyone's eyes looked up to where the light had been hanging. There, dangling from the hole in the ceiling, was Joel's leg. When I saw it, I knew exactly what had happened.

Uncle Clif bounded up the stairs to find out why his son's leg was hanging from the ceiling. I knew Joel was in trouble. We all began quietly cleaning up the glass. It was one of those times when you feel really bad and you wish someone would say something funny. I was feeling bad for Joel when Uncle Mike piped up and said, "I've been wanting to take that light down for a long time."

Everyone laughed. Nobody liked that old light, anyway. We swept up the glass, and Grandpa hauled the mutilated relic out to the barn. Grandma announced dinner was ready.

# tour three

tennessee

florida

alabama

mississippi

louisiana

texas

new mexico

arizona

hawaii

california

# 21

# arctic inn

We said good-bye to Traverse City a few days after Christmas and left to begin our third tour. It would be the longest one we'd planned, and we wouldn't be coming back for almost five months.

I was still confused about my last visit with Melisa and Brittany. It made me sad to think about them. I was afraid they didn't care about me anymore, and that scared me. It was like wanting to open the mysterious box in the junkyard back home. I just felt better leaving it alone. I didn't even talk with Mom about it. Instead, I tried to think about all the new places I was going to visit.

I thought our car had been loaded down before Christmas, but after packing up all the gifts we'd received, I could hardly move. It was going to be a very long trip back to Florida.

We spent our first night at a hotel in Tennessee. The snow was sparkling, and it crunched under my feet as I carried our luggage to the room. I was exhausted from all the holiday parties and from the fourteen-hour ride in the cramped car. The next morning, I had a meeting with Governor Sundquist in Nashville, so I wanted to sleep well that night. One of the things I've learned from traveling, however, is things don't always go the way you expect.

Dad turned on the heater to warm up the room. I washed my face and collapsed on the bed. Just then, the heater kicked off.

"What's going on?" Mom asked. Dad walked over to the heater and pushed the "on" button. Nothing happened.

"You'd better call the front desk," Dad stated.

"They're moving us to another room," Mom groaned, after hanging up the phone. "Honey, go down to the front desk and get the key. We'll meet you at the other room with the luggage."

We were all tired, and the last thing we wanted to do was move our luggage again. Plus, there was Shasta with her kennel. We hauled everything outside, to the stairs, and up to the second floor. Dad was there with the key. The room looked exactly like the other one. Dad checked the heater, it worked. It was almost midnight. Jonathan climbed into bed. As we snuggled into our beds, the lights flickered.

"Oh no, not again," I moaned. The heater shut off.

"They should change the name of this place to the 'Arctic Inn', " Jon said sleepily.

"I'm too tired for this tonight," Mom said. She picked up the phone to call the front desk again. "They're having electrical problems and are working on it right now," she reported. "The whole hotel is down. They're asking everyone to keep the heaters on low, because it's overloading their circuit."

"Maybe we should find another hotel for the night," I suggested.

"I have a better idea," Mom said. "Amy, go down to the car and bring up the sleeping bags to put over our beds. That will keep us warm, besides Jon is already asleep." I looked over enviously. He was in dreamland. I dragged the sleeping bags from the car. Too tired and cold to put on my pajamas, I climbed into bed in my clothes. I just wanted to sleep. I missed our motorhome.

The next morning, we woke up to a warm room. We repacked the car for the second leg of our journey south. We weren't far from Nashville, so I worked on my questions for Governor Don Sundquist.

Nashville's capitol building sits at the top of a hill. Once inside, we found our way to the governor's office. Every capitol is so different, and we never know where the governor will be. The secretary told us to wait in the rotunda, the governor would be out soon. I found this a little odd. Usually, I met the governors in their offices. We waited anxiously for Governor Sundquist to arrive. Finally, I saw him walking down the hall toward us. His light brown hair was neatly combed and his suit pressed. He greeted me in the hall.

"Welcome to Tennessee, Amy," Governor Sundquist said warmly. We shook hands. "I heard you're on quite an adventure this year."

"Yes, it's been great so far."

"Well, I'd like to give you something, Amy, because I'm very impressed with what you're doing." He presented me with a certificate appointing me a Tennessee Ambassador of Goodwill. My role was to carry the best wishes and the message of Tennessee's hospitality to all people of other states and other lands. It had the state seal embossed in gold on the bottom, and it was signed by Governor Sundquist.

"Thank you," I said, as he signed the sweatshirts.

*In the library at the Capitol.*

I crouched in the back seat of our car, trying to find a comfortable spot. It would be another 12-hour ride before we arrived at our motorhome in Florida. I couldn't wait to get there. Driving through Georgia, I realized I wasn't feeling well. Mom felt my forehead.

"You have a fever," she sighed.

None of us wanted to spend another night in a hotel. I just wanted to sleep in my own bed. We arrived at the motorhome at one o'clock, and I felt as though I had the flu. Mom made up my bed.

"I'll pray for you tonight," she said. She kissed my cheek and tucked the blankets around me.

My fever broke the next day, and I was feeling better by evening. We were back at the Fort Wilderness Campground in Disney World, and Dad said we could stay a few extra days until I felt stronger.

# 22

# captain vectra

Since I was sick for a few days, we lost some travel time, and we weren't able to visit the Florida Keys. I was disappointed because I'd read great things about the Keys in our travel brochures. I added the Florida Keys to my dream list.

After we left Orlando, we stopped by the capitol in Tallahassee to see the governor. When Mom told the secretary why we were there, the secretary replied, "You'll have to schedule a meeting ahead of time."

"I tried to schedule a meeting nine months ago, how much more time do you need?" Mom asked.

The secretary blushed. "I'm sorry, I'll see what I can do." She exited through the door beside her desk and appeared a minute later. "If you would like, I can take the shirts in to have them signed for you."

"Thanks, that would be great," Mom said, frustrated once again by bureaucratic red tape.

It seemed kind of silly. We were right there, and the governor was right there, but the staff couldn't work out a brief introduction. I wondered if the governor even knew about it.

Later that day, we drove to a campground in Destin, Florida. The place brought back memories of a family vacation we'd taken a year earlier. During that trip, we camped at the Holiday Travel Park and had a beautiful campsite right next to the ocean. We were traveling in a little Minnie Winnie motorhome then, which was about half the size of our new motorhome. I remember being surrounded by big diesel buses and joking about feeling like the poor kid on the block.

Dad dreamed of traveling in one of the diesel buses. He had an RV book that listed all the big rigs, and every time one came rolling into the campground, Dad would grunt like Tim Allen on the TV show, *Home Improvement*, and grab his book to look up the model. That's how we met Memphis Ben. That wasn't his real name. We made it up as part of a game we like to play. The object of the game is to create names for people we see during our travels, based on what we observe about them. It taught me to notice more details, which is a good thing for a writer to learn.

Memphis Ben was a nice guy from Tennessee. We met him the first day he drove into the campground. He was driving one of those big diesel buses. Dad ran to get his book. Sitting outside in his lawn chair, Dad explained every little detail of the rig to Jon and me. Distracted by the sound of the diesel engine, Dad looked up from his book to see Memphis Ben's bus stuck in soft sand.

"Houston, we've got a problem," Dad said.

Memphis Ben had driven too far forward. We watched as he tried rocking the bus back and forth, but that just made him sink deeper. Dad shook his head.

"Maybe he can afford to own one of those big rigs, but that doesn't mean he can drive one," Dad said.

Dad went over to join the other campers who'd noticed the problem. They all grabbed shovels to move the sand and then lay down boards for traction. Eventually, Memphis Ben's bus was freed from the sand.

A few sites over from ours was Bobby Big Screen. Bobby had a TV the size of a billboard. Our TV's reception wasn't very good, all we could get was a fuzzy picture in black and white. So at night, Mom and Dad would turn on the sound of our TV and watch the evening news with Tom Brokaw on Bobby Big Screen's TV from across the campground.

Camping next to Memphis Ben was another character, Inspector Vectra. We'd been watching this guy for a few days. He was camping in a blue and silver Vectra motorhome. Every day, he came outside in his khaki shirt and pants and a brown leather hat like Indiana Jones. With a pipe clenched between his teeth, he tinkered with all of his gadgets in the outdoor compartments. He had everything. One day, he pulled out a boat, unfolded it, put a motor on it and went fishing out in the ocean for hours. He was fun to watch. He reminded us of the cartoon character, Inspector Gadget, so we named him Inspector Vectra.

One day at the campground, the wind picked up. Jon and I ran to get our kites. After about 45 minutes, it started raining.

"Amy, I'm getting wet, let's go inside," Jon said.

"You go ahead, I'm going to stay out a while longer."

Jon ran back to the camper. The wind blew harder and harder. My kite was out to the end of its line. I tried to roll it back in on the little plastic spool, but it hurt my hand. I was getting soaked from the rain, and the wind whipped my wet shirt against my skin. I kept trying to pull my kite in, but I lost my grip on the string, and it slipped through my fingers. I thought my kite was long gone, but somehow I caught the string. Just then, out of the corner of my eye, I caught a glimpse of someone. I turned to get a better look. It was Inspector Vectra. His skin was very tan, his hair was long and bushy, and he was walking in large strides toward me. In his hand was a block of wood. I was scared. My heart raced. I didn't know what he was doing. I glanced up and down the deserted beach. There was no one around. I knew Mom and Dad couldn't see me, because several straw beach huts blocked their view.

The kite string was cutting off the circulation in my hand. I wasn't sure if I should let it go or not. The wind and the noise from the waves crashing on shore were almost deafening. Even if I tried to yell, I realized no one would hear me. Suddenly, Inspector Vectra was standing next to me. I froze. He reached out his hand toward me, and without saying a word, took the string out of my hand and wound it around the board. I never guessed he was coming out to help me. He brought the kite all the way in and handed the board to me. In a gruff voice, he yelled, "There you go!"

I don't remember thanking him. All I could think about was getting back to the motorhome. I ran all the way without looking back. I slammed the door behind me and stood against it for a moment to catch my breath.

"Did you have fun, Amy?" Mom asked. *Fun?* I thought. Exasperated, I told them what had happened to me, how Inspector Vectra saw I was having trouble and rescued me and my kite. I could hardly speak a whole sentence at once, because my heart was still pounding wildly.

"Why didn't you come and help me?"

"We didn't know you were having any trouble," Dad said. "We thought you were staying out in the rain just because it was so much fun."

"Since when is it fun to stand in the pouring rain and fly a kite that's all the way out on its string?" I asked. They laughed at me.

"Amy," Mom smiled, "you're so adventurous, we never know what you're going to do next."

That night, we went to thank Inspector Vectra for saving my kite. He invited us in, and we visited with him and his friend, Doris. We told him that we'd nicknamed him Inspector Vectra. He laughed at his new name, but asked if we wouldn't mind calling him Captain Vectra. "You see," he explained, "I'm the captain of a boat in Baltimore harbor." From then on we referred to him as Captain Vectra.

Nearly a year later, Mom called him and asked him to meet us for lunch. I thought it would be funny to return the board he used to rescue my kite. We had a plaque inscribed with "Captain Vectra," and I glued it on the board. I also made a Certificate of Merit commending him for rescuing

*Captain Vectra and the board that saved my kite.*

me and my kite from the fierce Florida winds. He couldn't believe I'd saved the original board for so long.

"I've been looking for that board, I couldn't remember where I'd put it," he laughed. "I'm going to hang this on my boat."

*January 15... Went to the beach and collected sand dollars. Saw the destruction from hurricane Opal. It was sad to see so many homes destroyed and lives affected from one storm.*

# 23

# surprise party!

"**D**ad, is this our campground?"

"Yeah," he said bleakly.

"Do we have to stay here for my birthday?"

"We don't have much choice, it's the only place around." The campground was a dusty field that looked like an abandoned drive-in movie theater. There wasn't a swimming pool or recreation room anywhere. The only thing I saw was an ugly little bath house painted like Neapolitan ice cream. It was not the luxury campground I'd planned on for my birthday.

"**H**appy Birthday, Amy," Mom said, shaking me gently. It took a moment to wake up, but then I realized my 13th birthday had finally arrived. I was now officially a teenager! Despite the less-than-great campground, I was feeling pretty good about the day, until I heard Mom's desperate call from the bathroom.

"Kurt, the water won't come on!"

Mom was about to climb into the shower, but nothing was coming out of the faucets. Dad jumped out of bed and checked the kitchen faucets. "The pipes are frozen," he said. "It must have gotten pretty cold last night." He looked out the window at the thermometer. "Well, no wonder, it's only eighteen degrees! I guess you girls will have to take your showers in that pretty little cement building," he said sarcastically. Jon laughed. He knew how much we didn't want to go to that shower house. I gazed around the dreary campground and saw a few people thawing their outdoor hook-ups with hair dryers.

"Dad, why don't you do what they're doing?" I asked, pointing out what I saw as the perfect solution.

"Because we don't have time for that, Amy. We need to get going or you'll be late for your meeting with Governor James."

Of all days for this to happen, I thought. On my birthday and a day that I had an interview scheduled. On top of that, I had a bad cold. Mom and I didn't want to go to the disgusting-looking shower house. We weren't sure it had hot water, or any running water for that matter. I wondered what we'd do if the pipes in the shower house were frozen, too. We didn't have much time to discuss it. Dad was pushing us along, trying to convince us it would be okay. Mom and I put on our robes and sandals. Reluctantly, we stepped out the door. I shuttered from the cold. We ran toward the building. All the little puddles of water on the gravel road were iced over. When we got to the shower house, it didn't look much better inside. With cement walls and floors, each corner housed a resident spider with an elaborate web.

Mom turned on the fluorescent light. It strained and flickered before it lit up with a buzz. "Well, that's a good sign," she joked, "let's check the showers."

Of the two shower stalls, only one worked, so we had to share. That meant one of us had to stand aside and freeze while the other showered.

"Let's make this quick," Mom said.

Shivering and shaking, we quickly washed and ran back to the warmth of our motorhome. We drank the hot coffee Dad had made.

"I bet that was the quickest shower you ever took," Dad teased.

"What I don't go through for these governors' meetings."

We were expecting someone from a local television station to be at the interview that day, but when we checked in at the governor's office in Montgomery, nine or ten reporters stood around the room, waiting. I was surprised. The media people bustled around the small room, setting up their cameras and untangling cords. When they realized who I was, they began asking me questions.

"Amy, what's been your favorite state?"

"So far, probably Vermont."

"Who is your favorite governor so far?"

"There have been quite a few, it would be hard to name just one," I said.

"Have you gotten answers from the governors that have been just yes-and-no answers?"

"No," I paused, "I try not to ask yes-and-no questions." Everyone in the room laughed when they realized the reporter had just asked me one.

At that point, Governor Fob James entered the room. He stood by the door for a moment while someone straightened his tie. He was short and stocky, with thin brown hair. He was warm and friendly, greeting everyone around the room.

When he came to Jon, he rubbed Jon's head and said, "I like a man with a good haircut!" Jon always had his hair buzzed short, because it was coarse and grew straight out.

"Hi, Amy. I'm Governor James." He spoke slowly and his southern accent was very heavy. I liked the way he talked. The cameras began flashing as the report-

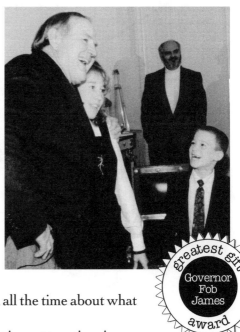

ers took pictures of our hand-shake.

"Nice to meet you."

He invited me to sit in a nearby chair, and we began the interview. My head was stuffed up from my cold, and I didn't like the way my voice sounded.

"Did you want to be governor when you were my age?"

"No, I wanted to be a sea captain, then a soldier, and then a professional baseball and football player." I could relate to that. I change my mind all the time about what I want to be.

"What's the most fascinating attraction in your state?"

He took a deep breath, held it for a second, then let it out with a sigh. "Boy, that's a tough question, Amy. That's a tough political question," he repeated, as he rubbed his chin with his hand. Everyone laughed. I think they enjoyed seeing a dignitary stumped by a kid.

"I would say the personality of our population."

"What is the most interesting historical site in Alabama?"

"Montgomery is a very historical city. The orders for the first shots to be fired for the Civil War were issued here."

At the end of the interview, he signed the sweatshirts and handed me a big blue Alabama beach bag containing a cooler and a thermos.

"Amy, this is for you. Happy birthday."

I was surprised. I smiled and shot a glance at Mom. Governor James and the media all sang "Happy Birthday." It was cool to have a governor give me a gift and sing to me. I couldn't have asked for a better birthday celebration.

After the interview, a reporter from television station WSFA Channel 12 News invited us to the studio to watch my interview on the news broadcast. While we were there, he gave us a tour of the station. I watched the behind-the-scenes action and how the reporters put their stories together. The station crew even let Jon and me sit behind the news desk. I saw the teleprompter. It's a little television in front of the newscasters, and they read their stories from the screen. I always thought newscasters had that stuff memorized, because they're usually looking right at the camera. Knowing they had a little help made me feel better about sometimes forgetting my interview questions.

# 24

# convict cafe

"**A**ren't you afraid you're going to be expelled from school, being out there on the road all year?"

I had just met Mississippi's Governor Kirk Fordice, and he was interested in my adventure.

"Well, I'm homeschooled."

"Good for you," he said, giving me the thumbs-up sign. "We have a lot of homeschoolers in Mississippi. I have to give your parents a lot of credit for taking on that huge responsibility," he said, glancing over at Mom and Dad.

The governor then invited Jon and me to have a seat on the leather couch near him.

"So, what did you want to know, Amy?" the governor asked in a heavy southern drawl. He was an older man with white hair.

"Can you tell me what is the most important industry in Mississippi?"

"I guess I would have to say the biggest industry by far would be agriculture. It brings in a lot of money for our state. And second would probably be shipbuilding. We make a lot of war ships here."

"What do you like most about being governor?"

"The best part is being able to do something that makes the state better as a whole."

He explained that he used to be in the construction business, but when he moved into politics, he realized he couldn't run government like he did his business. "It's a slower pace and takes more time to get things done," he said.

Mississippi's lieutenant governor is not part of the governor's cabinet, and can be affiliated with a different political party. The decision-making process is slower than in some states. That was one of things I'd been learning through my interviews with governors. I thought every state was like Michigan, with a governor and a lieutenant governor of the same political party, but that's not always the case. Some states have a Republican for governor and a Democrat as the lieutenant governor. Governor Fordice seemed to like the diversity.

"Each state is different," he said. "That's part of the beauty of the United States, that each state has its own power."

Before we left Jackson, Mississippi's capital, we visited the Museum of Agriculture. Mom and Dad were taking us to many historical sites and museums on this trip, and I expected this to be another boring tour. I was wrong.

First, we went into the museum store where we discovered a great collection of Indian items for sale. Jon and I love things like tomahawks and arrowheads. We're always trying to make them. This museum offered a walking tour that took us through the 1800s and introduced us to the "good old days." What's so good about washing your clothes by hand, anyway? Or hauling wood in the winter? Or having to go outside in the bitter cold to use the outhouse? I hear people say "life back then was so simple," but to me it sounds like a lot of work just to survive.

I've heard stories from Dad about what it was like when he was growing up on a cherry farm. Actually, I do think life was simpler back then, but hard. Life is easier now, but more complicated. I wonder what the next century will bring to make our lives simpler, or would that be more complicated?

After we left the museum, we walked back to the motorhome. On the way, I saw a sign that read *cafe*. It was a small building that looked like a cabin, and something smelled really good. We convinced Dad to let us stop there for lunch. Inside, it was rustic looking. We were told to seat ourselves, so we found an empty table and sat down.

While we waited to order, I noticed Mom and Dad were whispering to each other. I tried to get their attention.

"What are you talking about?" I asked.

They didn't answer. They were too busy looking at the waiters and waitresses. It did seem odd, they were all wearing the same strange uniform. The uniforms included green and white striped pants and white t-shirts with big black letters on the back that read MDOC. I leaned over the table toward Mom.

"Mom, why are they dressed like that?" She looked over her shoulder and leaned my way. "Those aren't regular waitresses."

"What do you mean?"

"Those letters on the back of their shirts stand for Mississippi Department of Corrections," Dad explained.

"What does that mean?" Dad put his arm around my shoulder and pulled me toward him.

"It means they're convicts," he said, quietly in my ear.

"What? You mean criminals?"

"Yes."

"Oh my gosh," I said slowly.

"What are conviks?" Jon asked loudly.

"Shh, Jon, be quiet, they might hear you." Suddenly I felt very weird.

Just then a waitress came to our table. "Ya'll want the boofey?" she asked in a strong southern drawl.

"Yes, we'll all have the same," Dad told her.

"Okay, jus hep yosef."

Jon waited for her to walk away and then asked me again, "Amy, what's a convik?"

"A prisoner," I whispered in his ear. He gasped. His eyes opened wide and he sat up straight in his chair.

"Why are they here and not in jail?"

"This is probably part of their punishment," Dad explained. "C'mon, let's go get our food." Jon didn't budge.

"I don't want to eat here, Dad. Can we leave?"

"Jon," Dad said, looking him in the eye, "you don't need to be afraid, these aren't dangerous prisoners."

"Do you think they killed people?"

"No, they probably stole things or something like that."

We all went to the buffet together and filled our plates. Jon was very quiet through the rest of our meal. I've never seen him so well-behaved. I think he was relieved when we were back in the motorhome and on our way out of the parking lot. Although it was a strange situation, I thought it was a good idea to have prisoners working instead of just sitting in a jail cell watching television. I think it's important for people to pay their debt to society when they've broken the law.

Still, that was a meal I'll never forget.

*January 20...Drove the Natchez Trace Parkway, nice drive. Saw antebellum homes of the south.*

# 25

# off the hook

We began studying the westward expansion and the Louisiana Purchase as we headed into Louisiana. When President Jefferson decided to buy Louisiana from the French in 1803, he doubled the size of the United States. For $15 million, that was a good deal. The funny thing about it was, he didn't know exactly what the United States had purchased. That's why he sent Lewis and Clark out on their famous expedition to explore the new territory of the west. The state of Louisiana was eventually carved out of this huge chunk of land, and the remainder became the states of Arkansas, Iowa, Missouri, Nebraska, North and South Dakota, and most of Kansas, Minnesota, Colorado, Montana, and Wyoming.

One afternoon, after we were done with school and our chores, we decided to get a taste of Louisiana's famous Cajun food. Miss Helen's Restaurant was located just a mile down the road from our campground. Jon had catfish, and I had alligator soup and crawfish. We tried a little bit of everything. Shrimp, stuffed shrimp, catfish, crawfish, crawfish gumbo, seafood gumbo, shrimp gumbo, fried oysters, crawfish ettouffe' (pronounced a-too-FAY), and alligator soup. I liked

*Mmm. Alligator soup!*

everything, except for the gumbo which was like thick soup. It tasted a little too fishy for me. The other thing I didn't like were the oysters. I didn't like oysters in Maine, and I didn't like them in Louisiana, either.

The Lafayette KOA was home base for our week in Louisiana. The campground boasted a stocked fishing pond, and I had big plans to catch a fish. I went fishing several times, but I didn't catch anything. I was beginning to wonder if there really were any fish in the pond.

The campground hosted a Crawfish Night for the guests. We wanted to check it out. Crawfish is a big thing in Louisiana, kind of like lobster in Maine. Jay, one of the campground owners, said some people like to suck the brains out of the boiled crawfish, it was considered a delicacy. He convinced me to try it. Mom just about threw up when she saw me do it, and she couldn't eat anymore. Actually, it wasn't so terrible, although I probably wouldn't jump at the chance to do it again.

"Are you sure there's fish in that pond?" I asked Jay, after filling myself with crawfish.

"Yeah, I put 'em there myself," he said.

"Well, I'm not having any luck."

"Maybe you're not using the right lure."

"Can you show me your best lure?"

Jay smiled and motioned for me to follow him. As I tried to keep up with him, I noticed the long strides in his walk. He was tall and slender and probably about Dad's age. With his deeply tanned skin and brown hair highlighted by the sun, Jay looked like he spent a lot of time fishing. He took me into the campground store, to a wall of dangling tackle and pulled a shiny lure off the rack.

"This is what you need," he said.

I looked at the lure. It was orange, blue and yellow, and it had three hooks attached to each end. It looked like a fish, and, at the least, it looked like it would catch something. When I checked the price tag, I flinched. Five dollars! I paused for a moment, trying to decide how badly I wanted to catch a fish and if it was worth the five dollars. I glanced up at Jay.

"How confident are you that this lure will catch a fish?"

"I think it'll work," he said.

"Are you so confident that if it doesn't, you'll buy it back?" I asked him. A big smile came across his face.

"Sure, I need one of those in my tackle box, anyway!"

That night I tried the lure. No luck. The next day I went out again. Jay walked by.

"Catchin' any?"

"No, not yet."

"Keep tryin'."

Finally, the next afternoon I caught a fish. It was only three inches long, but it was still a fish. The funny thing was, I didn't catch it with the fancy five dollar lure I bought, I was just using a worm. I decided to keep the lure and let Jay off the hook. Besides, I liked the way it looked in my tackle box. Dad showed me how to scale the

fish and clean it, then we fried it for dinner. It was small, but tasty.

My interview with Louisiana Governor Mike Foster would mark my first meeting with a governor west of the Mississippi River. I was surprised when I saw Louisiana's capitol in Baton Rouge. It doesn't look like the other capitol buildings. It looks more like the Empire State Building. The capitol stands 450 feet tall, has 34 stories, and cost five million dollars to build.

Governor Foster had won the election for governor of Louisiana in November and had just been inaugurated. The press secretary, Marsanne, told me there would be a press conference after my interview with the governor, and the media would probably ask me some questions about our trip.

Marsanne escorted us into Governor Foster's office and introduced us. The governor was a husky man with a salt and pepper beard. As soon as I sat down, he began telling me about Louisiana.

"If I had a small business, why would I want to bring it to Louisiana?" I asked him.

"I'm not so sure you would. Come back in six months or so and ask me again."

He made it clear to me that Louisiana was a poor state and he was there to try and make it a better place in which to live and work.

"I'm not a politician by trade. I ran for office because I didn't like the way things were."

I found myself thinking how much courage it took to stand up and face the challenges he was facing. I hope Louisiana will become a better state as a result.

"What do you think will be your greatest challenge as governor?"

"Getting most of the things that I ran on into law."

"What is your favorite place in Louisiana?"

"To what?"

"Just your favorite place to be."

"Either it'd be out in the gulf fishing or out in the marsh huntin' ducks."

"If you could be anything you wanted to be or do anything you wanted to do, what would you do?"

"You know the strangest part, I've always done the things I've wanted to do and gotten away with it," he joked. "As I decided I wanted to do something with my life, I was able to do it, so for the time being this is what I want to do."

The press was waiting, and Marsanne said we needed to wrap up the interview. We had our picture taken with Governor Foster and headed out to the press conference. A mass of media began asking both me and the governor questions. One of the reporters asked what I liked about Louisiana.

"I like the food down here because we don't have this stuff in Michigan."

They all thought it was a pretty funny answer, and I was red with embarrassment that night when it was broadcast on the evening news. I guess I can relate to politicians who say things that don't come out just right, but have to live with it being aired on the news or printed in the papers. Oh well, I probably won't see those people again.

Mom invited Marsanne over for dinner. She came bearing gifts: a copy of a book written about the Louisiana State University baseball coach for me, and a LSU baseball cap for Jon. We enjoyed our time with her.

*January 26...We are now officially halfway through the trip. Awesome! Bought an alligator head at the camp store, I went over on my Louisiana budget, spent ten dollars.*

Later that week we took an airboat ride at Marshall Landing with Airboat Tours, Inc. It was only thirty degrees outside, and we were going to be cruising through the swamps at speeds up to forty miles per hour. We had our winter coats and gloves on to keep warm. Our driver was a friendly Cajun named Mike. He started the huge fan behind us. It sounded like an airplane. He handed us headsets to cover our ears and protect them from the deafening noise. The faster we went, the colder it felt and the stiffer I became. I was glad we brought a blanket with us. I wrapped it as tightly as I could around Jon and me.

We saw lots of different birds: white pelican, blue heron, coot, kingfisher, white ingrid, owl, and tons of ducks. There were also lots of cypress trees. At one point, Mike shut off the engine.

"Don't worry," he said, "the carburetor is just freezin' over. We have to let it cool down." That didn't make any sense to me; if something is freezing, why do you have to let it cool down?

We were hoping to see some alligators, but it was too cold for them to come out. Some of the cypress trees growing in the swamp are over 200 years old. Most of them are hollow and the wood ducks like to make nests in them. It was an awesome ride, but by the time we got back to the car, I was numb.

Laundry day is my least favorite day of the week, but in Louisiana, Mom helped us. In the campground laundry room, a young guy with dark hair was folding his clothes. Mom was being nice and chatting with him. She learned he was from Canada. When I came back from the motorhome with hangers Mom needed, she sent me back to let Dad know we'd be having company for dinner.

"Dad," I yelled, as I opened the motorhome door, "we're having company for dinner."

"What? Who is it?"

"Some French guy Mom met in the laundry room."

"Oh great, when is he going to be here?"

"I don't know. Mom will be back from the laundry room in a few minutes, and she'll let you know the details."

Dad was getting used to unexpected company. Mom was always inviting strangers over for dinner or coffee. She loved to entertain, but because Dad was in charge of the cooking, it sometimes drove him crazy.

When Mom returned to the motorhome, she explained to Dad that she had befriended a man from Canada who was traveling throughout the United States on a journey similar to ours.

"He's traveling by car and sleeping in a tent. Honey, can you believe that? And the weather forecast said that temperatures are going to be dropping below freezing tonight, so he decided to go to a motel. When I realized he'd just be sitting in a motel room by himself, I invited him to come and have dinner with us. I'm sure you'll like him, it'll be fun." Mom could be so convincing.

Dad managed to throw together a nice pasta dinner, and Robert told us about his life in Quebec. He was a teacher who'd taken the year off to see the United States. He was keeping in touch with his class back in Quebec through the Internet. He would send the information back to them from each place he visited, so they could learn right along with him. It was interesting, because his trip was similar to ours, and he was visiting many of the same places we were. When dinner was over, we exchanged addresses and wished each other well on our journeys.

*February 3... Went to New Orleans. Smelled lots of good food and heard some cool music while driving through downtown.*

# 26

# amy for governor?

"They aren't kidding when they say everything in Texas is big," I said to Mom and Dad, as we walked through the massive doors of the capitol building in Austin.

We checked in with the receptionist to let her know we'd arrived. Standing in the hall, I noticed several camera crews arriving, which added to my anxiety. I was already nervous enough about meeting Governor George Bush, Jr. *This was more than just interviewing a governor,* I thought. *I would be talking to someone whose father had been the President of the United States.*

"Mom, I'm so nervous."

She pulled me aside and gave me a pep talk. "Now, Amy, remember that Governor Bush is a regular person just like you. He puts his pants on the same way you do. He just happens to be the governor of Texas."

I laughed at the funny way Mom was trying to calm my nerves, but it worked. She was right. He is just another person—an important one—but just another person.

We made one final trip to the bathroom before it was time to meet Governor Bush. Mom had to make sure every hair was in place, and I had to wash my sweaty palms. I didn't want to shake his hand and gross him out. Finally, they called my name. I took a deep breath as I walked through the door to the reception room. Governor Bush reached out his hand and welcomed me with a big Texas handshake. He turned to the press and explained that I would be interviewing him.

"I'm a little nervous," he said. I felt better knowing he was nervous, too.

One of the reporters asked me to state my full name.

"It's Amy Burritt, that's A-M-Y-B-U-R-R-I-T-T," I said. Everyone laughed, and Governor Bush put his arm around me.

"I like this girl," he said with a smile. "Don't be surprised if she becomes the first woman president." Whoa, slow down Governor, I thought. I just want to make it through this interview.

"This is a private interview," he told the press, as we left the reception room. I was really glad I didn't have to interview him in front of the media. We sat down in Governor Bush's office.

"You were very articulate in front of the press," he told me. "I was very impressed by that. I must tell you, that's not easy. That was the capitol press corps. Those are the most sophisticated reporters we have, and you stood up there and spoke clearly. It was very good."

"Thank you," I said. "You can relax now."

"Thank you," he laughed. "I appreciate that." He looked over to the man standing at the door and asked, "How much time do we have?"

"Five minutes," the man replied.

"We'll need ten," the governor said, as he sat down on the couch. I like this guy, I thought.

"Well," I said, beginning the interview, "my goals this year are to meet and interview all the governors and the President. Can you tell me, what are your personal goals?"

"My personal goals are to be a good father and husband, to worship my Lord, to live a decent life caring for other people. My goals as governor…," he paused. "One of the things I try to do as governor of the United States, I mean of Texas…" I started to laugh when he said governor of the United States. He paused, laughed at himself and said, "We kinda think we're a special country." Then he became serious again.

"The goal I have set for Texas is to make sure that every child can read. My philosophy is government ought to do a few things and do them well. I don't have any political goals, and I will tell you this, I will never seek office unless I have enthusiasm for the job."

"Who has most shaped your political career?"

"My father, by far. I look up to him not because he was President, I look up to him in spite of the fact that he was President, he was still a great father. He had his priorities absolutely straight, and his

131

family came first before everything. That's why I respect him. He also came into the process with his integrity and left with his integrity. My mother also shaped my life. She was a great first lady and a terrific mother."

"What was it like to be the son of a President?"

"First of all, there were a lot of really neat things: Christmas at Camp David, going to the White House any time I wanted to go, eating dinner one night with Gorbachev, Jim Bakker, my Dad, and mother. It was just fascinating. I got to see history like no one else did. I learned a lot, but the stressful part was the press, at times. They tried to damage George Bush by damaging his children. I didn't like some of the characterizations of a good man, and yet there was very little I could do about it. But, that's politics. But, if you're honest with people and straightforward, and just be yourself, generally things work out pretty well in life, whether you're in politics or not."

"I kind of half expected you to be wearing cowboy boots, being the governor of Texas," I commented. I was getting better at letting the interview flow naturally and not asking only my written questions. I think it made the interviews more interesting.

"Well I wore 'em yesterday. You missed me. I had a nice pair on in Washington. But," the governor continued, "Texas is a great place, it's a neat state. You know we were a separate nation, and Texans have the reputation of being braggadocios. And we are, about our own state, because we really have something special. We have a unique history and legacy. And the topography is so unique; West Texas is desert and there are no native trees, and east Texas is called the Piney Woods."

Governor Bush continued to talk about his state and his job as governor. It was great, because he was answering my questions. I didn't even have to ask them.

"If you ever want to be anything politically, run for the governor of your state, because the governor is the chief executive officer and gets to make interesting decisions every day. I know I'm talking too much and not answering your questions," he smiled, "but let me just give you a piece of advice about making decisions."

He paused for a moment, as if searching for just the right words. "If you set your principles in place—what you believe—decision-making becomes pretty easy. See, if you make decisions based on politics, then you foul up, because you send contradictory signals, you look wishy-washy, which you would be. But, if you make decisions based on your principles, the decision-making process is not only fun, but it's really rewarding. That's why you ought to run for governor."

I laughed at the thought.

After he signed our sweatshirts, Governor Bush put on his cowboy hat and said, "Let's get a picture." I stood next to him, and Jon stood on the other side. Governor Bush was tall and thin, and he had a great smile. He showed us pictures of his family and explained the paintings on the wall.

I really liked this man. He was down-to-earth, and I left his office feeling great. I think he inspired me. I never really thought about it before, but maybe I will think about running for governor. After I graduate.

heart of texas
Governor
George
Bush, Jr.
award

During our visit to San Antonio, we toured the infamous Alamo. I learned about the legendary Davy Crockett, who lost his life defending Texas from Mexico at the Alamo in 1836. I remembered a song about Davy Crockett, something about being king of the wild frontier. I started singing it. I would have liked Davy Crockett. I stood at the Alamo and tried to imagine what it was like for him in those last hours. Later, I wrote a story in my journal.

"Are you going to be all right, Jim?"

"Yeah, yeah. It's only a leg wound, Davy."

Jim Bowie was one of my best friends. I wrapped his wounded leg with bandages. I needed to get back to my post, but I hated to leave Jim alone.

The shots of rifles and the thunderous roar of the cannons were almost deafening.

"Get back to your post, Crockett," Colonel Travis shouted. "We need you!"

"Get some rest," I said to Jim as I headed for my post. Even though some men have been fighting for two days straight, no one is allowed to leave their position defending the Alamo, no matter how tired he is.

From my post I can see some four, five, or maybe six thousand Mexican soldiers closing in on our makeshift fort. The odds seem impossible, and most of us Texans believe we are going to die, considering that there are thousands of them and only two hundred of us, but we will fight for our freedom to the end.

Mexico's Constitution says that we have the right to vote for our leaders, but when a man named Antonio Lopez de Santa Anna became President of Mexico, he threw out the Constitution, declaring we no longer have the right to vote. That is why we are fighting the Mexicans.

Every day, there are less and less Texans and seemingly more Mexicans. Someone went to notify Sam Houston that we need more soldiers. Sam reported back, he had no men to spare.

Most of the time I use my gun, but every couple of days Colonel Travis puts me behind a cannon and today is one of those days. Standing behind this cannon packing gunpowder isn't exactly one of the safest places to be. I dodge bullets most of the time. Some men aren't so lucky. Most of us realize what the future holds, nevertheless, we will fight until the end.

A few days later, we packed up the motorhome and headed for Big Bend National Park in southern Texas. Along the way, we stopped at a store to buy some groceries. A group of people were staring at me while I walked Shasta in the parking lot.

"Are you Amy Burritt?" one of them asked.

"Uh, yeah, I am," I said. I didn't recognize any of them.

"We saw your picture in the newspaper," a lady explained, showing me the article. "We think it's great what you're doing. I can't believe we met you."

"What an incredible year you must be having," another person commented.

"It is," I nodded.

"How did you like Governor Bush?" they asked.

"He was great. I really liked him." Just then, Mom and Dad came out of the store.

"Are these your parents?" the lady with the newspaper asked.

"Yes."

"Oh, hello," she said. "We just read about your trip in the paper. We're so excited to meet you."

When Mom, Dad, Jon, and I finally climbed back into the motorhome, we talked about how unbelievable it was that out in the middle of nowhere someone recognized me from the newspaper. I could almost imagine what life must be like for high-profile politicians and celebrities. It would be hard to protect your privacy.

We spent eight hours driving to Big Bend, only to find there wasn't a single campsite available in all three campgrounds. We backtracked to the Stillwell Ranch about ten miles away where we found a place to camp for the night. It was a big open gravel lot with little posts sticking out of the ground for water and electricity.

The southern part of Texas is pretty flat. You can see a long way. That night, we stood outside and gazed at the billions of stars surrounding us in the black sky. I'd never seen the sky so dark. I realized that's what the real cowboys see every night as they roam the range. In the distance, we could hear the calls of coyotes, crying like a litter of pups. I was thankful to be sleeping in a motorhome.

*February 9... Saw javelinas for the first time. They look like wild boars with coarse hair, kind of like hairy pigs.*

**W**e woke up early the next morning and drove back to Big Bend. This time, we found a campsite. I liked this part of the country. There were some big mountains, and Mexico was just across the border. After talking to several campers who'd crossed the border, we decided to make the trip, too. Dad paid two Mexican men to take us across the Rio Grande River in a little rowboat. The river wasn't as big as I'd imagined. With a name like Rio Grande, I expected it to be huge, with raging waters. It was orange and murky, nothing like the crystal clear rivers I was used to in Michigan. In some places, it's very wide, but where we crossed, it was narrow enough to toss a stone across the river.

When we landed on the other side, we were approached by more Mexicans who wanted to rent us their burros for the ride up the hill. Mom thought it would be a fun experience for us, so Dad forked

over the money. The donkey ride was fun, but they sure did smell. We didn't even have to steer the donkeys They'd made the trip so many times, they could've done it in their sleep. In fact, I think mine was asleep!

There were several small stands along the winding, dusty road. Mexicans were selling their goods. They had rocks from the mines in Mexico, little scorpions made out of wire, and bracelets that said *"Mexico"* and *"Boquillas."* Boquillas was the town we were approaching.

As we rounded the last corner, I caught sight of the first houses in the desolate village. They were built from mud and clay. Dad said it helped keep the houses cool during the summer heat since they didn't have air conditioning. There were openings for windows and doors but no screens or glass to cover them. I wondered about bugs.

I saw little children running barefoot on the rocks and hot sand. Their worn clothes were stained and ripped. I looked down at my brand name clothing and new tennis shoes. I began to feel a little overwhelmed at the amount of nice things I owned. These kids seemed to have so little.

We dismounted our burros at the top of a hill. A bunch of kids with shiny rocks in their hands ran over to us. They held out their rocks and begged, "One dollar, one dollar!" I leaned over and looked at the rocks. They were quartz. I asked Dad if I could buy one. Since he objected to spending a dollar on a rock, we started to walk away. The children followed, insisting we buy a rock. Dad told us they expected people to bargain with them, so we said, "A quarter?" They nodded and traded the purple quartz rock for a quarter.

We walked around Boquillas. It looked like a ghost town. We saw an old church locked with chains to keep out vandals and a barren-looking one-room schoolhouse. The town didn't look like it had much to offer for recreation. There weren't any playgrounds or gymnasiums where the children could play sports. I didn't even see any balls or toys. I did see a lot of trash blowing around, though.

It was hot, probably around 95 degrees. There weren't many trees for shade, just old cement buildings lining the streets. All the dust in the air made me thirsty, and I was getting hungry. There was only one place in the village that served food, but I wasn't sure I wanted to eat there. It looked like an abandoned house turned into a store. There were several outside tables to choose from, so we sat down at one under the shade of the building. A Mexican woman promptly attended our table and asked us what we wanted for lunch.

"What do you have?" Mom asked.

"Tacos and burritos. They come three on a plate."

"We'll have a plate of each and four Cokes, please."

Since that was the only food and drink they served, it was an easy decision to make. Dad had also told us not to drink any water, because it might not be sanitized and could make us sick.

The Cokes came in large glass bottles, but the bottles were chipped and scratched. They looked as if they'd been recycled a million times. Yuck. Still, it felt good to have something cold to drink. The waitress brought our lunch and set it on the table. We all stared at it for a minute, surprised. We thought three tacos and three burritos would be enough for the four of us, but there on the plate were three tiny little tacos and three mini-burritos. They looked more like an appetizer. We looked at the plates, then at each other. Finally, we all just laughed at the sight of the miniature food.

"Well, dig in!" Dad exclaimed.

I wanted to order more, but Mom and Dad were anxious to get back to American soil. The donkeys took us back down the hill. Mom bought one of the little wire scorpions and a few bracelets with the word *"Boquillas"* on them to send to my cousins.

*February 11...Drove through Fort Stockton, Fabens and El Paso. Bought cowboy boots for fifty dollars at the last stop. My most expensive souvenir yet.*

# 27

# see you at
# the top

"Amy," Mom said, interrupting the math problem I was trying to finish. "Guess what?"

"What?" I could tell by the look on Mom's face, she had something exciting to tell me.

"Do you remember one of the things on your dream list that you really, really want to do?"

Puzzled, I set my pencil down and turned to the notebook with my dream list. I started rattling off several things on my list.

"Climb a mountain?" I asked.

"No."

"Go parasailing?"

"No."

"Bungee jumping, go to Australia, meet the President?"

"No, no, no." It was driving Mom crazy. She couldn't wait any longer to tell me. "Swim with the dolphins!" she blurted. "The Hilton Wiakaloa in Hawaii just called to let me know you were accepted into the dolphin program!"

"Wow! I can't believe it, that's awesome!"

I jumped out of my seat and gave Mom a big hug. Swimming with the dolphins was a dream I didn't think I'd accomplish for a long time, but we'd be going to Hawaii as soon as we finished our travels through New Mexico and Arizona.

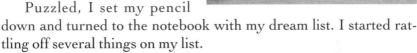

The weather was beautiful in New Mexico. Living in Michigan, I wasn't used to 65 degree temperatures in the middle of February, so it was hard to concentrate on my school work. And with my mind now focused on the dolphins, it was nearly impossible. I just wanted to be outside.

We were staying at the All-American RV Park, just outside Albuquerque. The park sat on the top of a hill overlooking the city, and at night the lights of Albuquerque were a beautiful sight to see.

As we headed to Santa Fe, I realized what a neat state New Mexico is. A large portion of the land is desert, but we passed by some big mountains where it snows and people can ski.

Santa Fe, New Mexico's capital, has one of the most unique capitol buildings. It's round and looks like the clay pies Jon likes to make in the mud. The "Round House," as it's called, was noisy and crowded the day we went for my interview with Governor Gary Johnson. The governor's press secretary explained they only had one day left of the legislative session and the governor's time was very limited.

"Try and keep the interview under ten minutes," she asked.

"No problem," I said. I was happy with ten minutes.

While I waited, I read the governor's biography. I learned he likes to ski and climb mountains. He is also a triathlete. I thought it would be fun to talk with a governor who likes sports like I do.

The press secretary motioned for us to follow her. Entering the governor's office, I noticed several reporters. Governor Johnson hobbled over and welcomed me to his office. His leg was wrapped in a blue splint.

"Hello, Amy. Welcome to Santa Fe."

"Thank you, Governor."

"You're welcome.

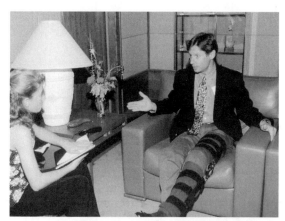

*Interviewing Governor Gary Johnson.*

Why don't you have a seat over here," he said, pointing to a couch. I didn't want to waste any time, so I jumped right into my questions.

"What are your personal and political goals?"

"I've based my life on a few things: always tell the truth and always keep my word. And, from a personal standpoint, goalwise, I have some athletic goals. I'd like to climb Mount Everest. I'd like to be world triathelon champion in my age group. Those are my goals, all in the context of telling the truth and keeping my word."

I realized I had some things in common with this governor. Climbing a mountain is on my dream list. Maybe I'll see him at the top someday.

"Kids my age are looking into different careers and thinking about what they want to be when they grow up. What did you want to be when you were my age?"

"I wanted to be President of the United States, but I also realized that I would have to accomplish things business-wise, and, of course I would have to be having fun along the way." That reminded me of another one of Dad's motto's, "Find something you like to do and make a career out of it."

Realizing my ten minutes were almost up, I thanked him for his time and asked him to sign the sweatshirts.

"Sure," he said. "What do you plan to do? Do you have any aspirations?"

"Well, I'm really enjoying learning about government, but the good thing is, I don't have to make that decision right now."

There was a TV journalist and a newspaper reporter waiting to ask me questions after I finished my interview. The governor's press secretary asked me if I had everything I needed from the governor. When I answered "yes," I heard the two media people ask, "How'd she do that?" Maybe one of my aspirations should be to be a reporter.

*February 12... Went digging for geodes at Rockhound State Park. Mom let me call Melisa and Brittany. I couldn't wait to tell them about the dolphins. They didn't seem excited about my news. I almost wished I hadn't called.*

# 28

# stupid day

It's a good thing Arizona has an eye-catching welcome sign. From the terrain, I never would've guessed we had crossed the border.

Our first planned stop was the Petrified Forest. We drove through it, and later, at the visitors center, Jon and I bought some petrified wood. I discovered in many of the other national and state parks, collecting rock or petrified wood was not allowed, so I was glad we could buy some for a souvenir.

After that excursion, we drove through the Painted Desert near Holbrook. I never could've imagined how beautiful and almost unreal this desert would look. It really does look like someone dropped pastel-colored paint all over the desert. The name fits!

We also stopped along the way to look at some petroglyphs (a carving or inscription made on rocks) created by the Mojave and Pueblo Indians. One petroglyph showed a giant prehistoric bird with a man in its mouth. There were also a bunch of smaller pictures of men and stairs. I'm sure the pictures told some very interesting stories. Maybe the picture of the men going up and down the stairs was telling a story about an underground world. The one with the giant bird could mean long ago there were huge birds that watched the Indians at work. When a bird saw a man alone, it would swoop down and snatch up the frightened Indian in its large beak and carry him to a nest high above the land. Yes, I'm sure they all meant something, but until I learn to read petroglyphs, I could only imagine the stories they told.

It rained on the only day we had to see the Grand Canyon. We ran to the overlook, but fog made it difficult to see. Clouds hung heavy over the canyon as we stood in the rain, trying to get a glimpse of the spectacular natural wonder. Back at the gift shop, people crowded in, browsing through bins of souvenirs and collectibles until the rain stopped. Someone suggested we go to the Imax Theater and see a movie about the Grand Canyon. Imax is a gigantic screen, and you feel like you're right inside the picture when you watch. We bought tickets, deciding it would probably be the best way for us to see the Grand Canyon that day.

The theater parking lot was full of touring buses loaded with Japanese tourists. I've seen many Japanese people at the national parks and tourist attractions, and I've never seen people who take so many pictures. They must really like America. Shoulder to shoulder, we inched our way into the theater. I was listening to the tourists talk to each other while we waited for the movie to begin. It was fun to listen to the Japanese language, but it sounded confusing and different. There was no way I could figure out what people were saying.

The Imax screen made me feel like I was in the canyon, soaring over the Colorado River, whitewater rafting and hangliding. I'm sure I was able to see parts of the Grand Canyon I wouldn't have been able to see outside, even on a sunny day.

The rain stopped the next morning, and we headed for the little town of Sedona. We didn't know what a stupid day it was going to be. That's what Dad calls a day when we don't use common sense, and we do something stupid—a stupid day.

Mom and Dad had their usual cup of coffee for the road, and I finished securing the motorhome for travel. The sun was shining, so Mom set up the video camera on the dash to tape our descent down the mountain. The red rocks were amazing.

"Amy, will you get Shasta off the dash?" Mom asked, as she was trying to video tape. "She's in the way of the camera." That was Shasta's favorite seat. She would sit there and look out the window while we traveled down the highway.

"C'mon Shasta, get out of Mom's way," I said, leaning forward to grab Shasta. I heard something splash beneath me.

"Amy!" Dad yelled. "You spilled my coffee! Hurry, get a towel." I ran to the cupboard to grab a towel.

"Oh no!" Mom gasped.

"What?" Dad asked, while trying to steer the motorhome on the narrow mountain road. She looked at Dad with a blank stare, as if she was trying to word the next sentence in a way that would keep Dad in his seat.

"The coffee spilled on your camera." I suddenly got a very sick feeling in my stomach.

"What? How bad is it?" Mom lifted Dad's $1,800 camera up where he could see it. Coffee dripped out the sides as she turned it around.

"It's soaked," Mom said, wiping it with the towel. Dad had a look on his face that I've only seen a few times in my life.

"Doggonit, Amy, how many times do I have to remind you to use common sense? You don't reach over a hot cup of coffee."

"I didn't mean to do it. I'm sorry," my shaky voice pleaded.

"Amy, it's not your fault, honey, I told you to reach up here and get Shasta. I know you didn't mean it." Mom's consoling words didn't make me feel any better. I knew if that camera got wet, it was ruined. Dad's friend, Bud, a professional photographer, and Melisa and Brittany's father, had picked out that one because Dad wanted a dummy-proof camera for the trip. It did everything; at least, it used to do everything.

I sat on the couch behind Dad's seat. At that point, I was wishing he had a "kid-proof" camera instead. Tears welled up in my eyes. I knew Dad was upset. It seemed like it took forever to get to the bottom of the mountain. Somehow, the beautiful red rocks didn't seem so pretty anymore. Dad pulled off to the side of the road in downtown Sedona and picked up his coffee-logged camera. He fidgeted with the buttons and dials checking for damage.

"It won't turn on," he said grimly.

"I'm sorry, Dad," I repeated, as the tears streamed down my face.

"That's all right, Amy. It could have been any one of us." I realized when Dad saw my tears, he felt bad for scolding me. He set the camera on the dash.

"Let's go walk around town. This looks like a neat place," he said.

I tried to enjoy the sights and shops of the cute mountain town, but I was still shaken from spilling the coffee. There was something very peculiar about this place. Looming over the town was a huge red rock formed in the shape of a coffee pot. Life can be so cruel.

The camera incident added to my feeling of homesickness. We'd been gone for eight weeks. After that amount of time, we would usually be heading home. Instead, we were going farther west. After my last call to the girls, I didn't feel like calling them again, and we'd stopped writing letters weeks ago. I felt we were drifting further and further apart, in more ways than one.

The next attraction we visited in Arizona was Biosphere 2. This huge glass dome sits out in the Arizona desert like a golf ball in a sand trap. It is considered by many to be a $150 million scientific flop. The building was designed to look "space age," but the idea for the experiment just didn't work. The idea was conceived by a group of scientists who wanted to create a totally airtight facility where humans, animals, and plants could live independently from the rest of the world. When it was completed, four men, four women, several chickens, goats, fish, and other critters were sent to live in the building for two years without any physical contact outside the Biosphere.

All the different ecosystems of the world were represented. There was a desert, a rain forest, a million dollar man-made ocean, and swamp lands. The inhabitants grew cacti, banana trees, and coffee trees. The artificial world even had ants. I learned about how the group used goats for garbage disposals and fish manure to help the rice grow. I thought about all the other animals that play an important role on Earth. We sometimes forget that every single animal and insect is a necessary part of an ecosystem and the food chain.

The scientists also created rain that would fall from the roof of the greenhouse. It was monitored and regulated by a state-of-the-art computerized control system. The system was used to manipulate the environment by controlling carbon monoxide, oxygen, humidity, and other environmental variables.

They forgot one important variable, however. The wind. The experiment proved that without wind, the trees were not as strong, so as they grew taller, they began to bend and eventually snap in half and fall to the ground. There were other things they didn't consider.

The condensation on the glass roof dripped down onto their desert and caused it to grow vegetation.

When we visited, I expected to see people living inside, but the experiment had ended in 1993, nearly three years before our trip. Columbia University was taking over the project to use for educational purposes.

I give the scientists credit for trying, but I don't think any one can recreate the wonderful world God made for us.

*February 22...While in Arizona we traveled through Flagstaff, Tucson, Yuma and Casa Grande. Over 700 miles this week.*

# 29

# coconut delight

I was excited as we drove on Interstate 8 into southern California. We had plans to visit the San Diego Zoo, one of the biggest zoos in the country. Mom and Dad found a campground for the night, and we went to bed early, anticipating our big day at the zoo.

The next morning, we sat in a restaurant looking out the window, our long faces reflected back at us. Outside, it was raining cats and dogs. That was the only day we were able to visit the zoo, but the rain didn't look like it had any intention of stopping. Dad assured us that *someday* we would come back to San Diego. Little did we know how soon that someday would be, and never in a million years could I have guessed what would bring us back.

The next day, we made the long, 170-mile drive north to Newbury Park. Dad's brother, Craig, his half-sister, Debbie, and their mother, Grandma Joyce, lived there. Aunt Debbie had offered to take care of Shasta for us while we were in Hawaii. We also left our motorhome there. We planned to fly to Honolulu and stay in the Aloha State for three weeks. March seemed like the perfect time to visit Hawaii.

"Hi!" Aunt Debbie squealed, in a high-pitched voice when we arrived. She hadn't seen me in twelve years. "Oh, look at you, Amy. You've grown up so much! And Jonny, you're so cute," she told him, rubbing his hair.

Jon hated it when people did that to him, but Aunt Debbie had such a bubbly personality, you couldn't help but like her. She also had red hair that reminded me of Melisa and Brittany.

We spent the next several days packing for our trip to the Hawaiian Islands. Dad had ordered a new camera to take with us, and it was delivered the night before we left. Uncle Craig drove us to the airport and helped us unload our luggage.

"Something's wrong with this picture," Uncle Craig said, looking at us standing on the curb in our vacation clothes. "You guys get to go to Hawaii, and I have to go to work." I like Uncle Craig, he's a lot of fun. With his huge muscles and his crew cut, Uncle Craig looks like a body builder. We waved good-bye, anxious to board our plane.

We were flying United Airlines, on a 747 doubledecker that looked like a big ship. When the attendant announced it was time for takeoff, we went to our assigned seats. Jon was sitting with Dad, and I was with Mom. Dad reminded us to set our watches back, again. Since we began heading west, we'd already changed our clocks three times. It was easy gaining the time, but coming back east would be a drag.

The six-hour flight went by fast, and the stewardesses made Jon and me very comfortable. They kept bringing him the extra brownies from lunch, and they gave him a handful of pins. We were finally flying, so Jon was happy. Before I knew it, the pilot was making his announcement.

"Ladies and gentlemen, this is the captain speaking. Welcome to Honolulu, it's a balmy 82 degrees outside. Enjoy your stay in the islands." We were finally in Hawaii!

I'd never seen such beautiful blue water. I stood on the 17th floor balcony of the Hilton Hawaiian Village and gazed at the Pacific Ocean. I could see all the way down the sandy beach to Diamond Head, an inactive volcano that's the trademark of Waikiki beach. Three weeks of sunshine and palm trees. I could handle it. I ran back into the room, threw on my swim-

*The view from the Hilton Hawaiian Village.*

suit and made a beeline for the beach with the rest of my family. The hot sand felt great on my feet. I ran to the water and jumped in; it was warm. I splashed around for awhile, throwing water on Jon and running from him. We lay in the sand making "angels" the same way we did in the snow in Michigan. Then, I remembered something.

"Mom, can I have one of those special coconut drinks I've always wanted? Please?" She handed me a five dollar bill.

"Only if it's under five dollars."

"Okay."

I brushed the sand off my legs and walked over to a little beach hut where all kinds of special drinks were served. My eyes scanned the price list and stopped at the Coconut Delight. It cost seven dollars. I frowned, but then I noticed a small chalkboard off to the side. It read, "Special of the Day, Coconut Delight, $3.50." My lucky day.

"I'll take the special, please," I said with a smile. I carried my drink back to the beach and sipped it slowly. Palm trees, sandy beach, sunshine, and a tropical drink. It felt like a scene out of a television commercial. In fact, I think that's where I got the idea for the drink in the first place.

We did so much in Honolulu over the next five days, I probably checked off at least a half-dozen things on my dream list. We went to a Polynesian dinner and magic show at our hotel. Jon and I attended the Rainbow Express Kids Program offered by the Hilton, while Mom and Dad spent the day together. Nancy, the teacher we spent the day with, was a lot of fun. She took us in a limousine to the aquarium, we went shelling at the ocean, she taught us how to make leis (the flower necklaces people wear in Hawaii), and she helped us make picture frames with the shells we collected at the beach. Jon and I had a blast. The day went by quickly.

Our hotel also offered scuba diving, another big thing on my dream list. I knew Mom and Dad wouldn't let me go alone, so I started working on Mom right away. After some heavy duty convincing, she agreed to go with me. We took a brief lesson in the pool before taking the plunge into the ocean. I couldn't wait to dive in, but Mom wasn't sure she was ready.

Our dive instructor, Brent, gave us instructions on the boat.

"Breathe steadily and slowly, and don't hold your breath when you're coming to the surface or else your lungs will explode." *Whoa*, I thought, *better remember that detail.* "Don't touch the coral because, one, it's very sharp, and two, if everyone who came down here touched it, the coral would die off. And last, but definitely not least, clear your ears as you're going to the bottom, otherwise your eardrums will explode."

I remembered how Brent explained to clear my ears, "Plug your nose, keep your mouth closed and blow until you feel your ears fill with air." I sure didn't want to forget that lesson, either.

Of the twelve students in the class, I was first to volunteer to dive in the water. For me, this was a once-in-a-lifetime opportunity, and I wanted it to last as long as possible. Mom, on the other hand, was the last one in. I had a feeling she would be.

I held my breath and jumped into the water. The weight of the air tank on my back disappeared. I exhaled and bubbles floated past my mask to the surface. I inhaled slowly to make sure my regulator worked. It did. I sounded like Darth Vader. Brent took me to the bottom and motioned for me to get on my knees. He handed me a shell and made a stop sign with his hand. I think the shell was a ploy to keep me occupied and out of trouble while he was bringing the other divers down.

After a few seconds, my body began to float up toward the surface. I swam back down and dug my feet into the sand to keep from floating away again. Then I noticed a fat, little tan-colored fish swimming around me, checking me out.

How cute, I thought. Just as I reached my hand out to touch it, the fish exploded into the size of a beach ball with spikes. I almost screamed. I launched myself off the bottom of the ocean floor and sand flew everywhere. My heart was beating a hundred miles an hour. At that moment, I thought I would never touch anything else.

I was right, Mom was the last diver to be brought down. Even if she was chicken, I thought it was cool I had a Mom who was willing to try some new adventures. It took her four times to clear her ears, and when she finally reached me, I could see a concerned look in her eyes.

"Okay?" she asked with her hands. We'd learned special signs on the boat to help us communicate with each other underwater.

Putting your thumb and index finger together in the shape of a circle meant "okay."

"Okay," I motioned back. In my excitement, I moved on ahead, anticipating all the wonders of the ocean. During the dive, I saw all kinds of brightly colored fish and coral, but the highlight was the big green sea turtle that glided by me. I couldn't resist rubbing its shell with my hand. It was hard and slimy, covered with algae, and little fish were swimming all around it, eating the green, mossy carpet off its back.

I turned around to see how Mom was doing. She was gone. I wondered what happened to her. Our instructor motioned us on. A school of shiny, silver fish swam by us. They moved together in a certain rhythm, as if they were listening to the same music.

Everything was going great. I was having the time of my life. Suddenly, the girl in front of me accidently kicked the regulator out of my mouth with her fin. The force of the fin hitting my face pushed me backwards. I realized my only source of oxygen was floating somewhere around me. Frantic, I reached back, waving my arms wildly and searching for my regulator. I felt the hose floating behind me. Just as Brent had taught me earlier, I stuffed it back into my mouth and cleared the water. Everything happened so fast. I looked around to see if Mom was watching, but she still wasn't there. Brent noticed my tank was low on air and motioned for me to surface. Slowly, I began my ascent. Take it slow, I told myself. I didn't want my lungs to explode. Back on the boat, I unloaded the heavy gear off my shoulders, my face stinging from my encounter with the fin. I noticed Mom just climbing back on the boat.

"Where did you go?" I asked her.

"I panicked."

"What do you mean you panicked?"

"I started breathing heavily and felt like I had to get to the surface for air, so I did. The only problem was, when I surfaced, I was a long way from the boat and I had to swim all the way here in those big waves. I'm exhausted," she said, slumping into a chair on the deck.

"Well, you missed out on the excitement below," I said, drying my hair with a towel. "I got the regulator kicked out of my mouth."

"What?" Mom exclaimed.

"It's okay, Mom, I put it back in and I didn't drown. See!" I said with a shrug of my shoulders.

"Amy, you and water just don't seem to mix," referring to my experiences in Maine and Vermont. Mom can be so overprotective sometimes.

*March 2...Visited Mom and Dad's friends, Loren and Betty Jean. Had fun with their daughter, Angelise. She's about my age and is homeschooled, too.*

Hawaii has many islands. The seven main islands are the biggest. They are Hawaii, then Maui, Oahu, Kauai, Molokai, Lanai, and Nihau, but we were only going to three of them, Oahu, Kauai, and Hawaii. Hawaii is the one with the big volcano. I couldn't wait to stay at the Hilton Waikoloa Village. It was the hotel with the Dolphin Quest program. I had read about Dolphin Quest. It's a marine research and education center that allows hotel guests the chance to swim with dolphins. Another once-in-a-lifetime adventure!

We checked in at the front desk, and I was amazed at all the beautiful flowers in the lobby. They were so big, they almost looked fake. The place was awesome. It had its own tram and a boat that takes guests around the 62 acres of hotel property. When we arrived at our room, Mom walked over to the balcony and opened the slider.

"Amy, come here and look at this." I walked out onto the balcony and looked down. There, right below us, were the dolphins, swimming and playing in the lagoon just outside our room. I could almost reach out and touch them. A tropical breeze was blowing through the palm trees surrounding the pools, and just beyond the palms was the ocean. It was like a dream. I would swim with the dolphins the next day. I was so excited, I didn't sleep much that night.

I was up early the next morning, waiting in line for my chance to play with one of the six Atlantic bottle-nose dolphins. They looked like little kids playing in the water, jumping up in the air and squealing to each other.

"My name is Dana," the instructor said. "I am one of the dolphin trainers here at Dolphin Quest. I want you to meet my friend, Lokahi." A dolphin swam up to her side. Even though Lokahi was only two years old, he was big, about six feet long.

I watched as Lokahi moved around in the water next to Dana, making a clicking noise like a little kid trying to get attention. She instructed Lokahi to swim by me and three other girls who were in my group. She said we could touch Lokahi's fin. It was hard and felt like rubber. Dana gave him a fish and waved him off to jump up in the air. Lokahi was back in a split second, wanting more fish. Dana called me out of the line to pet him. I could feel his strong body as he swam around me. There is a certain magic you feel being next to dolphins. Lokahi was so gentle, and I loved the way he whistled and squeaked. He seemed to be communicating with me, but I didn't understand what he was saying.

Dana sent us back to shore to get a fish from the cooler. It was cold and slimy. I laid it across my hand. I would need the fish to bribe Lokahi for a kiss. Dana explained how to lay the fish flat in the palm of my hand to feed Lokahi. Thinking about his eighty-eight sharp teeth, I wanted to make sure I did it right. One by one, the girls and I stepped forward to give Lokahi our token as we leaned our faces down toward him. He was cold and wet, and he snorted after I kissed him. Dana said he liked me.

My favorite part was when I put on my mask and watched while he maneuvered under the water and around obstacles like me. Dolphins don't see color, they see in shades of gray. But they do have 20/20 vision, so I knew he could see me. One time, he came swimming past me with such speed, I thought he would run right into me, but he didn't.

*March 5...I was amazed to discover that you can ski on the big island. Not just water ski, either!*

*March 8...Flew to Kauai, the island that gets the most rainfall in the world. Found a tide pool by the ocean that had sea cucumbers. Jon and I had another water fight like the one in Maine!*

After four days on Kauai, we flew back to Oahu for my interview with Governor Benjamin Cayatano. We filed into the governor's office. Governor Cayatano was a short man with dark skin and black hair. "Aloha," he said, meeting us at the door with the traditional Hawaiian word of greeting and departure.

"Aloha, nice to meet you," I said. He motioned to a set of burgundy chairs.

"Sit here," he said. His office had high ceilings, and the walls were a brown-colored wood. I expected the place to look more tropical, but it was very plain.

I learned that Hawaii used to be a kingdom founded by King Kamehameha, until it became a state in 1959. Governor Cayatano is only the fifth governor of Hawaii and the very first Filipino governor.

"Thank you for taking the time to let me interview you."

"My pleasure. Are you enjoying your stay here in the islands?"

"Yes, very much." Governor Cayatano was quieter and more reserved than the other governors I'd interviewed. "Governor, what would you say is the most interesting historical site in Hawaii?"

"Well, I think the governor's mansion is certainly an interesting place, because it housed the last reigning monarch that Hawaii had, and when her [Queen Lileokalani] reign was overthrown by a group of civilians, she was placed in house arrest, and she spent her time at the mansion. It's called Washington Place. The other is the palace. We are the only state in the Union which has a palace, because we once had a king and we once had a queen. The other thing I would say is the Pali. Follow the old Pali road and it will take you to a lookout which was the site of a major battle of King Kamehameha."

"What is Hawaii's main industry?"

"Well, as you may have guessed, our main industry is tourism."

"There is so much to do here and the people are so friendly, I guess I don't even need to ask you why someone would want to come and live here."

"Yes. There are many different cultures represented in Hawaii, and the people get along with each other better than any other country or state, because everyone who comes here embraces what we call the "Aloha Spirit." This is a process where the people possess a great deal of tolerance, sensitivity, and care for each other."

When the interview was over, Governor Cayatano offered to give us a personal tour of his state house.

"Hawaii's capitol building is very different from all the others," he explained during the tour. "You see the building is open in the center to the sky. It was designed to be like a volcano. And if you look at the corners, the tall white pillars represent the palm trees. Well, enjoy your stay in the islands, and I hope you will come back," he said, shaking my hand. "Aloha."

"Aloha."

*March 14...Went on a submarine dive 180 feet below the surface. Saw shipwrecks, plane crashes and tons of tropical fish. What an experience!*

# 30

# leavenworth
# & greenwich

$B$ack in California, we picked up Shasta. She was very happy to see us. As Dad drove the motorhome down the freeway, I laid on the back bed, exhausted from everything we had done in Hawaii.

Southern California is so crowded, and the traffic is awful. Some days, the smog is so thick the sky is brown. I couldn't believe people breathe that disgusting air every day. It wasn't really the sunny image I had of California. As we drove north, the traffic im-proved and the scenery began to change. It went from pavement and ce-ment to beautiful green mountains and lakes.

We drove north to Sacramento, California's capital. The governor's staff told us to come to the capitol building, and they would try to work out a meeting with Gov-ernor Pete Wilson. The governor's reception room was as busy as the freeways of southern California. I'd never before seen so much

activity in a governor's office. People were coming and going through several large wooden doors in the room. After watching awhile, I decided they should put in a traffic light, because people kept bumping into each other. Somehow, that would seem fitting for the state of California.

"Hi, Amy, nice to meet you," the governor's aide said. "I'm sorry Governor Wilson is not available right now. He's on his way to the airport to meet with Senator Dole."

Because this was a campaign year, we seemed to be traveling to many of the places Bob Dole was visiting during his presidential campaign. I was beginning to wish I could meet this man, but that would have to wait.

"Do you think Governor Wilson could sign my sweatshirts for me?" I asked the aide.

"Sure, I'm on my way there now. Why don't you leave them with me and pick them up later?"

"Okay, that's great." I smiled, relieved that at least I would be able to accomplish my signature goal, even if I couldn't meet him personally.

We camped in Vallejo that night. From there, we were able to take car trips to San Francisco and the Napa Valley. In the Napa Valley, which is famous for all the wine produced there, we toured some of the vineyards and wineries. We ate lunch at a great restaurant.

The next morning, we were up early and on our way to San Francisco. As we crossed over the famous Golden Gate Bridge, we could see Alcatraz in the distance. It used to be a maximum security prison set on an island, and even though it is no longer used, it still looks eerie.

Who says you can't learn things from video games? Our video expertise actually helped us navigate some of the crazy San Francisco streets. On our computer, Jon and I have a car racing game set in San Francisco, so we'd already driven all over the city before we had even arrived there. In the game, there's a street called Lombard, which is known as "the crookedest street in the world."

"Dad, follow this street for two blocks and then turn left, it will take us to Lombard Street," Jon said. Dad looked at him like he was crazy. "No, really, I've been here before," Jon explained.

"He's right," I told Dad. "This is the way to Lombard." Dad didn't believe we knew how to get there.

"That's just a video game, you guys."

"Oh, Dad," Jon persisted, "please turn here." Dad finally decided to make the turn, if only to prove we were wrong. After a few more turns and directions from us, we came to Leavenworth and Greenwich, which is exactly where Lombard Street is located in the game.

"Sure enough, here it is," Dad said in amazement. The little brick road zig-zagged back and forth down a steep hill.

"We told you so, Dad," Jon said proudly.

Dad parked the car near San Francisco's famous Fisherman's Wharf, and we walked around. Musicians were standing along the streets playing instruments, and people could put money into little cans next to them. I especially liked a saxophone player we heard. I had "learn to play an alto sax" on my dream list.

*The crookedest street in the world.*

It was a cold day with a brisk breeze blowing off San Francisco Bay. We planned to ride a trolley, but the line was long, and it was too cold to wait. It's funny: living in Michigan I never imagined anyone could be cold in sunny California.

*March 20...Went to Bodie Ghost Town. Traveled through King City, San Jose. We're headed north.*

# tour four

oregon

washington

alaska

idaho

nevada

utah

colorado

oklahoma

arkansas

missouri

# 31

# i could've worn jeans

I couldn't deny the truth any longer. It was an ugly sight. It wasn't just one thing; it all looked bad. Mom and Dad were right, something had to change. The whole family stared at me. I began to laugh uncontrollably. I never realized how funny I looked when I chewed food.

"Mom, do I have to sit here and watch myself eat?"

"Yes, Amy." My shoulders dropped. I continued eating. "Slow down!" Mom said. "You're eating too fast, chew your food twenty times before you swallow, and sit up straight. Have you forgotten all the manners we taught you?"

"But, Mom, nobody can chew rice twenty times," I complained.

"Don't scrape your fork across your teeth," Dad reminded me for the third time.

The whole incident reminded me of the book I was reading, *Anne Frank, Diary of a Young Girl*. It's a true story taken from the diaries of a 13-year-old Jewish girl who hid from the Germans during the Holocaust. She was like me in a lot of ways, including having bad habits that her parents tried to break. For Anne, it was talking too much. For me, it's biting my nails and eating like a slob.

I tried to convince Mom to let me wear something other than a dress for my interview with Oregon's Governor John Kitzhaber.

"No, this is a formal meeting, and you need to wear dress clothes. It's very important to dress respectfully for someone as important as a governor. Besides, all of the governors wear dress clothes."

"Yeah, but they're the governors, they have to wear nice clothes," I argued. Reluctantly, I pulled out a dress for the meeting.

After a short drive to Salem, Dad parked the car in front of the capitol. We grabbed our assigned piece of equipment. Mine was the video camera bag and the tripod. Sometimes, my interviews take place in the governors' offices, but since we were going to be meeting Oregon's governor in his conference room, and we were early, we had plenty of time to set up the camera.

Governor Kitzhaber walked into the room. I didn't realize he was the governor until his aide introduced him. The governor was the person wearing jeans and cowboy boots. I couldn't resist whispering in Mom's ear.

"I could've worn jeans."

The governor handed me a packet of information about Oregon, and we sat down to begin the interview. He was relaxed, sitting in a wingback chair.

"When you were a kid my age, what did you want to be when you grew up?"

"I wanted to be a naturalist like Dr. Dolittle." I laughed at his answer. "How did you go from wanting to be Dr. Dolittle to being governor of Oregon?"

"Well, I went far astray," he said, putting his elbows on the arm of the chair and folding his hands. "I started out going to medical school and practiced emergency medicine. Then, I got involved in legislature, and, then," he said, opening his hands wide and grinning, "look what happened."

I was having a good time with Governor Kitzhaber, because I knew he was enjoying the interview.

"What is the most interesting historical sight in Oregon?"

"Probably the Oregon Trail. You can still see the ruts that the wagons made in the 1840s. We also have the Oregon Trail Interpretive Center."

Following the interview, we took one of our family sightseeing tours. We drove alongside a section of the Oregon Trail. From the comfort of our car, I tried to imagine what the pioneers endured on their long, treacherous journeys. As we zipped down the highway, I envisioned the car as a covered wagon.

*The hot sun beat down on the team of oxen; their nostrils flared as they gasped for air. They were pulling a heavy load through the mountains. Our wagon was laden with family heirlooms. Four weeks have passed since Father threw the paper on our round oak table back at home in Missouri. "There's Gold in California," the headlines read.*

*"All our dreams of fortune can come true in California," Father exclaimed. Mother's eyes scanned the newsprint. She looked up at Father, carefully studying his face. She wasn't a dreamer like him, but she loved Father dearly and believed in him. We packed what we could fit in a wagon and headed West on the Oregon Trail.*

*I was drawn out of my thoughts when the wagon slowed to a stop. I pulled back the canvas. Father stood behind the wagon, hands on his hips, surveying the steep incline ahead.*

*"Father, why have we stopped?"*

*"Our load is too heavy for the oxen."*

*I slumped back into the wagon, wondering what would have to be sacrificed this time. I gazed at the hope chest grandfather made for me for my thirteenth birthday, just four weeks before his sudden death. I had memorized every line in the grain of the oak wood. Inside were my dearest treasures. A lock of my baby hair, tied with a pink satin ribbon. Mother had saved it from my first haircut. An antique silver spoon from grandmother lay on top of a stack of neatly pressed linens. Great grandmother's china set, and around the scalloped edge of each plate was a gold ring. My favorite was the tea cup with the delicately shaped handle. But my most valued treasure was my Bible.*

*Once before, Father had to lighten the load, leaving the table, chairs and old dressers on the dusty trail. Father said these would*

be easy to replace with our fortunes in California. My box had been spared last time. I prayed that it would be left untouched once again. Father poked his head in the wagon, his eyes landed on my trunk.

My heart sunk as Father looked me in the eye. "No, Father, no! You know how much this means to me."

"We'll not make it over the mountain if it stays," Father insisted.

"I'll walk, Father, I'll push from behind," I pleaded as tears streamed down my cheeks.

"You're going to have to anyway," he answered. "You may keep your smaller treasures, but the box and the dishes have to go."

I opened the lid to my chest, and Mother helped me carefully put each item on a linen. I gently pulled the four corners of the soft cloth together and tied them.

Sobbing, I buried my head in Mother's arms as Father tossed my precious china set to the ground, I couldn't bear to watch. Mother stroked my hair as she tried to comfort me, knowing the sacrifice I was making. The sound of the trunk hitting the ground pierced my heart. I never realized how much we would have to sacrifice to reach our dream.

# 32

# t.h.i.n.k. a.p.p.l.e.s.

"**J**obs ... education ... quality of life. If I hear those same answers one more time, I'm going to scream," I told Mom, as we headed for the state of Washington in our motorhome.

"Amy, maybe you need to change your questions."

"I don't know, but I have to do something to make these governor interviews more interesting. I am really getting tired of the same boring questions and answers."

"I don't think it's the questions, I think it's that piece of paper that holds you back from having more conversation," Dad said. "I've told you this before, Amy. You have to memorize those questions. Why don't you try the system we talked about?"

"Because I haven't worked on it enough," I muttered, realizing how weak my excuse sounded. Dad just shrugged his shoulders. I knew it was up to me to make a change, not Mom and Dad. They couldn't memorize the questions for me. Only I could make the difference. I was beginning to feel frustrated with the whole thing. The interviews, the traveling, the close quarters, everything.

**I**t was early morning when we arrived in Olympia, Washington's capital. We went immediately to the governor's office. Mom talked with the scheduler there and explained how we'd been trying to arrange a meeting with Governor Mike Lowry for almost a year. The woman apologized and asked us to have a seat while she did some checking. We said we'd wait in the cafeteria.

Mom checked our voice mail and learned our meeting with the governor of Alaska was scheduled. While we waited in the cafeteria, Mom spent a long time on the telephone, making plane reservations and searching for a place to stay in Alaska. It was our next state. She returned with a big smile on her face.

"You won't believe it," Mom said excitedly. "I found a woman who owns a bed and breakfast in Juneau. She said she'd let us stay there for free."

I couldn't believe our good fortune. I was excited about the awesome time we'd have in Alaska. I thought of it as one of the last great frontiers.

Our thoughts of Alaska were interrupted when Governor Lowry's secretary told us they were still working on arranging a meeting with the governor. Another couple hours went by, we checked back again. Still no answer. We'd already been waiting three hours. We took a tour of the capitol to kill some more time and returned again to the governor's office about noon. We were finally able to talk with the governor's personal aide, Jordan, who told us he was meeting with the governor at four o'clock that afternoon. Jordan said he would ask Governor Lowry about an interview then.

The waiting thing was beginning to annoy me. We sat around for another four hours hoping the governor would see me. It seemed as though the day would never end. Finally, at four o'clock, Jordan made another appearance and announced that Governor Lowry would be happy to meet with me at five o'clock. I worried that after waiting all day, I might not be at my best for the interview.

There was one good thing about waiting. I decided to take advantage of the time, and I spent most of the day working on a new interview technique. Dad and I created a system we called T.H.I.N.K. A.P.P.L.E.S. We took the first letter of the key word in each of the questions and organized them to spell two words, T.H.I.N.K. A.P.P.L.E.S. These letters stood for: Thank you, History, Industry, Needs, Kid, Attraction, Personal, Political, Live, Enjoy, Shape.

The interview hour arrived, and I sat down with Governor Lowry. I was tired after my nine-hour wait and nervous about my new approach.

**T**    "*Thank you*, governor, for giving me this time to meet with you."

**H**    I thought for a second. "What is the most interesting *historical* site in your state?"

"Probably the Whitman Mission in Walla Walla."

**I**    "What is the most important *industry* in your state?"

"High technology, Boeing, Microsoft, and many, many others. We also have a large international trade business."

**N**    "What are your state's greatest *needs* and how do you plan on taking care of them?"

"It would be for quality education. It's not as good as it needs to be for the future."

I couldn't believe how well it was working. I hadn't forgotten to ask any questions and they all came more naturally than when I read from a piece of paper.

**K**    "When you were a *kid*, what did you want to be when you grew up?"

"I wanted to be a pilot."

**A**    "What is the most fascinating *attraction* in your state?"

"Probably Mount Ranier, Mount Saint Helens, Puget Sound, we just have so much natural beauty."

**P**    "What is your most important *personal* goal?"

"My personal goal is to be a good person."

**P**    "And what about your *political* goal?"

"I want to help people rebuild their confidence in our goverment. There is a lack of confidence in government, and I believe it's very misplaced."

**L**    "Why would someone want to come and *live* in your state?"

"It's a good place to get a good job. We have a high quality of life. The environment, safety, and education make it a great place to raise a family."

**E**    "What do you *enjoy* most about being governor?"

"Working with young people."

**S**    "What person or event most *shaped* your political career?"

"My father definitely is the person who most shaped me. As far as an event, probably I would have to say what happened in

Germany when the Nazis took over. It was an absolutely terrible infringement on individual rights, so I am very sensitive about the government or society using the government to invade privacy decisions and infringe on people's rights."

Wow, this was an easier interview than I thought it would be. I asked all of my questions with no problem, and I was even relaxed enough to listen to some of his answers.

"Well, that's all the questions I have, Governor. I wondered if you would sign my sweatshirts?"

"Sure, I'd be happy to."

When I finished, Jordan told Mom he would like a copy of the tape, because the governor did so well. I thought, well, what about me? I didn't do so bad either. Mom and Dad agreed that my new interview approach probably helped make the governor look good, too. I realized what a difference the interviewer can make. After that experience, I enjoyed watching the news and grading reporters on their interview styles.

*April 3... Will be leaving for AK tomorrow. I can't wait to get on the plane, I love flying.* The Gig Harbor Campground *we're staying at in Washington has tons of Reader's Digest magazines —my favorite. Saw Mt. St. Helens, and toured the town of Gig Harbor, reminded me of Traverse City.*

# 33

# i just want to go home

I watched as luggage handlers loaded live albino bunnies into the same Alaskan Airlines jet I would soon be boarding. I stood inside the airport terminal in Seattle staring at the strange bunnies, wondering how spending Easter in Alaska would feel. I was homesick. We'd already been gone thirteen weeks and wouldn't return home for eight more. I hoped the great adventure in Alaska would be enough to keep me from thinking too much about Traverse City, and Melisa and Brittany. At one time, the three of us had talked about opening the box in the junkyard when spring arrived. I wondered if they'd do it without me. They'd been able to go on with all the other parts of their lives without me, why not that?

We boarded the plane. As I settled into my seat with the latest issue of *Reader's Digest,* the flight attendants began their familiar routine of acting out the emergency procedures. Our DC-10 lifted off the runway, and I could feel the difference between this plane and the jumbo jet we flew to Hawaii. The jumbo jet had a smoother ride. I was nervous as our plane bounced around in the air. I wondered how the bunnies were doing in the baggage compartment.

Mom was excited about the bed and breakfast we planned to stay at when we arrived in Juneau, Alaska's capital.

"I can't wait," she said. "I've always wanted to stay in a bed and breakfast."

I laid the magazine on my lap, "Mom, what do you think it's going to look like?"

"I think it's going to be a quaint Victorian house surrounded by beautiful flower gardens."

"No, no, no. You've got it all wrong," Dad interrupted from across the aisle. "It's going to be a magnificent mountain lodge, overlooking a pristine lake, with large windows for viewing the moose and bear roaming the property. It's going to be great."

Two and a half hours later, we began a bumpy, but beautiful, descent into Juneau. From my seat by the window, I peered through the clouds and caught glimpses of a chain of small islands. In the distance, I saw Mendenhall Glacier, a huge river of minty blue ice. Suddenly, the plane dropped. It was like a ride on a roller coaster. My stomach was in my throat. I looked at Mom. She was gripping the arm on her seat so tightly, her knuckles were white. After a few more dips, the plane bounced onto the runway and finally came to a stop. I let out a sigh of relief. I was glad I didn't need to use any of the emergency procedures, because I hadn't been paying attention to them anyway.

We hailed a cab and gave the driver the address of the bed and breakfast. The weather was dreary.

"Where's a good place to eat?" Dad asked the driver.

"There isn't any," he replied. We all laughed, amused by his humor.

"No, really, where's a good restaurant?"

"Trust me. I'm from Chicago, I know good food, and you won't find any here." The cab came to a stop in front of an old brown ranch-style house. It sat up up on a hill with other rundown houses.

"Here you are," the cab driver stated flatly.

"Are you sure this is the place?" Mom questioned.

"Yep, this is it," he answered, nodding his head slowly.

We stared at the lackluster home. It wasn't at all what we'd envisioned. Reluctantly, we unloaded our luggage and walked slowly up the steep steps.

We knocked on the door and waited. A few moments later, the door opened and an old woman peered through the crack in the door.

"Listen, I've changed my mind," she growled. She obviously knew who we were. "I can't keep you here for the whole week, you'll have to find another place to stay. If I have to, I'll keep you for a couple days."

She turned around and walked into the house, leaving the door ajar, probably expecting us to follow her. Mom and Dad stood at the door in shock. They didn't know what to say. We stepped inside to escape the rain while we tried to gather our thoughts. She hastily pointed out the bedrooms and the bathroom.

"Breakfast is at eight o'clock," she said, and without another word, she disappeared up the stairs.

I walked into the room that was supposed to be for Jon and me. It smelled musty. The furniture was old and rickety, and the carpet was a dirty brown shag. I didn't want to stay there. I walked into the other bedroom where Mom was sitting on the edge of the twin bed. She was upset.

"I'm not staying here," Mom said, and she picked up the telephone. I was relieved to hear her decision. She started calling hotels from the yellow pages. After several calls, she found a room. It happened to be at the Baranof Hotel, the most expensive place in town.

"It figures," Dad said.

We called for another cab to take us to the hotel. Mom opened the door to the upper level.

"Uh, ma'am, we, um ... we found another place to stay." She waited for a response, but there was none.

"Um ...we'll be leaving now. Okay? Bye." Mom shut the door.

We picked up our luggage, went outside, and stood in the rain waiting for the cab. It was the same driver who'd just dropped us off. We didn't say much, but I knew he was wondering what happened. So much for the bed and breakfast idea, and so much for gracious hospitality. Our room at the hotel was great, though. It was a king suite with nice furniture and clean carpet.

*April 5...The cab driver was right, it's really hard to find good food, and it's so expensive. So far there's McDonald's.*

The State Museum of Alaska was located just down the street from our hotel. We dashed through the cold rain to the museum entrance. Inside we discovered displays of native artifacts. One was a small tool called an ulu (pronounced OO-loo) that the Eskimos use to skin whales. It had a wooden handle with a sharp curved blade. I wanted to buy one, but it cost twenty dollars. I had budgeted fifteen dollars for Alaska and, since I'd already spent some money on a totem pole, I decided to pass on the ulu.

Handmade articles of clothing with detailed beading hung throughout the museum. We also saw pottery with intricate designs, little moccasins, and baby carriers. Many of the items were made from the hides of animals; even parkas were made from waterproof seal guts. The Eskimos were resourceful. They didn't waste anything.

*April 6...We found a another restaurant, Taco Bell.*

The next morning, I slept until eight o'clock. I went into Mom and Dad's room.

"Did you hear that pitter patter this morning?" Mom asked. "It woke me up."

"Huh?" I said sleepily. I didn't know what she was talking about.

"Did you hear that pitter patter?" she repeated. Then it hit me.

Oh, my gosh," I said, "It's Easter, isn't it?" I ran back into our room where Jon was sleeping. I shook him.

"Jon, wake up, it's Easter, we gotta find our baskets!" He bounded out of bed and began his search.

Jon was having a hard time finding his basket. I knew where it was hidden, but I didn't give it away. He found it behind the television in Mom and Dad's room. Mine was more difficult to find. There weren't many places to hide a basket in a hotel room. After a few clues from Mom, I found it hidden in the closet, on a hanger underneath her jacket.

We organized our candy in neat little piles on the bed. "Oh Mom, I wish we were home for the egg hunt," I said, popping a jelly bean into my mouth.

"Yeah, me too," Jon said. "I wanted to find the Golden Egg this year 'cause Grandpa said it was going to be worth ten dollars."

"Oh, that's right," I said. "I wonder who found it this year?"

"I'm going to miss dinner the most," Mom said.

For as long as I can remember, Grandma and Grandpa Peckham have held an Easter egg hunt and cookout at their house. Every Easter, Grandpa gets up early in the morning and digs a hole in the ground and builds a fire. He lowers a cast iron kettle filled with beef, carrots, onions, and baked beans into the pit and buries it. Eight hours later, everyone gathers around to watch him dig up our dinner.

"Remember last year, when it rained so hard and we were running through the woods trying to find the eggs?" Dad asked. "Nothing stopped us from having our egg hunt."

"Yeah, Grandpa painted the Golden Egg with spray paint," Mom laughed, "and when I found it, the paint was running down my arm."

"Then after the rain stopped, Grandpa built a huge bonfire and we all stood around it to dry off. That was fun," I said.

"I bet they're all having fun right now at Grandpa's," Jon said solemnly.

We all became very quiet, lost in our own thoughts about past Easter celebrations. It's hard to be away from home during a holiday.

"Mom, can I call Melisa and Brittany to wish them a Happy Easter?" I asked.

"Sure."

I ran to the other room and dialed the phone. Our conversation was short, and we didn't seem to have anything to say to each other. I felt as though I was talking to strangers. I couldn't understand it. Were they forgetting about me? I'd hoped talking to them would make me feel better, but it didn't. I felt worse. The only close friends I had were slipping away from me, and there was nothing I could do about it.

I sat on the green, overstuffed chair in our room. With my arms folded, I stared down at the floor. *I'm sick of traveling. I don't want to do it anymore. I just want to go back to the life I had before, a life with my friends.*

Mom interrupted my thoughts. "Amy, why don't you and I go down to the lobby and have a cup of coffee together?"

Mom knew how hard this was for me. I wasn't sure a cup of coffee was going to make me feel better, but I needed to get out of the hotel room. I nodded my head and wiped my tears away. As we stepped into the elevator, I felt a hard lump in my throat.

The lobby was bustling with people dressed in their Sunday best. We found an empty couch in a quiet corner. I was tired and confused. I wanted to avoid a conversation with Mom, so I looked around the room. The walls were a dark, stained wood with pictures of Alaskan scenery. The room was dimly lit by small candles burning on each table. I sat with my arms folded and watched the happy families around us.

"I know you're having a hard time with this, Amy ..."

"I don't want to finish the trip," I interrupted. "I just want to go home."

"Amy, I miss my friends, too, but we made a commitment. You made a commitment."

"But why can't we just quit?" I asked. I stared at the floor, my vision blurred from the tears welling up in my eyes.

"We could quit," Mom said. "We could pack it all up and go home right now, but we aren't quitters."

I felt trapped. My eyes scanned the room. I felt like I was locked in a cage, just like the albino bunnies on the plane, and Mom and Dad had the key.

"What would we be teaching you if we gave up now and went back home? This was something you wanted to do, too, Amy. Remember how excited you were to take this trip?"

"But, I didn't know how hard it was going to be." Tears streamed down my face. Mom reached into her purse and handed me a Kleenex.

She put her hand on my shoulder and looked me in the eye. "Remember the goal you set for yourself at the beginning? You are more than halfway through now. Do you really want to quit when you've come so far?"

I thought about it for a moment. *Yes, I did want to quit.* At that moment, I felt lonely and defeated. I wanted to go home and forget the whole thing. Then I thought about facing my family, not to mention the media who'd been following my story. I took a sip of coffee and felt it slowly run down my throat. I stared at the people crowding in the lobby. Mom's words, "You made a commitment," echoed through my head. She was right. I'd made a promise to myself.

"I can't quit," I blurted out. "I ... I ... I can't go back home and tell everyone that I gave up." I took a deep breath and glanced at Mom. She looked puzzled.

"Where did that come from?" she asked.

"I guess ..." I sighed, looking down at the busy design in the carpet. "I guess I was just thinking about myself. I hadn't thought about how my quitting might affect other people."

That Easter morning in Alaska, I made up my mind. From that point on, I was going to take charge. I realized it was my project, and I would reach my goal, no matter how difficult things were.

It rained almost the entire week we were in Juneau. During the off-season, which is early spring, there isn't much to do. We went to the library quite a few times. One option we had was to rent a car and drive the fifty-mile stretch of highway from Mendenhall Glacier to Douglas Island. It only took a couple hours, even with Mom and Dad stopping every two minutes to take a picture.

The highlight of the drive was seeing bald eagles soaring across the sky. It was the first time I'd ever seen them flying free. Until then, I'd only seen one in a cage at the zoo. Eagles just aren't as magnificent in captivity as they are flying free in the wild.

My renewed conviction to make my interviews the best they could be filled me with confidence. I was ready for the interview with Alaska's Governor Tony Knowles.

"Hello Amy, how are you?"

"Great," I said, shaking his hand.

"Would you like some coffee?" His offer made me feel important.

"No, thank you." We sat down next to a coffee table and began talking.

"Some of my goals are to meet all the governors, meet and interview the President, and get my book published. What are your personal goals?"

"Gosh, I feel intimidated, because you expressed yours so well," he said laughing. "My goal is to never forget who it is that I am serving and to do it with honesty and integrity."

"What would you want people to see when they come to Alaska?"

"Well," he hesitated for a moment, "what's the most fascinating thing that you've seen here?" I thought he was clever for turning the question around.

After thinking about it for a moment, I said, "For me, the bald eagles were the neatest thing. It was cool to see hundreds of them flying all over, free to do as they pleased."

"I would have to agree with you on that."

I was feeling good about how the interview was going. I thought perhaps the governor sensed my newly found confidence when he made his next statement.

"You're a great interviewer. You express yourself very well. I'm completely impressed."

"Thank you."

"...And, I'm sure I'll be seeing you in media journalism. I think you have a great career ahead of you."

*April 10... Wish I could see the rest of Alaska, the real Frontier. Mom says there's so much more to explore than just the capital city. Maybe we'll come back someday.*

# 34

# the promise

Potatoes. Mom's favorite food. She likes them cooked a hundred different ways. This was the topic of our conversation as we drove into Idaho.

"I think I'll write a cookbook just for potatoes." Mom said. "There'll be baked, fried, french-fried, spiral-sliced, twice-baked, American-fried, and my favorite, wrapped in foil and thrown into a campfire."

Mom drove Dad crazy with potatoes. Because he did the majority of the cooking on this trip, most mornings Dad just wanted a simple breakfast, but Mom would always ask him to fry her some potatoes.

"What's wrong with cereal?" he would ask.

My meeting with the governor of the potato state, Philip Batt, actually began with the governor interviewing me. He was a short, older man with fine hair and a cheerful disposition. As he leaned back in his burgundy leather chair, he asked me question after question. He wanted to know how many states I'd been to, how long we'd been on the road, how much was left to see, and more. I began to wonder if he was ever going to let me ask him anything! When I finally had the chance, I started with my most important questions first, just in case I didn't have time to ask all of them.

"What are Idaho's greatest needs and how do you plan on taking care of them?"

In a self-composed manner, he answered, "Well, it's important to create jobs for our young folks. It's only been, like, ten to fifteen years ago, when we had a "brain drain" goin' out of Idaho. The most talented people were going elsewhere to find jobs, because they couldn't find them so well here. We have corrected that to a great degree." I laughed to myself over the governor's statement about the "brain drain". I'd never heard it phrased that way before.

"What is your greatest political goal?" I asked him.

"Well, I've reached the climax of my political career here, I suppose. I don't think I'll run for President, even though Bob Dole, who is my choice, is a little older than I am, but he can have it," he laughed. "Your Governor Engler is a fine feller, I like him."

"So do I," I said, remembering the many governors who'd said the same thing about my governor.

At the end of my week in Idaho, I decided to write a letter to President Clinton. I really wanted to interview him for my book, and a letter seemed the best place to start. Soon afterward, I received this letter in the mail:

*A space reserved for the President.*

*May 29, 1996*

*Amy Burritt*
*Post Office Box 4651*
*Traverse City, Michigan 49685-4651*

*Dear Amy:*

*Thanks so much for asking to speak with me in person. I always enjoy meeting with young people from all over our country and hearing their thoughts and concerns about America and the world. Unfortunately, because of the many demands on my time, I am unable to meet with you now. Maybe someday we'll have an opportunity to visit with each other.*

*I encourage you to continue setting high goals for yourself throughout your life. By working hard in school and making your voice heard, you are preparing yourself for the time when your generation will be leading America into the 21st century.*

*Best wishes for every future success.*

*Sincerely,*

*President Bill Clinton*

I knew something was up one evening when Dad asked all of us to dress up for a special dinner and told me to choose the restaurant. I picked the Olive Garden. It's my favorite. Mom and Dad were acting very secretive about the whole thing. It wasn't my birthday or anything special, so I was curious.

After we ordered our meal, Mom and Dad explained why we were having a special celebration.

"Amy," Mom began, "Dad and I believe in celebrating a child's passage into adulthood. Over the last few weeks, you've shown us that you're ready to handle some of the responsibilities of being an adult."

"You mean so much to us, Amy," Dad said. "We have watched you grow from a small baby into a mature young woman. Remember the bald eagles in Alaska and how magnificent they were flying free? Now, we believe you're at the time in your life when we must give you to God, and allow you to grow and handle the responsibility of your own life and your relationship with Him. We believe you are ready to fly."

Dad handed me a small black velvet box.

"What's this?" I asked, still trying to absorb everything they'd said.

"I bought this for you a year ago and was waiting for the right time to give it to you," Dad said.

Surprised, I slowly opened the box. I saw something shiny inside. It was a ring. A beautiful gold ring with a heart. In the center of the heart was a silver cross with a diamond. I stared at it for a moment before I pulled it out. I couldn't believe Dad bought me a special ring. I looked at him, tears welling up in my eyes.

"What's this for?"

"It's called a promise ring."

"What's that?"

"The diamond is a precious stone, which represents you," Dad explained, his voice cracking a little as he looked at me. I wasn't used to seeing Dad so emotional. "The cross means that you belong to Jesus, and the heart is your promise to keep your heart and body pure until marriage. The unending circle of the ring represents the circle of love in our family and that we'll always be here for you."

I was so overcome with emotion, I was speechless. I couldn't stop crying, realizing the strength of Mom and Dad's love for me. I slid the ring on my finger and just stared at it. It was the best gift I'd ever received. That night, in my heart, I made my own promise to God.

*April 19...Spent all day rollerblading and biking at the Playground Sports and RV Park.*

# 35

# the loneliest road

"**I**'m only two inches shorter than Michael Jordan," Governor Bob Miller told me, after he noticed my mouth gaping. I don't know if it did that because I was surprised at how tall the governor was, or because I had to lean my head back so far to look up at him. Whatever the reason, my mouth fell wide open.

Governor Miller walked with me around his office, and showed me pictures of the many famous people he'd met. I saw a picture of him swimming with dolphins in Hawaii. I told him I'd done the same. I felt more relaxed knowing we had something in common. During our meeting, the governor told me if Nevada were a country, it would be the second largest mining country in the world, lagging only behind South Africa. He also said many people believe Nevada's money from silver mining is what built San Francisco.

Governor Miller invited me back to meet with him the next day. It was the first time a governor wanted to meet with me twice! The second time, there was a television crew and a newspaper reporter there to interview me.

"Amy, what do you think about the seven-year-old girl named Jessica who just died in a plane crash while attempting to set a new record?" I'd heard about the terrible accident and was saddened by her death.

"I don't see anything wrong with kids pursuing their dreams, but I wouldn't want a seven-year-old driving a car down the highway just because she wanted to, either."

When the media finished their questions, I invited Governor Miller to visit our motorhome parked in front of the state house. To my surprise, he agreed. He had to duck his head to get inside. We talked about the trip while I gave him a quick tour and showed him where I did my schoolwork. He was the only governor who took time

to visit with me in the motorhome. I think that was really cool, and if I'm ever elected to public office, I would like to be that personable.

During that second visit, Governor Miller told us about a long stretch of highway called the Loneliest Road. It goes right through the middle of Nevada, through desert salt flats and mountain ranges. He sent us to the Chamber of Commerce to pick up a packet of information. We received a piece of paper showing the name of each city along the road. Travelers along the road get a stamp under each city's name. After you've traveled the entire road, and have all the stamps, you can send the paper back to the Chamber of Commerce. In turn, they send a postcard and a pin with a certificate that reads, *"I survived the loneliest road in America."*

It really was a long, lonely road. We drove for hours and hours, and it seemed as though we didn't go anywhere. The scenery still looked the same a hundred miles down the road. When evening came, we pulled off the highway in a little town called Austin. There were just a few stores, a restaurant and a gas station, but they were all closed for the night. Dad parked the motorhome along the side of the road and we went to bed.

The next morning, we walked to the International Cafe for break-fast. I thought it was a pretty optimistic name for a restaurant in the middle of nowhere. The restaurant was housed in an old building along the main street. It looked like it might have been a general store at one time. Inside, the walls were covered with handmade items for sale. We chose a table and looked around for a waitress. A group of men sat at a table near the back. They were carrying on a lively conversation. One man realized the waitress was busy in the kitchen, so he walked over to the coffee pot behind the counter.

"Ya'll want some coffee?" he asked. Mom and Dad nodded, and with one hand tucked in the pocket of his bib overalls, the man poured coffee for them.

"Am I going to have to tip you, too?" Mom teased.

He chuckled. "The waitress'll be with ya'll in a minute."

We finished our waffles and walked along the street looking at the dilapidated buildings. One store caught my interest. It was an old wooden shack with stockpiles of rocks and animal bones out front. Cattle skulls hung on the building, and an old wagon wheel leaned against a rusted barrel. I wanted to go inside, but it was closed.

We were about to climb back into the motorhome when we noticed a young couple walking toward us. Both were carrying big packs, and the guy had a guitar. They motioned to Dad as though they wanted to talk with him. Dad told us to go inside. We watched curiously through the window to see what was happening.

*Lizzy and Andy.*

The man had short brown hair. He was wearing gray sweats and a blue-hooded sweatshirt with the words "Lake Tahoe" on the front. The girl had long, thin brown hair, and she wore jeans and a big baggy sweater. After exchanging a few words with them, Dad stepped into the motorhome.

"What did he say?" I asked, as Dad hopped up the steps.

"He wants to know if we'll give them a ride through the desert."

"Cool!" I shouted. Dad gave me a funny look. We'd never picked up hitchhikers before, and he wasn't sure about the idea. Mom and Dad sat on the couch and discussed it.

"They're foreigners," Dad said.

"Where do you think they're from?"

"I don't know. I didn't recognize his accent."

As I listened to Mom and Dad's discussion, I looked out the window. I saw the two strangers sitting and sipping coffee outside the gas station. They looked harmless to me. I thought how great it'd be to meet someone from another country. Dad seemed uncomfortable with the idea, but, surprisingly, Mom thought it would be okay. Finally, Dad agreed to allow them to ride with us until we reached the end of the Loneliest Road. Dad stepped out the door and motioned for them to come inside.

"Hi, I'm Emily," Mom said, shaking the girl's hand.

"My name is Lizzy," the girl replied softly.

"Welcome to our home, Lizzy. This is Kurt, Amy, and Jonathan."

"Hello, nice to meet you. Thank you so much for giving us a ride. This is Andy," she said, motioning to her friend. Andy's hair was messy, and his skin was tanned like Lizzy's. We all said hello to him.

"Are you hungry?" Mom asked.

"We had some cheese this morning. I was carrying it in my pocket, but it got soft and mushy from sleeping on it," Lizzy said in her English accent, moving her fingers as if she was squeezing the cheese.

"Where did you sleep last night?" Mom asked, always inquisitive.

"We found a small bush off the side of the road and slept there. It was pretty cold, though."

"Would you like some breakfast?" Mom asked. Andy and Lizzy looked at each other and then smiled at Mom. She knew what that meant. She opened the fridge, checking the inventory.

"Do you like ham and eggs?" They nodded their heads eagerly.

Mom cooked them a breakfast fit for a king and queen with ham and eggs, toast, yogurt, bananas, orange juice, and coffee. I couldn't believe how much they ate. They must've been starving. During breakfast, we learned Lizzy was from London, England, and Andy came from Slovakia. They'd come to explore America.

After they finished eating, we started back out on the Loneliest Road. Thanks to the turn in events, however, it wasn't going to be so lonely.

Mom invited Andy to sit up front with Dad, so she could visit with Lizzy. Her face lit up as she began telling us about her adventures. They'd come from San Francisco and were going to New Orleans and then New York City. The two first met in San Francisco when Lizzy's plans to ride with some friends didn't work out. The friends left her alone to fend for herself. She met Andy while he played his guitar on one of the piers, which was how he financed his travels. After Andy and Lizzy decided to travel together, they mapped out their route and began their journey across America. Andy was teaching Lizzy to speak Slovakian while they traveled. They hoped it would help them communicate better.

"I've always wanted to see America, so I worked hard to save enough money to fly from England to San Francisco. I've been all over the world, China, India, and even Africa." Her life sounded so exciting. How cool it would be to travel all around the world. "My mother wishes I would get married and have a family," she said, "but I want to see more of the world before I settle down."

I liked the way she talked. Her British accent made all her words seem more interesting as she told stories of her travels. I noticed a bracelet she was wearing.

"Where did you get your bracelet?" I asked her.

"I made it, would you like to learn how?"

"Sure."

From her grungy backpack, Lizzy pulled out some string and proceeded to twist the ends together and pinned it to my jeans. She showed me how to braid them together, then she let me take over. She took a pair of worn patchwork jeans out of her bag and laid them on her lap. They were covered with neat designs.

"Tell me the story of your jeans," Mom said.

"Well, I started with my sunshine," Lizzy said, smiling and pointing to the big yellow sun embroidered on the front. "I used to sew under the reception desk at work while I was on the telly," she explained, leaning her head down to her shoulder as though she was holding a telephone. "So, then I thought I had to do the moon. And I am forever fighting with the material splitting. Then I put bluebells here, because I love the bluebells of England. Now, I just keep adding things as I travel, like the mushrooms here and a little pocket here."

Sewn onto the front pocket was a friendship bracelet given to her by someone she met traveling.

"Now, I'll have to add a big motorhome here," she said, pointing to a worn spot in the fabric.

Andy didn't understand much English, so I don't think he understood what Dad was saying to him. Andy just nodded his head when Dad asked him a question. Every few minutes, Andy would grab his camera and take a picture of the scenery, which hadn't changed much. At one point Dad told Andy a joke, but he didn't get it. Mom and I thought it was funny that Andy didn't have a clue Dad was even telling him a joke, but Dad just kept on talking. They seemed to make a good pair.

Andy and Lizzy rode with us for about seven hours, stopping at Eureka and then Ely. Together, we watched the video footage of me swimming with dolphins in Hawaii on the television in the bedroom. Then we sat at the table making animals out of Fimo dough, laughing about the silly things we could do with it.

"Being around your family makes me homesick for mine back in England," Lizzy said. "I miss my mother." She looked down at the little blue dolphin she'd created with the dough. I knew how it felt to miss your friends and your family. I wished there was something I could do to make her feel better.

After we ate dinner together, we stopped to let Andy and Lizzy off along the side of the road. They were headed south, and we had to go north. Mom loaded their backpacks with goodies. We sat and watched them walk away. After a few minutes, Dad turned the motorhome northward.

# 36

# lickety-split

"**J**on, quick, go get the camera," I whispered.

"Okay." Jon took off down the steep boulder we'd been climbing. He ran toward the car. Near the bottom he slipped and fell a few feet to the ground.

"Are you okay, Jon?" I yelled, peering over the edge of the steep rock. He stood up slowly and brushed the dirt off his clothes.

"Yeah, I'm alright." He took off running again. Jon was a good runner, and over the last few months, his thirst for adventure had grown as much as he had. I couldn't believe my little brother was already eight years old and had grown a good inch taller in just a few months.

I waited at the top of the red rock, watching a lizard closely. This one was brightly colored with bulging eyes that seemed to warn me not to get too close. I wondered if he was poisonous. He was only about six inches long, including his tail. On the ends of his feet were suction cups that helped him hang on to the rock. He was so cute. I wanted to take him home, but I knew Mom and Dad wouldn't allow it, so I decided a picture would be the next best thing.

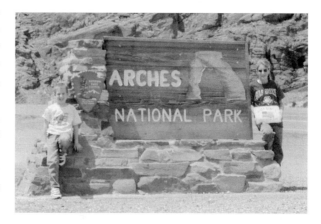

I scanned the desert from the top of my perch. We were in Arches National Park, surrounded by piles of red boulders stacked on top of each other. There were huge arches that looked as though someone had carved them out of the stacks of oddly shaped rock. It reminded me of Fred Flintstone's town of Bedrock.

"Here, Amy," Jon said, handing me the camera. I zoomed the lens in on the lizard. The noise startled him, and he darted about a foot away. I thought this must be the kind of challenge a photographer for *National Geographic* faces. I crawled very slowly toward the lizard, I wanted to get a close shot. Click.

"Got it," I said, as the lizard took off running again. This time he crawled around the other side of the boulder and was gone.

"Man, he's fast," Jon said.

"Yeah, I'll name him Lickety-Split."

Dad honked the horn, signaling it was time to leave. "C'mon, Jon, let's go."

Utah was the most beautiful state I'd seen. It was spring when we arrived, and all the flowers were in bloom, giving the air a sweet, invigorating smell. Utah has so many national parks and monuments, we had a hard time deciding which ones to visit. Like many others, we needed more than a week for this state. We did make it to Arches National Park, Bryce Canyon, and the Capitol Reef National Park. My favorite place was Arches; I even got a bag full of the red sand to take with me.

Salt Lake City is the capital of Utah and home to the Mormon Tabernacle. The Tabernacle sits in the center of this mostly Mormon town, and its towering white spires can be seen from miles away.

In the capitol, Governor Mike Leavitt welcomed me with a sturdy handshake.

"Hello, Amy. Welcome to Utah," the governor said. "I understand you've been seeing a lot of territory these days. How long have you been at it?"

"Thirty-six weeks."

"Wow, that's pretty ambitious."

"Yeah, and a lot of fun."

"Well, as I understand it, you have some things you want to accomplish here today."

"Yes, I have these sweatshirts all the governors have been signing for me. If you would do the same, I would appreciate it."

"Okay. I understand you have also been asking the governors some questions?"

"That's right." I told him.

"What would you like to know about Utah?" he asked me. I knew he only had a few minutes to meet with me, so I chose to ask just one question.

"What would you say is the biggest problem you face as governor?"

"Coping with the growth of the state and making sure there are enough jobs for everyone. I come from the baby boom generation. The children of the baby boomers are having their own children, so we're struggling to get everyone educated and get them jobs."

I was surprised he didn't say "water," as some of the governors in other western states had said when asked about big problems. The governor thanked me for stopping by.

The next day, we were leaving Utah and heading to Colorado. As we drove down the highway, Dad ran over a lizard that tried to cross the road.

"Oh," I gasped. "I hope that wasn't Lickety-Split."

"Well," Dad laughed, "if it was, we're going to have to change his name to Lickety-Splat."

*April 30...Drove through Salt Lake City, Provo, Cedar City and St. George. Jon and I made Indian war paint by mixing water with the red sand. It stained our skin.*

# 37

# my first ballgame

Spring in Colorado is full of contrasts. Snow had fallen the night before we drove through the mountains and over Loveland Pass, at an elevation of nearly twelve-thousand feet. The trees looked as though they'd been sprinkled with powdered sugar. The scenery was pretty, but it seemed strange to see snow in May. This was the first time Dad had driven the motorhome through snow. The roads were slippery, and driving on the winding mountain roads was precarious at times. As we descended into Denver, however, the snow disappeared and the weather turned warm and sunny, a near-perfect day to visit my Dad's sister.

We pulled up in front of Aunt Linda's house. She walked out the door with a Coke in one hand and a cigarette in the other.

"Where you guys been? I've been waitin' all day!" She said, grabbing me and giving me a big hug. She wasn't much taller than me, but very strong.

"It took a little longer than we expected, because we hit snow coming over Loveland Pass," Dad explained while he hugged her.

"Yeah, yeah, yeah! Excuses, excuses," Aunt Linda said in a raspy voice.

I was anxious to see my cousin, Katie. I hadn't seen her in two years. I ran up the stairs and peeked into her bedroom. She liked to collect dolls, and her room was full of them. Everything was pink. I heard humming in her bathroom, so I walked over to the open door. There she was, standing in front of the mirror, brushing her long brown hair. Katie was always concerned about how she looked.

"Amy!" she yelled, when she noticed me.

We hugged each other, and it didn't take long to become reacquainted. We sat in her room for a while, catching up on the latest fads, the best music, and the boys at her school. It really seemed good to be with family again.

The next morning was the first Tuesday of the month, and Mom was supposed to make her monthly telephone call to Jack O'Malley, the deejay of the morning show for WTCM. Because of the time difference between Colorado and Michigan, we had to call bright and early at six o'clock. When I tried to wake up Mom, she said it was my turn to call in the update, she was too tired to get out of bed. A few months before, I would have been too nervous to call Jack myself, but things had changed. I made the call. Jack was easy to talk with, and we had a great conversation. I also enjoyed the opportunity to tell everyone in northern Michigan that my Mom couldn't call, because she didn't want to get out of bed.

Once again, the sweatshirts prevailed in helping me make contact with a governor. After Governor Roy Romer's press coordinator saw our sweatshirts and all the governors' signatures, he suddenly managed to find a few minutes for me to see the governor.

"Amy, this is Governor Romer," the press coordinator said.

"Hi, Governor."

"Hello, Amy," he said, shaking my hand. He pointed to Jon.

"Who is this?"

"Jon," my brother answered shyly.

"Jon, are you related?" the governor asked.

"Yeah." Jon smiled.

"And is this your brother and sister?" Governor Romer asked, pointing to Mom and Dad. We all laughed.

"Did you want me to sign these?" He looked at the sweatshirts.

"Yes, that would be great."

The meeting was fairly brief, and the governor apologized for not being able to have a full interview with me. He explained the legislative session was just winding up, and he was very busy. I thanked him for taking time to meet with me.

Dad promised to take Jon and me to a baseball game sometime during our trip, so I was thrilled when Uncle Dave, who lives and breathes baseball, bought tickets to a Rockies game. He's a big fan of the Colorado Rockies, and he wanted us to see his team play. Jon was excited, too. He hoped to catch a ball during the game. Mom and Aunt Linda decided they'd rather go out to dinner.

On the way to the stadium, Uncle Dave told us we were going to be spoiled for our first game, because he had tickets to the V.I.P. section where the celebrities sit.

The new Coors' Stadium was awesome. It was designed to be like an old-fashioned stadium, but with all the modern conveniences like shops, restaurants, and food vendors set up all around the building. Every seat in the stadium was taken. Every game had been sold out since the stadium first opened.

The Rockies were playing the San Diego Padres. The Rockies were behind for most of the game. To rev up the team, we passed out letters Katie and I had made earlier. The letters read, "GO ROCKIES!" At the bottom of the ninth inning, things started to heat up. The Rockies got a run that tied them with the Padres. The game went into a tenth inning. When player number 10, Dante Bichette, walked up to the plate, the crowd went crazy. He was a favorite, everybody loved him. It was the bottom of the tenth, with two outs and two men on base. Bichette's first swing was a strike. The organ player played the charge song, and everyone stood up. The second pitch came, he swung. It was a fly ball. It went long and it was GONE! A home run to win the game! Uncle Dave couldn't believe what an incredible game we'd seen. His Rockies really came through for us.

*May 4...Saw another Rockies game, this time we sat in the rock pile.*

# 38

# lasting impression

Walking alongside the fence surrounding the Oklahoma City bombing site left me speechless. There was nothing left on the site where the Murraugh Federal Building once stood in downtown Oklahoma City. It was just an empty, desolate-looking block of land. Flowers, teddy bears, ribbons, and gifts of condolence covered the fence. The day we were there, about a year after the tragedy, people were scattered about, quietly walking around the area and carefully studying each little note and ribbon tied to the fence. Looking across the street, I saw the effects of the blast. Blown-out windows, cracked bricks, and twisted metal all stood as a sad reminder of the bomb that shook the footings of the building and the foundation of America. It was unbelievable to see how much destruction one bomb could do. Seeing it all in person provoked a sense of outrage within me. I couldn't imagine the pain people suffered that day or the grief they'd have to live with forever because of someone's horrible actions. My heart went out to the victims' families and friends. Why would anyone want to cause such pain and suffering to innocent people?

Mom, Dad, Jon, and I held hands by the fence and prayed for the families of the victims.

Later that day, we toured the capitol. We

*Fence of memories.*

saw the special room set up for displaying letters, gifts, poems, and quilts people made after the bombing. All these things were sent to Oklahoma from people throughout the world. One quilt was titled, "God's Little Angels," and it listed all the names of the children who died in the bombing. Letters from school children were displayed on bulletin boards with phrases like, "I'm sorry for what happened."

It seems as though our entire nation was affected by this tragedy. I stood in front of the list of names of the people who died. I could feel the emotions welling up inside me. They weren't just names posted on a board, they were real people and they were gone. I was angry at whoever did this evil thing. I wanted to be able to do something to prevent it from happening again.

At two-thirty, we found our way to the governor's office. Governor Frank Keating was coming out to meet me.

"What a project you've got going here," Governor Keating said. "Where are you from?"

"Traverse City, Michigan."

"I know where that is. My daughter went to the Interlochen Arts Academy there. So, I understand you want to ask me some questions?"

"We just came from the bombing site. What an overwhelming thing to see."

"Yes, and we showed the world what a very good state we are following the bombing. Everybody came together as a community

of people, and we just want to continue that tradition beyond just the tragedy." With that statement, I sensed he knew what it meant to be a true leader. He was able to help his state out of the tragedy of the past and into hope for the future.

"I saw the oil rig in front of the capitol. Is that the most important industry in Oklahoma?"

"The oil business has always been an important industry in Oklahoma, but not as big as it used to be. We're a big aerospace state and telecommunications state, as well."

"What is your favorite part about being governor?"

"The food," he laughed. "I like the meals. I like to eat. When you're governor, you don't have to eat much fast food. I like to meet lots of people, like you, your Mom and Dad, and your little brother, but I really like the meals." I liked his sense of humor.

"What are your personal and political goals?"

"My political goal is to make the state of Oklahoma rich and a better state. My personal goal is to have a good night's sleep."

"What do you enjoy most about Oklahoma?"

"I like the weather. We have great golf courses. The people and the history of the state. The moral values are still very basic here. For example, when the bombing occurred, there was not one act of looting."

Our interview came to a close. "I have a couple of shirts, I wonder if you'd sign them."

"Sure." Just before he signed them, the governor looked at our video camera and said, "Go Michigan!" We all laughed. Governor Keating ended the interview with a bit of advice I really appreciated.

"Take every day as it comes, do the best you can every day, and get smarter and better every day. And always enjoy what you do."

Seems like sound advice to me.

*May 10...Oklahoma left a lasting impression on me. Dear God, please don't allow something like the bombing to happen again.*

# 39

# governor
# on trial

The courthouse in Little Rock, Arkansas, was surrounded by media when we arrived. Everyone wanted to talk to Governor Jim Guy Tucker, including me. Governor Tucker was under indictment for his involvement in a land scandal and was in the middle of his trial. The trial is why we had to go to the courthouse instead of the capitol. Big trucks, with satellite transmitters mounted on the tops, were parked along the street, and men with huge cameras were waiting outside the doors of the building. I walked around taking pictures of all the media people while we waited. One of the reporters asked me what I was doing there.

"I'm traveling around the country interviewing governors for a book I'm writing," I told him, "and I want to meet Governor Tucker."

"Well, the chances of you meeting this governor are pretty slim," he said, laughing at me. I knew he was probably thinking I would be the last person to get an interview with the governor, but that kind of skepticism didn't faze me anymore.

We waited a long time before Governor Tucker arrived at the courthouse. He rode up in a black limousine; the media swarmed around the car like flies. I tried to break through the crowd to see the governor. One of the reporters asked me to get out of the way. That was the last thing I was planning to do. I knew I had just as much right to see him as the media. His press secretary stepped out of the car first and saw me standing there. We'd met her at the capitol earlier that day, and she recognized me.

"Hi, Amy," she said. I was surprised she remembered my name.

"I can give you a few minutes with Governor Tucker if you want to come inside the courthouse with us."

"Really?" I said.

"Just follow me."

Governor Tucker stepped out of the limousine, and she motioned for us to follow. I smiled at the reporters as we were escorted past them. We walked through the large doors of the courthouse. The security guards shut the doors, leaving the press on the outside looking in. I had a private audience with Governor Tucker. Once inside, the press secretary introduced me to the governor, and we shook hands.

"Is this your family?"

"Yes, this is my brother, Jonathan." He gave Jon a high-five, then a low one and then laid his palm out for Jon to hit it. Governor Tucker pulled it back just as Jon was about to slap it. "Oops, too slow," he said, laughing. Jon's face turned red. The governor shook hands with Mom and Dad.

"It's a terrific thing you're doing," Governor Tucker said.

"Thank you," Mom replied.

"This is my wife, Betty."

"Hello, nice to meet you," Mrs. Tucker said, smiling. "What a wonderful family you have."

"We have four children," the governor began, "ranging from 14 to 35, two dogs, a cat, and a turtle that died last week."

He was very friendly. It was hard for me to imagine he could've done anything wrong. We talked for a few more minutes until it was time for him to go into the courtroom. We left the courthouse with big smiles on our faces. I didn't say a word to any of the reporters.

Later that week, I received Governor Tucker's answers to my other questions.

What are Arkansas' greatest needs?

"Better results from public education."

When you were a kid, what did you want to be when you grew up?

"President."

What is your state's most fascinating attraction?

"Whitewater streams, especially Buffalo National River."

What are your greatest personal and political goals?

"Be a good father and husband and prepare our state for the 21st century."

stiff upper lip
Governor
Jim Guy
Tucker
award

considering
the
circumstances

What person or event has most shaped your life?
"My mother."

We celebrated Mother's Day during our stay at a state park near Little Rock. In the late afternoon, Mom called Grandma Peckham and Grandma Kay from a pay phone and wished them a Happy Mother's Day. While she was gone, we cleaned the motorhome, put on some jazz music, lit a candle, and set out a special dessert we bought for her. When she came back, she was surprised. I made a pot of coffee to go with our dessert while Mom filled us in about her calls back home. She also told us she found a bag of money sitting inside the phone booth.

"I didn't know what to do with it," she said. "I opened the bag to see if there was a name or phone number inside, but it was just money."

"Did you keep it?" Jon asked. I could see the dollar signs flashing in his hazel eyes.

"No," Mom said, in a scolding tone. "I took it to the office."

"How much was there?" I asked.

"Oh, quite a bit. Whoever lost it will be happy to get it back, I'm sure." The chocolate cake we bought for Mom was good. We played Scrabble after dessert, and let Mom win.

Later that night, when Jon and I were getting settled into bed, he wanted to cash in one of his backscratch tickets. His back was itching badly. In the dark, I reached my hand over the booth and began scratching his back. It felt as though he had a bunch of scabs.

"Jon, have you been gouging your back when you scratch?"

"No, it just started itching tonight."

I turned on the light, curious about the lumps on his back. I looked closely. They weren't scabs, they looked like spiders.

"Mom! Dad!" I called back to their bedroom.

"What?" Dad asked sleepily.

"I think you should come and look at Jon's back. It looks like there is a spider or something on it, and it won't come off."

Dad immediately jumped out of bed and came to Jon's side to investigate. Jon freaked out when I said the word "spider," and before Dad could look at it, he had to calm Jon. Mom jumped out of bed, too, and wanted to see what I was talking about. Dad looked at the scab.

"It's not a spider," Dad assured Jon.

"It's not?" he asked, just to make sure.

"No," Dad repeated, "I think it's a tick."

"Oh, no!" Mom shrieked. "We're going to have to disinfect the entire motorhome!" Of course, this only made things worse.

"What's a tick?" Jon yelled. I knew what it was, but I'd never seen one before.

"Well," Dad said calmly, "it's a little bug that burrows its way into your skin, and you have to pull it out with tweezers."

"Will it hurt?" Jon cried.

"It shouldn't," Dad said, motioning to me to find the tweezers. I was grossed out. Frantically, I searched through the bathroom trying to locate the little metal object. When I came out from the bathroom with the tweezers in hand, Mom was searching through my sleeping bag.

"What are you doing, Mom?"

"I'm looking for more ticks."

"In my bed? Jon has the tick. Not me!"

"Amy, if there's one, there's bound to be more."

Sure enough, she found one in my sleeping bag. Then she checked Jon's. He had four in his. I was so disgusted. We started checking everything.

"How did I get 'em?" Jon asked, as Dad gently pulled at the tick.

"Probably when you were walking through the woods in the campground."

Jon winced as Dad accidentally pinched his skin. "Amy, get me the flashlight. I need to make sure I got all of it."

Dad proceeded to pull seven ticks from Jon, four on his back and three on his legs. I started itching everywhere. Mom took me into the bathroom and did a thorough examination. Thank goodness, I didn't have any. When we'd searched every nook and cranny, we went back to bed. There was no way I'd crawl back into my sleeping bag that night, so I slept without any blankets. I had a hard time falling asleep. Every time I had an itch, I would turn on the light, just to check. I can't remember having so many itches before in my life.

*May 13... Didn't get much sleep last night. Found a few more ticks today. Was very glad to leave that campground. Feel like I'm in the army. We get a thorough check every night.*

# 40

# double-dare

**M**issouri was the last state on our fourth tour. It was the longest tour, and we hadn't seen anyone from home for five months. We planned to travel through the beautiful mountains near Branson and Springfield, leading to Jefferson City, Missouri's capital. After that, we would head back to Michigan for a ten-day visit before our fifth and final tour.

We stopped by Governor Mel Carnahan's office to have him sign our sweatshirts. It was pouring rain when Dad drove the motorhome up to the capitol. Mom and I ran inside with the sweatshirts while Dad and Jon waited in the motorhome.

As she took the sweatshirts, the governor's scheduler apologized that Governor Carnahan wasn't able to meet with me. She asked us to wait a few minutes. It was frustrating, sometimes, to know that the governors could find time to sign my sweatshirts, but they couldn't take a few extra minutes to actually meet me, the person behind the whole project. Still, the signings were better than no response at all.

While we were waiting for the shirts, his secretary called me over to her desk. She must have thought I was only eight years old or something, because she asked me in that annoying adult voice used only on little kids, "Do you want a pencil and a bookmark?"

No, I thought, I don't want a bookmark or a pencil. *What I want is an interview with the governor.* Having learned to appreciate the art of diplomacy, however, I accepted the gifts and thanked her politely.

A picture of Governor Carnahan hung neatly over the secretary's desk. Two security guards sat against the wall eating their lunch. I wondered if they knew everything about us like the security guard in Connecticut.

Someone came out of the governor's office with my sweatshirts. Mom and I looked them over. The governor had signed both of them, so I packed the shirts into the bag, and we ran through the rain back to the motorhome.

It rained the entire day we traveled through Missouri. Mom sat in the front seat with the map on her lap, guiding Dad around St. Louis. Dad called her his "co-pilot." Mom was doing a good job navigating. She could even read the map right side up now.

I spent the time organizing my bin and cleaning the motorhome. I wanted to have all my chores done by the time we pulled into Traverse City, so I could play with my cousins. Jon was building things with his Legos, as usual. That was something he loved to do when we traveled. We encountered a huge thunderstorm in Illinois. The rain was coming down so hard Dad could hardly see the road. He pulled off the freeway into a Wal-Mart parking lot.

"This storm is too hard to drive in," Dad announced. "We'll have to spend the night here and drive home in the morning."

I was disappointed. I wished Dad would keep driving. I just wanted to get home. I set up my bed and snuggled into my sleeping bag. I couldn't wait for tomorrow.

Late that night, I was awakened by the sound of squealing tires. I sat up and lifted the shade a few inches to peer out my window. It was still raining. There were two cars racing around the parking lot, squealing their tires and circling our motorhome. I freaked. Dad came out of the bedroom and checked the door to make sure it was locked. He told me not to worry. About ten minutes later, they left the parking lot and sped down the highway. I was relieved and went back to sleep.

My first day home, I spent the afternoon with Melisa and Brittany. The girls wanted to talk about my trip this time, and they seemed excited about some of the things I'd done, especially swimming with the dolphins in Hawaii. We had a great time together. I think we'd all matured a little, and things between us actually felt better than they had since I first left home. Time has a funny way of working things out.

The following day we went to the farm for our family's annual summer picnic. The whole Burritt clan was there. It was great to be home with my cousins again. I'd missed being around kids my own age.

Joel, the cousin whose foot dangled from the ceiling at Christmas, and I have a history of trying to outdo each other, and we're always daring one another to do something crazy. Somehow, during the picnic, we started talking about worms.

"Joel," I said, "If you eat a worm, I will." He stood there for a second.

"You want me to eat a worm?" he asked, in disbelief.

"Yeah, why not? I mean, it's not going to kill us."

*Top row: Annie, Jim.*
*Middle row: Katie, Jake, me, Joel.*
*Bottom row: Audrey, Jon, Allie.*

He hesitated for a second. Then, realizing he didn't want to be outdone by a girl, he agreed to the dare. We had no idea what worms tasted like, so we agreed to dip them in whipped cream.

We rounded up our eight cousins and told them what we were about to do.

"Gross, you guys are sick," Audrey said, as she ran into the farmhouse to tell the adults. Out the door everyone came. They wanted to see if what they heard was really true. Mom had the video camera ready.

"Amy, are you really going to do this?" she asked.

"Of course, why not?"

"Because, it's disgusting," she answered, her face wrinkling.

Joel and I rinsed the dirt off the worms and dipped them in whipped cream.

"Hey, Grandma, could Joel and I have a glass of juice to swallow them with?" I asked.

Grandma opened the squeaky screen door and went inside. Joel and I put the worms in our hands and watched them wiggle around, proving to the rest of the family that the worms were real and still very much alive.

"Here you are," Grandma said, handing each of us a glass of orange juice.

"Thanks, Grandma."

When we were sure everyone was watching, we held the worms above our faces and counted, "One ...two ... three!" We dropped the

*Worms taste better than they look!*

worms in our mouths simultaneously. The whole family was disgusted, but nobody was more grossed out than Joel. His face turned colors as he swallowed the worm. I could feel mine wiggling as it slid down my throat. It was like slurping spaghetti that wiggled by itself. Everyone cheered when we successfully kept the worms down.

"I can't believe my little girl ate a worm," Mom said in shock.

"Mom, I'm not your little girl anymore," I reminded her.

"That's for sure. My little girl would never eat worms."

*June 5...Kept the worm down just fine, it didn't bother me at all.*

# tour five

illinois

iowa

kansas

nebraska

wyoming

montana

south dakota

north dakota

minnesota

wisconsin

# 41

# beginning
# of the end

"What's the worst thing that's happened to you so far?" the newspaper reporter from the *Traverse City Record-Eagle* asked me.

"Well, I'm not sure. Maybe when the motorhome almost hit a bridge in Delaware," I said. "We had to take a detour through a city, and as we came around a corner, there in front of us was a very low bridge. Dad slammed on the brakes and stopped just in time. If he hadn't, the bridge would've made a convertible out of the motorhome."

"Were you scared?"

"No, but we did stop traffic for awhile. That was pretty cool."

"How many governors do you have left to meet?"

"We have ten states left on this last tour, but I still have three governors from the other tours to interview."

"Do you think you will see all fifty?"

"I don't know, but that's my goal," I said.

As we left Traverse City for the last leg of our journey, I wondered how it was all going to work out in the end. Would I really reach my goal? How was I going to get Governor Pataki of New York and Voinovich from Ohio? Plus, we'd heard that Governor Symington of Arizona was facing legal problems. Would I have to meet him at a courthouse like Arkansas' Governor Tucker?

We crossed the Michigan border into Illinois. It was easier for me to leave this time than it had been all year, probably because I knew I'd soon be coming home for good. I was used to traveling ten weeks at a time and living in the motorhome. I was even a little sad knowing we were on our last tour. I'd changed a lot during the year, or maybe the year had changed me.

There is so much to remember about our trip. The smell of a campfire became as much a part of my life as wearing dresses. I remember when we first discovered "Creemies" in Vermont. Ice cream that tasted so rich, we had one almost every day. There's the time I played Queen Lileokalani's piano in Hawaii for a group of tourists visiting her royal house. One of my favorite memories will always be the incredible sunsets of the southwest. I loved watching that big orange sphere sink into the horizon, leaving only the silhouette of a lone cactus.

During our week in Illinois, we stayed at the Sangchris Lake State Park. It was close to the capitol, so we wouldn't have far to drive for my interview with Governor Jim Edgar. Jon and I had a great time at the campground. We fished and rode our bikes every day.

We were early for our appointment in Springfield, and like many times before, we went to the capitol cafeteria. This one was in the basement. With its brick walls and dim lighting, I felt like I was in the cellar of an old castle. Small wooden tables with upholstered chairs lined the brick wall, and the ceramic floors reflected the light of the lanterns hanging from the ceiling. We went through the cafeteria line and ordered our drinks. We enjoyed this free time. It was quiet. We were the only ones there.

"Be careful not to spill," Mom reminded me after we sat down.

"I know, I know ...," my voice echoed.

"I would like to build a house like this," Dad said, as his eyes wandered around the room.

"Yeah, this is cozy, and it would be nice with a fieldstone fireplace over there," Mom said, pointing to a dark corner.

"With a big castle door to my room," Jon piped up. I looked around, imagining what it would look like if I could decorate the place myself. I envisioned a huge candelabra lighting the room, a suit of armor hanging on the wall next to a shiny sword, cobblestone floors, and a fireplace with a huge wooden mantle covered with medieval battle weapons.

"Uh oh, we'd better go or we're going to be late," Dad said, glancing at his watch. We gathered up our equipment and took the elevator to the governor's office. We still had a few minutes before the governor would be ready for us, so we all sat on a striped sofa to wait.

"Jon, where's the sweatshirt bag?" I asked.

"It's right here," he said, reaching down by his side. Then he stared at me, his eyes growing wider. "Well, I thought it was."

"Mom, Jon doesn't have the sweatshirts!" I exclaimed. Jon had misplaced them before, and I worried one of these times he would lose them for good.

"Better check the men's bathroom," Mom told Jon, "that's where you left them last time, remember?"

Jon's shoulders dropped. "Oh, yeah."

"We never went to the bathroom," Dad said. "I bet they're in the cafeteria."

The guys went to retrieve the sweatshirts while Mom and I waited upstairs in the reception room. Five minutes later, just as Dad and Jon were returning with the bag, the governor's secretary announced it was time for the interview.

Governor Edgar greeted me in his office. He was a tall, slender man with graying hair and glasses. We sat down at a long rectangular table. Sunlight flooded the room from the large window behind Governor Edgar.

"What would you say is Illinois' most important industry?" I asked, after the formalities were concluded.

"Agriculture and manufacturing are major portions of the economy."

I nodded my head as if I knew what he was talking about and went on to my next question. I was having a hard time jumping back into the interview routine after my time off in Michigan.

"When you were my age, what did you want to be when you grew up?"

"I think from the third grade on, I knew that I wanted to be an elected official," he said, with a straight face. "Throughout grade school, I was always class officer. In high school, I was student council president. I was also class president. I always knew I wanted to go into politics."

"What is your greatest personal goal?"

"To be a good grandfather to my grandchildren," he said, smiling. I was surprised. He looked too young to be a grandpa.

"What draws people to want to live here?"

He gazed at the ceiling for a minute as if he could read the answers up there. Lips pursed, he folded his hands and leaned back in his chair.

"This is a good state for employment. We have good paying jobs. We have Chicago, one of the most beautiful metropolitan areas in the world, and some of the best farmland."

"I know what you mean," I told him. "I've been to downtown Chicago before and visited some of the museums. I think my favorite was the aquarium. I really liked the city. Well, thank you for giving me so much of your time. It was great."

"It was a pleasure meeting you, Amy. Good luck on the rest of your adventure."

*June 12...We went to Lincoln's law office in Springfield and saw where he began his practice as a lawyer. Mom wandered into a bookstore next door and hit the jackpot. She found over fifty Landmarks. I caught a huge frog at the campground.*

# 42

# you make me smile

I never thought much about Iowa before our trip. It seemed like one of those states that was flat, dull, and uninteresting. But, after meeting with the governor, I learned Iowa is a state with some significant history, and many of the important things we use every day are made right there in the heartland of America.

"Welcome, Amy," Governor Terry Branstad said, reaching his hand out to shake mine.

"Thank you."

"What part of Michigan are you from?" he asked.

"Traverse City."

"Oh, that's a beautiful place. We had a governor's conference there once." Governor Branstad invited me to sit next to his desk. I began my interview.

"What do you enjoy most about Iowa?"

He leaned his arms on the desk. "Iowans are very friendly and hospitable people, whether going to the county fairs or visiting the schools or factories. We have a slogan we use now that says, 'Iowa, you make me smile.'" Governor Branstad said, grinning. "Because the people of Iowa just make you smile."

"What are your political goals?"

"Improving education and providing good jobs for those who live in Iowa are some of my goals. I spend a lot of time working to attract companies to Iowa. We have a number of companies that are making products like biodegradable detergents, breath mints, and toothpaste out of corn."

The bright light from the flash of a camera distracted me. There was a photographer in the room taking pictures for an article that was going to be in Focus On The Family's *Citizen* magazine. The governor must be a Republican, I thought, admiring the elephant collection displayed on his desk.

"What would you say is the most interesting historical site in Iowa?"

"Boy, that's a tough question, Amy," Governor Branstad said. "There are lots of historical places, but the Mississippi River played a major role in the history of the state, and Mark Twain, in his writings, made it famous."

I remembered visiting Mark Twain's house when we were in Connecticut. He'd lived there when he was married. It was a very unusual house with lots of small oddly shaped rooms that were dimly lit.

"And also," the governor continued, "Lewis and Clark and their famous expedition over the Missouri River was a great and important historical landmark of Iowa."

"Governor, we're out of time," his assistant announced. The photographer took a few more pictures, and Governor Branstad signed our sweatshirts. We took a quick tour of the capitol before we left.

On our way back to the motorhome, I thought about the Lewis and Clark Expedition. I'd studied it earlier in the year, so it was fun to be at the actual sites where the history took place. It made the facts and dates real and believable.

In 1804, when President Thomas Jefferson commissioned Lewis and Clark to explore the new territory he'd just purchased, they selected about thirty men to go with them. When the group left, they had no idea what they were going to encounter. Along the way, they saw antelope, big horn sheep, and grizzlies, animals they'd never seen before. Their journey was long and difficult, and everyone rejoiced when they finally returned to St. Louis over two years later. Talk about adventure!

I stared out our motorhome window, watching the landscape roll by, and I thought about how much Grandpa Peckham would have liked the Lewis and Clark expedition. Grandpa loves to explore. When I was seven years old, he told me the story of an expedition he once took to Alaska with the entire family.

I was sitting on Grandpa's lap as he relayed the adventure to me.

"Your mother," Grandpa began, "was a little older than you, when I sold our house and bought a camper and a van to take to Alaska." I remember watching Grandpa's eyes light up as he reminisced.

"I was excited about exploring the untamed lands of Alaska's frontier and had heard about people homesteading and living off the land. It had been a dream of mine for a long time."

"Did it take a long time to get there?" I asked.

"I didn't think it would, but along the way, we discovered that the van couldn't pull our heavy camper over the mountains."

"What did you do, Grandpa?"

"Well, we didn't have any choice but to sell the camper and buy a tent." Grandpa chuckled, as he reflected about that day. "Your mother was so mad when I told her that she had to give many of her things away. We all had to sacrifice. Without the camper, we couldn't take much with us. We donated everything, except the few things we had to have, to the Salvation Army and then hit the road for Alaska again. Finally, two weeks and a dozen or so flat tires later, we arrived."

"Was it exciting?"

"Very," Grandpa said, as his eyes widened. "It was the most beautiful place I'd ever seen, and we had some great adventures that summer."

"Did you see any bear?"

"Oh, yes. I remember one morning," Grandpa said, sitting back in his rocking chair. "It was very early. Grandma and I were asleep in the van, and your mother, Uncle Jim, and Aunt Sue were sleeping in the tent. I was awakened by the sound of someone yelling in the campground. I sat up and looked out the window. It was the park ranger warning everyone to seek shelter from a bear who was rummaging through the camp. She'd put her two cubs up a tree and gone looking for food. I jumped out of bed and called to the kids, telling them that a bear was coming. It didn't take long for your mother and Uncle Jim to scramble to the safety of the van.

"What about Aunt Sue?" I asked.

"I stuck my head out the door and saw the bear coming towards our site. I yelled to your Aunt Sue, 'Get out of the tent, Sue, get out of the tent!' She yelled back that she couldn't come out. I was really worried, and I was just about to jump out and snatch her from the tent, when she came hopping out on one foot."

"What happened to her, Grandpa?" I asked, wondering what in the world would have kept her from running to the van.

"Well," Grandpa continued his story, "she was hopping on one foot, because she couldn't find her other shoe! Can you believe that? I couldn't understand why she was so concerned about getting her shoes on at a time like that. She did finally make it safely into the van, and we all watched out the window as the bear sniffed around our site. Not finding anything to eat, she wandered to the site next to us where three guys were planning a hike across Alaska. They had boxes of food sitting all around their campsite. The mama had stumbled onto a bear's buffet. One guy was inside his tent when the bear clawed at the thin material, ripping it to shreds with her sharp claws. They'd broken the golden rule of camping, 'Never store food in your tent.' The park ranger managed to distract the hungry bear away from the tent, but she continued to overturn every single box until she'd demolished everything in sight. We were shaking in our shoes," Grandpa laughed. "Well, your Aunt Sue was shaking in one shoe, anyway. The ranger finally scared the bear off, and she summoned her cubs down from the tree and left the campground."

"Did the bear hurt anyone?"

"No, she was just looking for something to feed her cubs."

"Why didn't you stay in Alaska, Grandpa?"

"I realized how difficult it was going to be on my family, living off the land and trying to survive the harsh climate. Besides, every-one wanted to come back to Michigan. They missed their family and friends back home."

I remember smiling at that point and saying, "I'm glad you came back Grandpa, or else I wouldn't be here."

"You're right, Amy." Grandpa gave me a hug. "I'm glad I came back home, too."

Thinking about Grandpa's story made me realize that while some states may be more exciting than others, it's really the adventures you have along the way that make the difference. I looked at Iowa with a fresh perspective. It wasn't a dull state, it was the perfect place to enjoy some good daydreaming!

# 43

# here we go loopty-loo

I was beginning to feel like Dorothy in the *Wizard of Oz*, as though I'd landed in a strange land, with a very strange family. We were half-way through the five-hour drive to the capital, Topeka. Mom was sit-ting in the back seat, as she did on occasion so I could sit up front, and she wore her sunglasses upside down while she mouthed the words to *Here We Go Loopty Loo*. Dad wore his dark shades and pre-tended to be Elvis, while Jon sang in his "opera voice."

The craziness started after Mom purchased a Disney cassette tape. We all thought it was a good idea until we heard a couple of the songs and realized the tape was meant for preschoolers. Perfect, I thought, for the way my family was acting. After a few hours of listening to *Camptown Ladies, Three Blind Mice, Billy Boy,* and *Here We Go Loopty-Loo,* my family began to go a little "loopty-loo" themselves. I video taped their strange antics to document just how weird my family can be. They were driving me crazy. I began to wonder if we'd make it through the remainder of this tour without totally losing it. Maybe it was already too late. Maybe we'd been on the road a little too long.

When we arrived at the capitol in Topeka, I was hoping my fam-ily had fully recovered from our strange trip. If they hadn't, this was going to be a very interesting interview.

Governor Bill Graves of Kansas welcomed us to his office. He was tall and lanky, and I noticed he was wearing make-up. I thought it was kind of strange, but I didn't want to ask him about it. The way things were going, I'd already resigned myself to the fact that it was just going to be one of those days. Besides, maybe in Kansas it wasn't so strange!

"You're probably wondering why I'm wearing make-up," he said with a smile after we were introduced. "I don't usually wear make-up, but today I was filming a commercial and they just finished."

"Well," I said, "that explains it."

We sat at his desk for a moment talking about my trip while Mom set up the video camera. His office was big and bright, with lots of windows. Even the wood on the walls was a light color. Soon, Mom was ready for me to begin.

"What is the most important historical sight in Kansas?"

"The Dwight D. Eisenhower Museum in Abilene would probably be one of the places that I would certainly mention."

"What's your state's most important industry?"

"Well, it would obviously be agriculture. And, if I have permission to say, our second industry is aviation."

I was surprised to learn that aviation was so important to Kansas.

"What attraction would you want people to see when they to come to Kansas?"

"You might be surprised to know that we have a lot of tourists." He was right, I couldn't quite figure out why tourists would come to Kansas. "They should see the scenic Flint Hills, an area of high plains where buffalo used to roam. It's a native tall grass prairie and a very unique part of the country."

After a few more questions, I thanked Governor Graves for meeting with me, and he signed our shirts.

**W**hile we drove back to our campground from Topeka, Dad helped pass the time by telling us boyhood stories about his family's travels.

"When I was little, my family used to travel back and forth from California to Michigan every summer. We drove an old tour bus that Grandpa Gene bought from the movie studios in Hollywood and re-modeled into a camper. It was one of the first motorhomes on the road. It was called a house camper.

"Danny Bonaduce," Dad explained, "the actor who portrayed the red-headed trouble-maker on the show, *The Partridge Family*, was my friend. His parents were friends with my parents, and they used the idea of our family traveling in the bus for the television show.

"One summer, while we were in Michigan, we bought a cherry farm and moved from California to Cedar, Michigan. That ended our big trip every summer, because we had a farm to run. From a house in the city to the hardships of a rustic farmhouse, it was quite an adjustment to make," Dad said. He was only nine when they moved.

"That was in 1968, and we couldn't believe the house didn't have indoor plumbing," Dad continued, as he drove down the freeway. "When we had to go to the bathroom we went to the outhouse."

Oh boy, I thought, as I rolled my eyes, here goes Dad telling one of his sad growing-up stories.

"The outhouse," he continued, "sat down at the bottom of the hill. It was an old two-seater with a small window and a light."

I knew Dad wasn't exaggerating. I'd seen the outhouse at the farm myself. It was gross.

"In the winter, I'd put on my coat and slippers, you know the moccasins with the slippery leather bottoms?" Dad asked, as he looked at me in the rearview mirror. "Well, I would slide down the hill, and, reaching my arms out, I would grasp the door handle as my body flung into the air. If I missed, I'd slide right on past the old outhouse and it would take a lot of effort to get back up the hill."

"Cool, that sounds like fun," I said to Dad. He looked at me in the mirror.

"The only thing that was cool, was my rear end on the wooden toilet seat," Dad joked. He loved telling his stories. "One night, Uncle Ken and I discovered it was much more convenient to pee out the bedroom window, instead of braving the cold winter wind.

Eventually, though, the yellow icicles hanging below our window gave us away, and that was the end of our great idea."

Grandma and Grandpa still live on the farm in Cedar, and the old bus is still around. It sits out in the fields behind the farm, rusting into the ground, but it doesn't sit alone. Every chance we have, my cousins and I go visit the old bus and try to relive the adventures of our parents. Joel likes to sit in the driver's seat and mess around with

*The old studio house camper A.K.A. "the bus."*

the steering wheel and open and close the bus doors as if he's some cool bus driver. Audrey's little sister, Allie, likes to explore the bunkbeds in the back, while Jake and Jon curiously open drawers and cabinets, looking for old treasures. Audrey and I like to turn the dial that changes the sign on the front of the old studio bus. The "MGM Studios" sign is our favorite.

It seems like traveling adventures run in my family, I thought, staring out the car window. I knew I would have to travel again. The thirst for adventure was in my blood.

# 44

# the way west

"Chimney Rock," he said. "It's the most interesting historical sight in Nebraska. It stood as a symbol for 150 years as the way to the west. It was a landmark on old maps that could be seen from miles away."

Sitting in the capitol in Lincoln, Nebraska, I talked with Governor Benjamin Nelson. He had dark hair and a friendly face. As he rested in his chair, I could tell by his posture that he was relaxed.

"Our greatest need in the state is water for the agricultural industry," he said. I'd learned the western states didn't get much rain, which was a major factor in their water problem.

Governor Nelson wanted to be a lawyer. Then, later on, he decided to go into politics. "When you're involved in politics, you really need to put your personal life on hold, and your personal goals merge with your political goals."

Knowing he was in the middle of a campaign, running for the United States Senate, I decided to ask him about it, since he was the first governor I met who was actively pursuing another job.

"Why do you want to run for the Senate?"

"Because, I feel I can do more for the state of Nebraska at the federal level, by bringing more power back to the states."

"Who most shaped your political career?"

"The late Senator George W. Norris. He was one of the most important Senators in history, though not many people know his name. He got the Rural Electrification Act through Congress. It supplied electricity to the rural parts of America, which changed the face of America. He became a model that one person can make a difference."

"What do you like most about being governor?"

"Serving the people," he said.

The governor's secretary, who'd been in the room during the interview, asked the governor to tell me a story about the Christmas tree lighting. The governor leaned forward and folded his hands together, resting them on the table. He smiled and chuckled to himself.

"As governor, I was attending a Christmas tree lighting ceremony," he said, "and afterwards two junior high students asked for my autograph on their program. After I signed it, they turned and began walking away. One of the boys turned back, and holding up the program, he said to me, 'I'm going to hang on to this in case you become somebody.'" Governor Nelson smiled. "That really humbled me."

We traveled through many towns in Nebraska: Beatrice, Lincoln, Omaha. Even though southeastern Nebraska is mostly flat, just as Iowa and Kansas are, a few scattered hills helped break the monotonous landscape. Nebraska's had a lot of traffic, from the Lewis and Clark Expedition and the Oregon Trail, to the Mormon Trail and the building of the Union Pacific Railroad that started in Omaha and went westward. And, now, the expressway.

We'd been driving through the state for quite awhile, following the scenic road along the Missouri River. I was tired of playing Monopoly with Jon, so I went back to the bedroom and looked out the window at the cars below. People sure do travel differently than they did back on the Oregon Trail. What would we ever do without air conditioning? I liked watching people as they passed by our motorhome. I played detective by checking out the contents of the cars and then guessing the driver's occupation.

A suit, tie, and cell phone: probably a businessman. A suit, tie, cell phone, and a Twinkie: probably a businessman who doesn't care about his diet. The next car was a white four-door sedan. There was a brown leather briefcase on the passenger seat, a shaver on the dash, and a copy of the *Wall Street Journal* lying on the floor. The back seat was cluttered with newspapers and magazines. The driver looked as though he was on his lunch break and late for work. He chugged down his grape "Squeezit." It's amazing what people do while they drive. I saw a woman feeding her baby a bottle — not too difficult. A man shaving — I wouldn't take the risk. People reading the newspaper — not very wise. Girls putting on make-up — now that one really got me. How they can put on lipstick and mascara while they're driving down the road is beyond me. I can hardly put that stuff on when I'm standing still in front of a mirror. I wonder how many accidents happen because people are too preoccupied when they drive.

*Dad and his co-pilot, Shasta.*

*Jon plays another game of Monopoly by himself.*

218

# 45

# your word is good

Alightning storm lit up the sky, and I could see dark heavy clouds closing in on us. It was July 4th when we crossed the state line into Wyoming. Flash after flash of lightning welcomed us into the wild west. We couldn't have planned a better fireworks display ourselves.

Dad took the first exit, and we found a campsite at the Pine Bluff Campground.

Sitting inside the comfort of our motorhome, we watched the storm as it pounded from the sky. A lightning bolt flashed, and I counted, "One thousand, two thousand." Crack! I jumped when the sound of the thunder reached us.

"The storm's not very far away," I said, using an age-old method of counting the time between the lightning flash and the crack of thunder. Whatever number you reach is how many miles away the storm is.

"Now we can't do our fireworks," Jon whined.

"What are you talking about?" Mom asked. "Look at the fireworks show Wyoming is putting on for us!"

"But, Mom," Jon said sadly.

"How would you like to be that couple over there," Dad interrupted, pointing at the site across from us. It was a young couple in a tent. They looked troubled as they stuck their heads out to survey the storm.

The winds came. They beat against the side of the motorhome, and the rain on the rubber roof was so loud we couldn't hear the evening news. I went to the window and watched the couple in the tent. They were frantically trying to pack up and seek shelter from the storm. The rain came down so hard and fast that small lakes were forming around the campground. Their tent was in a low spot. They were stomping through the mud trying to keep their tent from blowing away. Just as I was about to ask permission to go help them, someone else drove up in a car and rescued the drenched couple.

The sun came out the next morning during our drive to the capitol in Cheyenne. I was meeting with Governor Jim Geringer. I noticed many pictures and statues around his office; I had the impression the governor was a cowboy. I looked up at him when he entered the room. He was a big man and talked in a deep, gentle voice as he answered my questions.

"We're the least populated state, yet one of the biggest geographically," said Governor Geringer.

"I come from a farming background. A lot of people in Wyoming, if they don't come from farming or agriculture, have roots in farming. And back on the farm, especially on the farm, but some on the ranch, too, if somebody happens to be driving by and they need to

talk, they just pull in the yard. You might put your foot on the bumper of the pick-up truck and talk. Leaning on the hood, you might swap stories and decide the issues of the day, or more'n likely, you'd go in the house." He paused, taking a deep breath. "But, the best thing about Wyoming, and a lot of the west, is, if you tell somebody you're going to do something, it's going to be done. Your word is good."

I felt as though the governor would've taken the whole day to talk with me. He didn't seem rushed at all.

"Wyoming also has some of the most interesting historical sites," he continued. "Yellowstone was the first national park in America, and the state of Wyoming was also the home of the first national monument, Devil's Tower."

After I finished asking my questions, the governor walked over to a small closet and pulled out two books.

"I want to give you something to remember Wyoming by," he smiled. They were big books with color pictures of the sights in Wyoming. He signed each of them, one for me and one for Jon. He wrote, *Amy, thanks for a great visit. Enjoy the rest of your time. Jim Geringer, Wyoming Governor.*

"Thank you for the books."

"You're welcome, Amy, and you come back anytime and see me."

"Thanks."

Later that week, we met Aunt Linda and Katie at Yellowstone National Park. We spent four days hiking and sightseeing in the mountains. I saw Old Faithful, a geyser that shoots water into the air about every forty-five minutes. It was awesome to watch. We went to the Grand Tetons, where we saw deer, moose, and tons of birds. We ate lunch at Bubba's in Jackson Hole, a place the governor had recommended. It was a great barbecue spot.

*Old Faithful*

# 46

# communication gap

Two motorhomes pulled into the site across from ours at the Bozeman KOA, where we camped during our trip to Montana. All the people in the motorhomes spoke a foreign language as they hollered back and forth to one another, trying to back up into their site. I like watching people set up their campers, and from what I could tell, it was a whole new experience for this group. I noticed a girl about my age sitting on the picnic table, watching all the commotion.

"Go say hi to her, Amy," Mom said.

"She doesn't speak English."

"That will make it more interesting." One of the things I did like about traveling was unexpected encounters with people I would've never met staying in one place. New people don't ever replace special friends like Melisa and Brittany, but new friends can give you special gifts, too. Gifts that come from the experiences you share with them and what they teach you about the world.

I listened to them talk a minute longer. It sounded like they spoke French. I'd studied French when I was seven, but after six years I only remembered a few words. I could count to ten, and I knew a few words such as *pain*, which means "bread". That should make a real interesting conversation, I thought, I could count out bread slices to her.

I walked slowly over to the campsite and stood there a minute until they noticed me. The girl was gone. She must have gone inside the motorhome. All of a sudden I felt silly.

*"Parlez vous Anglais?"* I asked the group outside. An older man said to me, "Yeah, I speak English."

I was surprised. I hadn't heard anyone speak a word of English the whole time they were setting up their campsite. I felt stupid for trying to speak French.

"Where are you from?" I asked.

"Switzerland," the man answered, "and I have a daughter your age." He called to her in French.

"I know. I was hoping to make friends with her," I told him. Out the door came the girl with brown hair who I'd seen on the picnic table. In her hand, she had a translation dictionary for French and English.

"What is your name?" the father asked me.

"Amy."

"'Deborah," he said to her, rattling off a bunch of French words. I didn't understand any of them until I heard him say, "Amy." The girl and I nodded hello to each other.

"She doesn't know any English, but she does have a dictionary that will help you two communicate," explained the father.

Deborah looked at me and I looked at her, trying to think of a way to break the ice. Then she motioned with her hands as if she was bouncing a ball and pointed to the basketball court in the campground. I nodded my head, and we headed for the court. We shot a few baskets, she pointed to the ball and said the French word for basketball.

"Basketball," I said to her. We continued this trading of words most of the afternoon. It was fun. We weren't speaking any sentences to each other, but we were communicating. With the help of Deborah's dictionary, I learned she loved horses and wanted to own one. I told her I liked dolphins, and I'd been able to swim with them in Hawaii. I could tell she thought that was cool, because her eyes opened wider, she smiled, and started nodding her head.

By the end of the day, the two of us were communicating pretty well. I'm sure we could've learned more from each other if we'd had more time. Her father gave Jon and me each a set of coins from Switzerland, and Deborah and I exchanged addresses. That night, I wrote on my dream list, "Switzerland, to see Deborah."

*July 18...We visited Montana State University and met Mike Malone, the President. The campus was awesome.*

Later in the week I met with the governor of Montana, Marc Rosciot. He was warm-hearted and compassionate as he spoke about his state during our interview at the capitol in Helena.

"The largest treasure of the Treasure State is its people," he said. "I think you'll find that you're warmly received. The people are the most valuable resource of the state of Montana."

The governor appeared sophisticated, and his speech was clear and concise. I felt slightly intimidated as I blurted out my questions. They seemed short and choppy compared to his fluent, well-spoken answers.

"Aside from the people," he continued, "You will find some un-believable differences in geography from one end of the state to the other. There's beauty virtually everywhere. The thing that I predict you will leave with is the memory of the big sky," he said slowly. "You can see more of the sky here than you can anyplace in the world. In fact in our view, we think everyone would have a richer and more blessed life if everyone had a Montana in their life."

When I asked him about his state's most important industry, he answered, "Agriculture remains our number one industry and has a dominance in terms of contributing to our way of life. You know we have a rural way of life here, where neighbors take care of neighbors, and being a good neighbor means more than just living next door to somebody." Governor Rosciot seemed to genuinely care about the people of Montana and the state's future.

"Thank you, Governor Rosciot."

"Well, Amy, it was a pure delight."

*July 21...Mom and Dad were asked to be cherry pie judges at the Bozeman County Fair because they're from the cherry capital of the world, Traverse City. They were even in the local paper.*

# 47

# there's no face like stone

George Washington, Thomas Jefferson, Teddy Roosevelt, and Abraham Lincoln. These four men all had one thing in common, other than each having been a United States President.

Somewhere in the Black Hills of South Dakota, there was a man who had a dream. Gutzon Borglum wanted to create a monument to these great men. He chose a mountain of granite and began pursuing his dream. He blasted the hillside to expose the stone and built special scaffolding to maneuver around the face of the mountain. People thought he was crazy, but that didn't stop him. He dynamited his way through the hard stone and was able to shape the granite to within one-quarter inch of his mark. He'd almost completed the project when he died at the age of seventy-four. His family and co-workers fulfilled his dream by finishing the work. Mt. Rushmore was complete.

We visited Mt. Rushmore during our trip through South Dakota. When I saw the mammoth faces jutting forth from the mountainside, I wanted to run up and climb them. It's amazing to think the world-famous monument was once only Gutzon's dream. I

would soon learn that sometimes fulfilling a dream requires a little help from friends.

We saw more wildlife in South Dakota than we did anywhere else on our trip. In Custer State Park, we came upon a herd of bighorn sheep. Dad stopped the car, and we watched them butt heads as they fought for the top spot on the rocks. Later, we saw mules standing in

the middle of the road. When we tried to drive slowly by them, one donkey stuck his head into the car through the open window. I think he was hungry.

**W**hen we arrived at the capitol in Pierre, Governor William Janklow's secretary explained that the governor was unexpectedly called out of the office due to flooding in the state. He was just leaving.

"Could you at least get him to sign the sweatshirts?"

"I'll see what I can do," she said. She stood up and took the sweatshirts.

"When can we pick them up?" Mom asked.

"Why don't you stop by later this afternoon, they should be back by then."

We never liked the idea of leaving the sweatshirts behind; we only did it five times during the entire trip. There was always the chance they'd get lost or damaged. We dropped by the office two hours later and picked up the signed sweatshirts. I was disappointed I hadn't been able to meet with Governor Janklow, but I realized his first priority had to be his state, and with all the flooding there was a lot of work to be done.

The afternoon before we left for North Dakota, Mom made more phone calls to the governors' offices in Minnesota and Wisconsin. She'd been trying to schedule meetings with them for quite some time, but hadn't been successful. They were the last two states we'd visit before the trip was over.

When she returned from the pay phone, she gave me the bad news. Both of the governors would be out of their states when we came through, because they would be attending the 1996 Republican National Convention in San Diego California. I was crushed. I'd come all this way, only to discover I was going to miss five governors. I sat on our couch pulling at the loose strings on our throw blanket, trying not to cry.

"Honey," Mom began.

*Oh no, not another make-me-feel-better talk.* I'd received many of those during the beginning of our trip, when things weren't going so well. I didn't want another one.

"You have nothing to feel badly about," Mom continued. "You'll have had 45 out of 50 governors participate in your project, Amy. That's really something to be proud of." She patted me on the knee.

"Maybe we should put you and Amy on a plane to Arizona, so she can try to meet Governor Symington one more time," Dad said, pointing to the map on the motorhome wall. "Then, we'll swing back through Ohio and New York to get those guys. By that time, the Minnesota and Wisconsin governors will be back in their own states."

"That's a lot of money to spend just to meet one governor," Mom said, referring to the flight to Arizona.

"Well, let's talk about this later," Dad yawned. "We need to get a good night's sleep before we go to North Dakota tomorrow."

*July 24...I realized today that we only have three states left to complete our goal of traveling through all fifty, but I still have five governors to meet after North Dakota. How am I going to pull this all together? What if I don't?*

227

# 48

# you've got a
# friend in me

The weather was warm and sunny as we cruised along Highway 85 toward Bismarck, North Dakota's capital. The fields along the road were covered with bright yellow sunflowers. We had the windows wide open, letting the warm summer breezes blow through the motorhome. I was trying to make a leash for Shasta on the knitting knobby Grandma Kay gave me. I figured I couldn't mess up a leash too badly. Jon was playing Monopoly with himself on the couch while Mom video taped the sunflowers along the highway. Dad put in the soundtrack from the movie *Toy Story* and cranked up the volume. We listened to this tape all the time during our trip. The song *"You've Got a Friend in Me"* was our favorite. We all sang along.

*"You've got a friend in me. You've got a friend in me. When the road is rough ahead, and you're miles and miles from your nice warm bed, you just remember what your old pal said, you've got a friend in me."*

We claimed this song as our own. I guess because we all discovered, being miles from home ourselves, we'd become best friends. We felt good when we sang it together.

I liked Governor Ed Schafer the moment I met him. He came out to greet me in the reception room. After a warm handshake and a friendly introduction, he led us into his office. He invited us to have a seat at his table, and we talked about our trip before I began my interview.

"What is the most interesting historical site in your state?" I asked him.

"Well, there are several, but probably the most important is

Medora. Teddy Roosevelt lived and ranched there for many years, and eventually he said, 'Had it not been for my life, living and working in North Dakota, I never would have been President.

"The other important event was about a man named Marquis DeMores. He had an idea that if you could process the beef on the range, instead of driving them all the way to Chicago to the big meat packing plants, that we would have better meat and better quality. He built a big processing plant there and invented the icebox car.

"Another historical event we're looking forward to is the centennial celebration of the Lewis and Clark Expedition."

"What is the most important industry in North Dakota?"

"Agriculture is the most important. We're the largest growers and exporters of wheat, honey, flax, sunflowers, and beans," he said. After seeing thousands of sunflowers along the highway, I wasn't surprised to learn they're one of the state's biggest crops.

"What did you want to be when you were a kid?" I asked him.

"When I was a kid about your age, I wanted to be a firemen," Governor Shafer said, "and I still kind of have that in me once in a while." Dad and I shared a smile over the firemen answer.

"What makes people want to visit or live in North Dakota?"

"The reason people live in North Dakota is because of the sense of community in the state. We have a lot of visitors who come from the crowded cities to just enjoy the wide open spaces, and the people who live here are very friendly."

"Who most influenced your life?"

"God gave me the ability to do what I do, but next in line I would have to say my parents. They taught me honesty and integrity, how to work hard, things that I didn't really appreciate then, but now I look back on it and see the values that they instilled in me are all very important."

"Are you going to the Republican Convention?" I asked him while he signed my sweatshirts.

"Yes, I'm planning on it. Are you going?"

I told him I wished I could be there. I explained that the last five governors on my list were Republicans and I'd had trouble getting in to see them.

"Why don't you let me see if there is anything I can do to help,"

229

Governor Schafer said.

"That would be great, thank you."

We left Governor Schafer's office, excited about the possibility of attending the convention. I wondered if the governor would really be able to help me find a way into the convention to meet the last five

governors on my list. If he did, then I might be able to accomplish my goal.

The next day, Mom came back from the pay phones and made an announcement.

"Governor Schafer called. He wasn't able to find any extra tickets to the convention, but he's willing to share his own with Amy."

"I had a feeling Governor Schafer would come through," I said, smiling.

"It would probably be our only chance to meet the rest of the governors," Mom said, considering our options.

helping hand
Governor
Ed
Schafer
award

"And, it would be a great learning experience for the kids," Dad added.

A few days later, when we were positive we wanted to go to the convention in San Diego, Mom called Governor Schafer to accept the offer and thank him.

We packed up the car and parked the motorhome in a secure place. We left the very next day. We had a week before the August convention was scheduled to begin. When we were in the car and heading south, it hit me. We were going to San Diego! I was determined to find a way to meet my last five governors. We made a quick stop in Denver and dropped Shasta off with Aunt Linda, who had volunteered to dog sit. We spent the night there, and we were on our way the next morning.

# 49

# via san diego

Three days later, we arrived in San Diego, along with thousands of other people. Dad dropped Mom and me off at the convention center the first night. Governor Schafer had managed to find two passes, so Mom could go with me. We went through the security gates and met Governor Schafer who was waiting outside the building for us.

"Governor, thank you so much for the passes."

"You're welcome, Amy. I'm sorry I couldn't get enough for your whole family."

"That's okay, you've done so much already. I can't thank you enough."

Shiny silver doors opened and we entered the convention center. I was wearing a new black business suit Mom bought for me, just for the convention. I felt confident.

The convention center was packed with politicians, reporters, and delegates. As we made our way through the crowds, I saw some of the governors I'd met before. Governor Whitman, Governor Geringer, and my governor, John Engler.

I didn't know the first thing about a political convention, but I was about to receive a hands-on lesson in convention politics. A National Convention is when each party

officially nominates their candidate to run for President of the United States. Our passes only allowed us to walk around the sides and back of what is known as the convention floor. You had to be a delegate or have a press pass to be admitted to the floor. The floor is where it all happens. Each state is represented by delegates who wait in state sections on the floor. Near the end of the convention, a vote is taken state by state for the candidate. At this convention, Bob Dole was the favored nominee, and by the end of convention week, Bob Dole would start his campaign as the Republican nominee for President.

Speaker after speaker stood at the podium and talked about issues such as family values and education, the same issues I'd heard about from my interviews with the governors. I wanted to meet the speakers, but I wasn't allowed on the convention floor.

There were several booths above the convention floor where the media sat, watched over the crowd, and provided live news broadcasts. All the major networks were there, and it was amazing to see news people in person rather than on television. I saw the people from CNN who'd reported my story.

The convention was so packed, I could barely see the red carpet below my feet. There were posters everywhere declaring things such as *Bob [Dole] is the Best, Dole, Kemp, '96* and *Speaker Newt*. There were so many things to absorb! If I hadn't been so excited, I might have gone into sensory overload. The floodlights above me were very bright, and loud music was blaring from the huge speakers surrounding the building. I wondered how I would find my five governors in the crowd.

While we were standing off to the side, I noticed a mob of people coming my way.

"There's President Ford!" Mom yelled, trying to be heard over the noise of the crowd.

She pointed to him. Gerald Ford was walking right toward me. I stuck my hand out, hoping our 38th President would see it. He did, and he shook it. Mom snapped a picture just as his hand shook mine. I couldn't believe it. I'd just shaken the hand of a President. A President who hailed from Michigan. I was in awe. I couldn't wait to tell Dad and Jon.

"It was so cool," I shouted to Dad, after he picked us up in front of the convention. "I wish you and Jon could have been in there with us."

The next day, some members of the Republican Governors Association invited us to a luncheon being held for some of the governors. At lunch, we met Paul Hatch, the Executive Director of the Republican Governors Association. When I explained to him what my project was about and why I was at the convention, he thought it was an interesting project.

"I'd like to help you out," Paul volunteered. "Hang around here after the luncheon, and maybe we can work something out."

"Sure. That would be great," I answered. I couldn't believe it. I was beginning to realize the value of persistence.

We found an empty table and made ourselves comfortable. I saw some of the governors I'd met before.

"Hey, Mom, look! It's Governor Beasley and Governor Sundquist and Mike Leavitt!"

"Go say hi to them, Amy."

"Are you sure it would be okay?"

"Yes, just go," Mom persisted. I wasn't sure they'd remember me, but to my relief, and pleasant surprise, they did.

"How's your project going, Amy?" Governor Leavitt asked.

"Great. I only need five more governors. That's why I'm here. They're all Republicans."

"Who are they?" asked Governor Sundquist.

"Symington, Carlson, Thompson, Voinovich, and Pataki."

"Ooh, Pataki will be a tough one." They all agreed with that fact.

"I know, my Mom's been trying for a year to reach him."

"Well, let us know if you need any help. We'll do what we can," said Governor Beasley.

I thanked all of them. Just then, Jonathan stepped up next to me. Governor Sundquist looked down at him, and noticed Jon had lost a front tooth.

"Did the tooth fairy bring you some money?"

"No, not yet," Jon said shyly. Governor Sundquist

reached into his pocket and pulled out a dollar and handed it to Jon.

"There."

Jon's face lit up and he grinned at the governor. "Thank you!"

"Hmm," Governor Leavitt smiled, "I think the going rate is five dollars, Governor Sundquist."

"Well, fork it over," challenged Governor Beasley, smiling.

We all laughed. Jonathan was thrilled with his dollar.

After the luncheon, Paul came over and handed me an envelope. I opened it and looked inside. I couldn't believe my eyes.

"What is it, Amy?" Mom asked.

"They're passes to the convention for all of us."

"Not just to the convention," Paul explained, "The ones marked *Hospitality Suite* give you access to the Governor's Suite at the convention. That's where the governors and their families hang out during the convention. I thought it would help you meet the last five."

"Oh, my gosh! This is so great. Thank you so much."

"You're welcome, kid. I'll see ya there."

This was awesome! When we came to San Diego, Governor Schafer was the only person who would help me; but after Paul's help, I felt as though the entire Governors Association was behind me. It felt like some kind of dream, but I knew perfectly well it was real. And, that was only the beginning of my convention experience.

On the long drive from North Dakota to San Diego, Mom and Dad had discussed the possibility of also attending the Democratic Convention. That afternoon, after our luncheon with the Republicans, Mom made some phone calls from our hotel room. Since the Republican Governors Association had been so helpful, she thought the Democratic Governors Association might do the same. I listened to her attempts to find passes while I watched the C-Span convention coverage on television. Mom made a lot of calls, but she couldn't get any passes. I'd hoped to have the chance to compare a Republican Convention to a Democratic Convention. I also thought I might've been able to meet the President there, but that wouldn't happen.

The next morning, Mom and I ate breakfast at the hotel restaurant. The Sheraton Grand Torrey Pines, where we were staying in San Diego, was a beautiful hotel. We overheard two men talking at the table next to us.

"Amy, I think those are Governor Carlson's security guards," Mom whispered.

"You really think so?"

"Well, there's only one way to find out," Mom stated. She stood up and walked over to their table. I followed her.

"Excuse me, do you work for Governor Carlson?" she asked.

"Yes, we do," they answered firmly.

"Oh, then I'd like to introduce you to my daughter, Amy."

"Hi." I said.

I explained I wanted to meet the governor and why. "Governor Carlson is one of the last five governors I have yet to meet."

"Give us a chance to talk with the governor and meet us back here in a few hours," one of them offered.

"Thank you."

After we finished eating, we walked around exploring the hotel. I wasn't surprised to discover Governor Carlson was staying there, as were many other governors such as Governor Beasley, Governor Schafer, and Governor Engler.

About two hours later, I was in the elevator on my way down to talk to Governor Carlson's security guards. A man in the elevator next to me broke the silence.

"Where are you from?"

"Michigan," I answered politely.

"I'm from Minnesota," he smiled. "Are you here on vacation?"

"Well, sort of. I'm attending the Republican Convention."

"Are you a politician?"

"No," I laughed, "Not yet."

Just then the elevator doors opened to reveal the two security guys.

"Oh," one of them remarked, "I see you two have already met." We both looked at each other, wondering what the guy was talking about. "Governor, this young lady wanted to know if she could interview you for a project she's doing."

I realized then that I'd been talking to Governor Carlson and didn't even know it. I turned to him, flushed, and formally introduced myself.

"Governor," I stammered, "I wondered if you'd be willing to let me interview you?"

He smiled, looked at his watch, and said, "Sure. I'm just heading down to the pool for a swim, why don't you meet me there and we can talk."

"Great, thanks."

My heart was racing as I hit the number four on the elevator key pad. When it finally reached our floor, I ran to our room and pounded on our door. Mom opened it cautiously, and I burst into the room. My mouth was moving as fast as my heart was beating while I explained what had just happened. I told Mom and Dad I would be doing a poolside interview, so we all scrambled to put on our swimsuits. When I was finally able to do a casual interview, I felt strange not wearing my dress clothes. Go figure.

Thank goodness we had our interview drill down to a science. We grabbed the camera bag and the sweatshirts, and moments later I was sitting in a lounge chair next to the governor of Minnesota.

That had to be the most unusual meeting of all. I wondered how many people interviewed a governor by a pool. Even though we were in a relaxed setting, the governor was still very businesslike and serious about the questions I asked. By his demeanor, you'd never guess he was sitting next to a pool in his swimming trunks.

"What are your state's greatest needs, and how can your administration help to take care of those needs?"

"I don't think we're any different than any other state. I think the biggest need in America today is to decide who we are, where we're going, and what price we're willing to pay to get there," he answered, adjusting his dark sunglasses.

"When you were my age, what did you want to be when you grew up?"

"I wanted to go into American government," he stated firmly.

"At age thirteen?"

"Yep," he answered.

"When we go to Minnesota, what do you think we should see? Is there any particular attraction?" The music blaring across the pool almost drowned out my question.

"I wouldn't recommend any one thing. I think what you want to pick up in any travel to any foreign country, to any state, is the flavor of the state. What is it about? Camping. If you like camping, you'll love Minnesota."

"What are your greatest personal and political goals?"

"Education. See, I can't give you an education. Seriously, I can give you a t-shirt, I can sign this," he said pointing to the sweatshirts. "I can buy you a Coke, but I can't give you an education. All I can do is give you the opportunity, and then hope that you'll be wise enough to seek an education. If you seek it, you'll do just fine, but if you think somebody can come along and give it to you," he said shaking his head, "can't do it. It's not possible."

When the interview was over, Jon and I jumped in the swimming pool with the governor.

That night, the convention center was under heavy security. We passed through a security system like the ones at an airport. Everything had to be checked. The security personnel looked through purses and camera bags. They even made us take a picture with the camera to make sure it was a real camera.

Once inside, we looked for the Hospitality Suite. We went through two more security checkpoints before we could get in the suite. It was very large, with three big screen televisions and several black leather couches. In the middle of the room, tables were set up with all kinds of food served on fancy silver trays. There was shrimp, spicy meatballs, egg rolls, and other finger foods I'd never seen before. Whatever they were, though, they tasted great.

I saw Governor Rowland. "Hi Governor, how are you doing?" I asked him, hoping he would remember me.

"Great, how is your trip going?"

"Good, I have just four governors left to meet."

"Congratulations!"

I also saw Governor Johnson. He remembered me too, and Governor Keating, who introduced me to his wife. I also met Governor Bush's wife, Governor Beasley's wife, and Mrs. Huckaby, the wife of the new governor of Arkansas. Mrs. Huckaby invited me to come back to Arkansas for tea. I told her I would sometime. It was a special reunion, and I was enjoying every minute of it. As I stood in line at the drink counter waiting for a Coke, the man in front of me turned around and asked my name.

"Amy Burritt," I said.

"Hi Amy, I'm Governor Symington of Arizona. Nice to meet you."

I thought I was hearing things. Could one of the governors I'd been searching for really be standing right in front of me?

"Uh, nice to meet you, too, Governor," I said, as I slowly stepped backwards. "Could you, uh, wait here just a minute?" I stammered. "I have something I'd like you to sign."

"Sure, no problem," he smiled.

I went over to my chair, grabbed the bag with the sweatshirts and

told Dad to bring the camera. I stood next to Governor Symington and watched him sign the shirts. I couldn't believe how things were coming together. Two down and only three to go.

# 50

# final challenge

Tommy Thompson, the governor of Wisconsin, was just finishing his speech to the convention. I watched on television from the Governor's Suite. Governor Thompson was one of the governors who wasn't going to be in his state when I planned to visit. Meeting him at the convention was the only way to get his signature on my sweatshirt. Paul, our friend from the Republican Governors Association, stood next to me with one hand in the pocket of his neatly pressed suit. He'd been asking me questions about my trip and the book I was planning to write. He pointed to the big screen in front of us.

"How bad do you want to meet Tommy?" he asked casually.

"Very badly," I said, surprised Paul would ask me.

"Do you think you can keep up with me?"

"Uh, yeah." I wasn't quite sure what he meant.

"Get your camera and follow me," he said. I looked at Mom. She just shrugged her shoulders and gave me a puzzled look. Well, I thought, what do I have to lose? I grabbed the camera bag. Mom told Dad to wait in the suite with Jon.

Paul started ahead, then looked back at us. "You're going to have to keep right with me or we won't make it on time."

"Okay," Mom hollered back.

We weaved in and out of the crowded hallways trying to keep up with Paul. We finally came to the security line behind the speaker's podium. Few people were allowed to enter this area. Paul waved to the men standing guard and said, "They're with me." The security men nodded their heads and let us go through. I couldn't believe it; maybe he would get me to Governor Thompson.

More crowded hallways and more security, but Paul seemed to know everyone. We eased our way to the back of the stage. Paul stopped and turned to me.

"Okay kid, I want to see how you work," he said, looking me in the eyes. "You're going to have to stop him yourself."

Nervous and excited, my adrenalin pumping, I stepped into the middle of the hall just as Governor Thompson stepped off the podium and began walking in my direction. My heart was pounding so hard, I was sure everyone could hear it above the applause.

"Governor Thompson, my name is Amy Burritt from Traverse City, Michigan," I said, shaking his hand.

"Yes," he said to me.

"I'm going to all fifty states this year, interviewing all the governors, and unfortunately I didn't get a chance to interview you, but I wondered if you would sign my sweatshirts?"

"Sure."

"Thank you." The governor patted me on the shoulder after he signed the sweatshirts, and he smiled as he walked away. He was pretty quiet. His mind must have been focused on the speech he'd just given to the convention.

"Good job, kid," Paul said, punching my shoulder with his fist. "You sure know how to stop 'em."

At the end of the night, after the delegates had left, we walked around the convention floor. It was littered with posters and hats. Jon and I rummaged through the discarded posters and party hats to find some souvenirs. Mom wanted a picture of us standing in front of the podium, holding onto our sweatshirts.

As we posed for the snapshot, a reporter asked, "What are those shirts all about?"

"I've been traveling around the country meeting the governors and forty-eight have signed my shirts."

"Can we film this?"

"Sure," Mom said. "What network are you with?"

"MTV."

Oh my gosh, I thought, I'm going to be on MTV. It was too good to be true!

A group of young reporters covering the convention came over to see what was going on. They also asked if they could interview me. The next thing I knew, C-Span's Steve Scully was pulling me away for a live interview.

"Okay, here we go," Steve said. "Amy Burritt, you won't be able to vote in the Presidential election, but already you're interested in politics. What are you doing?"

*Live interview with C-SPAN.*

"This year, I'm traveling to all fifty states and trying to meet the governors, and so far forty-eight have participated."

"Why are you doing it?"

"It's basically an extension of my education. I'm studying history and government, so I can share it with others through a book I'm writing," I answered. He rattled off tons of questions, and I answered each one with ease.

"What have you learned from politics?" he asked.

"I think the governors have been really great. They've helped form my views and it's been great to talk to all of them."

With only two governors left to complete my goal, I felt invincible. I still hoped to interview them, but even if they only participated in my project by signing the shirts, I would be happy.

We arrived at the convention the next night and tried to walk around the convention floor, but the crowds were heavier than before. Elizabeth Dole was speaking later that evening, so the hall was packed. Dad suggested we go up to the Governor's Suite and look for the remaining two governors there.

I was feeling frustrated as I watched the big television screen in the suite when I remembered Governor Beasley's words. "Amy, if you need my help, send a page to me on the floor and I will do what I can to help you," he'd said. I repeated those words to Mom and Dad and convinced them to come with me to look for Governor Beasley. I went to the first page I could find and sent a message to the governor.

The message read, "Governor Beasley, I need your help to meet Governor Voinovich and Governor Pataki, the last two on my list. Can you help me? Amy Burritt."

After twenty minutes or so, Mom and Dad tried to convince me that the governor really didn't have the time to help me. I insisted on waiting.

"Just a few more minutes, please?" I asked them.

Suddenly, a man appeared through the wall of security guards.

"Amy, hi, I'm Dewitt. Governor Beasley sent me over to get you. He's going to meet us in the middle of the floor and then he'll take you to meet those last two governors. C'mon, follow me."

Mom and Dad were astounded. I turned and smiled. "I told you he'd help me."

The security personnel weren't going to let us through, but Dewitt explained Governor Beasley requested that we meet him on the floor. They let us pass. I followed closely behind Dewitt. I didn't want to lose him or my fantastic opportunity. We finally reached the governor.

"You ready, Amy?" Governor Beasley asked.

"Yes, sir." I answered.

"Let's go. We're heading for Ohio first."

He turned and pressed through the crowd. I looked back to see if Mom, Dad, and Jon were keeping up. They lagged a little behind, but I could still see them. I could see the sign for Ohio. It was at the front, near the podium. As we got closer, security men were pushing the crowds back to clear the way for Elizabeth Dole. When Governor Beasley tried to get through, they said no one was allowed beyond that point.

"Listen," he told the big guard blocking our way, "I'm Governor Beasley of South Carolina and this girl has been on a mission during the past year, so we're going through."

He pushed his way past the man. I couldn't believe the governor was being so bold. I turned my head just in time to see my family cut off from following me. There was a lot of commotion around us in anticipation of Elizabeth Dole's speech. When we reached Ohio, I wasn't sure which person was the governor. Governor Beasley introduced me to him.

"Governor Voinovich, I'd like you to meet Amy."

Ohio's governor shook my hand. "Hello Amy."

"She's been traveling throughout the country this year meeting all the governors."

I looked at Governor Voinovich, "I wondered if you would sign my sweatshirts?"

"Sure, I'd be happy to." He smiled as he took the pen from my hand. Dewitt, who'd managed to get through security and follow us with Dad's camera, took our picture.

"Thank you, Governor Voinovich."

"Okay, now we have to get all the way over to New York," Governor Beasley said. "Stick close to me."

243

I felt like I was on *Mission Impossible* as we weaved in and out of the rows of chairs and crowded aisles. Mom and Jon had managed to catch up with us, but I didn't know what'd happened to Dad.

We passed by Michigan, and I accidentally stepped on Governor Engler's feet. "I'm sorry, Governor," I said, embarrassed that I was so clumsy.

"That's alright. How's your project going, Amy?" he asked.

"I'm on my way to New York to meet Governor Pataki, the last one!" I shouted excitedly. Mom and Jon stumbled over Governor Engler, too. We couldn't help it, it was so crowded. I could hear Mom apologizing to him. Because the crowds had been pushed back, it was shoulder to shoulder and no one was moving. It was hard to get anywhere, and people didn't want to let us pass.

We finally reached New York. Once again, Governor Beasley introduced me. At this point, we had to yell over the noise of the crowd.

"Governor Pataki!" I screamed, "I've been trying to meet you for a whole year. I've been traveling to all the states and meeting the governors and having them sign these sweatshirts. I wondered if you

*Mission accomplished.*

would sign them, too?" I showed him the shirts.

He glanced at the sweatshirts and then at me. "Sure," he said. "They look pretty full, how many do you have to go?"

"Governor Pataki, you're the last one." I smiled.

Across the sea of people, I saw Dad with his camera and he motioned to me that he wanted to get a picture. I pointed Dad out to Governor Pataki, who was kind enough to pose for a picture.

"Thank you so much, Governor," I said, shaking his hand.

I was turning to leave when I realized that I'd just completed my goal. All fifty governors had signed my sweatshirts. I was done.

Governor Beasley raised his hand for a high-five and I slapped it, laughing.

"Great job, Amy." Governor Beasley was laughing, too. Dewitt did the same. I turned to Mom for a hug, and tears streamed down my face. I wanted to get over to Dad so we could all celebrate the moment together. As I inched my way through the sweaty crowd, the security guys had heard about me through their little earphones, and they were all giving me high-fives as I passed by.

*my hero*
Governor
David
Beasley
*award*

Once again, I stumbled over Governor Engler as he congratulated me on the completion of my project. Governor Sundquist was next to him, and he gave me a high-five, too. By the time I reached Dad, I was flying. We all hugged and took a deep breath.

"Great job, Amy, you did it," Dad said with tears in his eyes.

"No, Dad, *we* did it."

I'd actually finished what I set out to do. What an awesome feeling. I'm not sure if it was just plain joy, relief, or pride, or a combination of all three, but whatever it was, I liked it. There was no way we were going anywhere with such a crowd, so we stayed on the floor to hear Elizabeth Dole speak. I was glad, because I wanted to see her. She came onto the podium, then walked down onto the convention floor. She stopped just a few feet from us and gave her speech.

*August 15...I did it! I got them all. I'm glad I didn't give up in Alaska.*

# one more thing

We drove into San Diego for the final night of the convention. I was still reeling from the excitement of the night before, when I'd snagged the last signature on my sweatshirts. The energy of all the people at the convention, combined with my success, fueled my confidence. I knew there was one more thing I had to do.

"I want to meet Bob Dole tonight," I blurted from the back seat. Mom turned back and looked at me with a blank stare.

"Amy, there are tens of thousands of people here who want to meet Bob Dole. Besides, I'm exhausted. You've met with almost every governor in the country, every single governor signed your sweatshirt, you have accomplished your goal. I'm really proud of you, but tonight I'm just going to sit down and relax in the Hospitality Suite. If you want to meet Bob Dole, you're going to have to do it yourself. I can't do any more work."

I couldn't believe what I was hearing. After a year of hard work and determination, we'd accomplished one of my goals, but now I had another one. I had the chance to meet Bob Dole, and Mom was giving up. After all the talks about at least trying. No, I thought, I wasn't going to let this opportunity slip through my fingers. At that very moment, I made up my mind. I was going to meet Bob Dole, with or without Mom and Dad's help.

Once inside the Governor's Suite, I decided to enjoy myself for awhile. I watched one of the big screen televisions just as Bob Dole walked onto the podium. His speech was great, the best I'd ever heard him give. As he came to the end of it, I knew if I wanted to meet him, it was going to have to happen that night.

"Dad, I want to go down there. I have to meet Bob Dole. He has to sign my sweatshirts."

Dad knew by the tone of my voice and the look on my face, I was going down there whether they wanted to or not. He looked at Mom.

"Honey, we're goin' down."

It was even more crowded than the previous nights. Red, white and blue balloons were falling from the ceiling as the song *I'm A Dole Man* blared over the loudspeaker. I inched as close as I could to the back of the podium. We'd gone as far as anyone could go around the perimeter without a pass. A huge crowd was positioned along the route where Bob Dole would be walking after his speech. Almost everyone wanted him to sign something.

I squeezed my way to the front. I showed a security guy the sweatshirts and asked him if there was a chance Bob Dole would sign them. Everyone around me started laughing. Instead of intimidating me, as it might have a year before, it made me even more determined. With my jaws clenched, I explained to the security guard what I'd been doing over the past year.

"Listen, I've been to forty-eight states, I've met forty-four governors. All fifty governors have signed this sweatshirt, and now I want Bob Dole to sign it."

He looked at me for a second with a scowl on his face. "No. You'll have to send them in to be signed."

The people around me seemed to laugh even harder. I moved down the line and told another security guy that I wanted my sweatshirts signed.

"No way," he said.

I moved further down, hoping to get a better view of Senator Dole. He was coming out and walking toward the noisy crowd. I knew I didn't have much time to get his attention before he was gone. I raised my voice over the crowd's enthusiastic cheering and shouted:

"Senator Dole! Senator Dole!" I waved a sweatshirt in the air to get his attention. I couldn't believe it, he was walking right toward me! "Senator Dole," I said as he looked at me, "All the governors have signed these sweatshirts, would you please sign them, too?"

"Sure."

Excited, I handed the first sweatshirt to him. Just then, I felt the bag with the other sweatshirt in it being pulled out from under my

*Bob Dole signs my sweatshirts.*

arm. I spun around in time to catch a security guy suspiciously checking out my bag. I shouted at him. "I need the other sweatshirt! Senator Dole has to sign both of them, please give me the sweatshirt!" I grabbed the shirt out of the bag and turned back. Senator Dole was still there, waiting patiently for the other sweatshirt.

"Thank you, Senator Dole, this means so much to me."

"You're welcome," he said.

We shook hands and he was gone. I slid out of the sweaty crowd. Mission accomplished. And, to all the people in the crowd who laughed at me, I got the last laugh. My persistence paid off. When I found Mom and Dad, I showed them the shirts. Ironically, Bob Dole had signed them in the spot reserved for the President.

# the last chapter?

After traveling through the last two states, Minnesota and Wisconsin, we were back home in Traverse City. I made one final call to Jack O'Malley at the radio station. "Hey, Jack," I said, "I just thought I'd let you know I did it. Fifty states, fifty weeks, fifty thousand miles and all fifty governors."

"Congratulations, Amy, great job. So what are you going to do now?"

"Take a break, for now, and then I'm going to write my book."

"Well, I wish you luck, Amy, and thanks for sharing your adventure with us. I'll be looking forward to reading your book."

Over the next few months, I concentrated on my school work, writing my book, and reconnecting with Melisa and Brittany. We were living in the motorhome until the renters moved out of our house. I went over to the girls' house as much as I could. At first, we were a little reserved with each other. It was hard to know what to talk about after so much time apart. There was one question I was dying to ask them, but I was afraid of their answer. I finally decided that after all I'd done over the last year, interviewing governors, pushing my way through convention crowds, and living in strange places, I could handle asking my best friends a question.

"So, did you ever open the box in the junkyard?" I braced myself for their response. I'd promised myself it would be okay if they'd gone ahead with their own adventures while I was away living mine.

"Are you kidding?" Melisa said.

"Yeah, why would we want to do that without you?" Brittany asked, looking at me like I was dense.

"Well, then, what are we waiting for? Let's go!" I said, as I jumped off Mel's bed and ran to put on my shoes.

"The time has come!" we yelled in unison.

All three of us were breathless by the time we made it to the junkyard. There would be no second thoughts this time. We ran down the hill to where the box lay. I leaned over and pulled at the lid. The girls stood there.

"Come on, you guys, we've waited too long. Besides, what's the worst that could happen when we open it?"

"Well, a dead body for starters," Melisa said grimly.

They knelt down to help me. Together, we pried the lid loose and opened it. I looked into the box. Melisa and I looked at each other.

"It's empty," I said, smiling. We all sat there a long time, staring at the emptiness in the box.

"Well," I said finally, "there's nothing to be afraid of anymore."

I realized all my worries about Melisa and Brittany not wanting to hang out with me were gone, too. I'd been afraid of the box's mysterious contents just as I'd been afraid of so many other things that year. As I peered into the empty box, I finally understood there'd never really been anything to worry about from the beginning.

*Brittany, me, and Melisa.*

"C'mon guys, let's go back to your house," I said.

We stood up and headed home.

# since then

I heard news reports about terrible flooding in North Dakota. As I sat and watched the devastation on television, my thoughts went to Governor Schafer. I remembered how kind he'd been to me. He'd helped so much on my project, I wondered if there was anything I could do in return.

"Mom," I asked, "would it be okay if I called Governor Schafer and asked him if there was anything I could do to help with the flooding?"

"Sure, Amy, if that's what you think you should do."

I picked up the phone and called the governor's office.

"He's in a meeting right now, can I take a message?" the secretary asked.

"Well, actually, I kinda wanted to talk to the governor himself. I was in North Dakota last July to meet with him for a project I was doing called *America Through the Eyes of A Student,* and I just heard about the flood. I wondered if there was anything I could do to help."

"Well," said the secretary, sounding a little skeptical, "I have a hotline number you can call to make a donation." She gave me the number.

"Would you at least tell him I called and give him my number?"

"Sure," she said.

"Okay. Thanks, bye." I realized the secretary probably received hundreds of calls from people who wanted to talk with the governor, and it must have seemed really strange to have a kid ask to speak to him.

"I hope the governor will call me back," I said to Mom and Dad.

"I think he will," Mom assured me.

"Well," Dad said, looking at his watch, "we can't wait around any longer for his call. Grandma is expecting us at the farm, but we'll bring the car phone, just in case."

It was a long drive to the farm, so Jon brought his backpack full of Legos to give us something to do in the car.

"Hey, Amy," he said, "do you think Grandpa will let us explore the barn today?"

"I doubt it. They have a lot of important things in there."

"Oh, yeah, but maybe they'll let us today," Jon said, hopeful. I liked having an optimistic brother.

"Jon, remember last time when we tried to sneak into the barn with Joel and got in trouble?"

"I know, Amy." He tinkered with his Legos. "There's always the bus to explore!"

The car phone startled me when it rang. Mom answered it.

"Hello?"

I listened from the back seat. Mom paused a second.

"Yes. Just a minute, Governor." With a big grin Mom handed me the phone.

"It's Governor Schafer," she whispered.

Already? I thought.

"How are you, Amy?" the governor asked.

"I'm great. Thanks for calling me back."

"When my secretary gave me the note, a smile came across my face, and I told her I would give you a call." We talked for a minute about how my project had gone and what I'd been involved in since I arrived home.

"So, what can I do for you, Amy?" Governor Schafer asked.

"Well, I saw the devastation from the flood in Grand Forks on the national news, and I wondered if there was anything I could do to help?" It still felt strange, even after this past year, to think a governor would call me and that I could talk to him like a regular person.

"Well, we need cleaning supplies and cash donations," Governor Schafer said.

"Okay, I'll do whatever I can to help."

After that phone call, I made it my personal mission to help the flood victims in North Dakota. I began by setting up drop locations around Traverse City for cleaning supplies and cash donations. I opened an account at the local bank so people could donate money. I sent out media releases to publicize the drive, and I called on my old friend, Jack O'Malley, to help me get the word out on the radio.

It didn't take long before I started receiving phone calls from people volunteering supplies and services. Consumers Energy and Ryder Truck Rental even donated trucks to haul the supplies to North Dakota. All I had to do was fill them.

*Me with Larry and Jim, the truck drivers.*

I organized a drive at the local Wal-Mart parking lot. The truck driver, Jim, my friend Aaron and his parents, Mark and Shelly, all helped take donations. It was a lot of work, but it was very rewarding, knowing I was helping Governor Schafer and the people of North Dakota.

From the donations we received, I was able to send over $35,000 in cash and cleaning supplies to North Dakota. It felt great knowing I could make a difference.

I guess I did learn some things about politics during my trip across America. I learned what it really comes

*Dad's friend, Chris loading the semi.*

down to is: politics is more than just working for the government or making government policies. politics has to do with relationships between people and being a responsible citizen with those relationships. And it doesn't take a person in an important position to accomplish something. Anybody can do anything, if they set their mind to it. Even a teenager.

A few weeks later I was sitting in the motorhome reading through my dream list. I couldn't believe everything I'd done in the past year and how many goals I'd accomplished.

"Amy," Mom interrupted, "I was just wondering, what would you think of *Europe Through the Eyes of a Student?*"

"Ahhhhhh!"